A Guide to Assertive Living

Your Perfect Right

by Robert E. Alberti, Ph.D.
and Michael L. Emmons, Ph.D.

Impact 🕸 Publishers
POST OFFICE BOX 1094
SAN LUIS OBISPO, CALIFORNIA 93406

Editions

First Edition, October, 1970
Second Edition, January, 1974
Third Edition, May, 1978
Fourth Edition, April, 1982
Fifth Printing, May, 1984
Sixth Printing, December, 1984

Copyright © 1970, 1974, 1978, 1982

by Robert E. Alberti and Michael L. Emmons

Library of Congress Cataloging in Publication Data

Alberti, Robert E.
    Your perfect right.

    Bibliography: p.
    1. Assertiveness (Psychology) I. Emmons, Michael L.
II. Title.
BF575.A85A43   1982   158'.1   81-20265
ISBN 0-915166-06-2   AACR2
ISBN 0-915166-05-4 (pbk.)

Impact ⚙ Publishers
POST OFFICE BOX 1094
SAN LUIS OBISPO, CALIFORNIA 93406

Acknowledgements

We are indebted to many, many people for the continuing success of this book. We had no idea in the summer of 1970 when we began this project that we would produce four editions, nearly half a million copies, and a successful publishing enterprise in the process. More important is the effect *Your Perfect Right* has had in the lives of hundreds of thousands of people. We are at once humbled and delighted with the results of our writing.

The response of our students and readers, both lay and professional, has been a major influence in keeping us "honest," and in keeping this book up to date.

Special appreciation is due Joseph Wolpe, and to the late Michael Serber, both of whom stimulated and encouraged our approach to assertiveness training. Cyril Franks offered us review space in *Behavior Therapy* when only a handful of people had ever *heard* of "assertive training."

Lachlan MacDonald edited the first two editions, and helped in many ways to launch this book, as well as serving for a time as agent and consultant for Impact Publishers.

Charles and Carita Merker gave generously of their time and talents to help make possible the publication of the first edition.

Deborah Alberti and Kay Emmons have been models of assertiveness. Both professionals in their own fields, they have given encouragement, love, and support. They made it all possible; without them there would have been no book. To them we rededicate this effort.

R.E.A.
M.L.E.

San Luis Obispo, California
December, 1981

CONTENTS

PUBLISHER'S NOTE

Part One

What Is Your Perfect Right?

Be fair with others, but then keep after them until they're fair with you.

—*Alan Alda*

Do you ever feel helpless, powerless, ineffective? Do you sometimes get pushy in an effort to make yourself heard? Is it difficult for you to make your wishes known to others? Do you often find yourself "low person on the totem pole"? Are you sometimes pushed around by others because of your own inability to stand up for yourself? Or do you frequently push others around in order to get your way?

The Assertive Alternative

This book offers an alternative to personal powerlessness and manipulation. You will find here a program which develops self-confidence AND respect for others. Based upon belief in the equal value of every human being, this book celebrates the unique value of each individual, and encourages positive relationships between and among persons who respect and value each other.

Over the past 10 to 15 years, noticeable progress has been made in the United States toward the development of a society based upon these values. Individuals have spoken out much more clearly, and some intolerable conditions have changed. Relationships, from the most intimate of love partners to the most distant of neighbors and co-workers, have begun to reflect a more equal valuing of both persons. A process called "assertiveness training" has had a good deal to do with some of those needed changes. This book, published in its first edition in 1970, has been a significant contributor to that process.

Popular ideas about what it means to be "assertive" cover an amazing range. A recent "Ziggy" cartoon illustrates the image many hold. The single-frame sketch shows our hero approaching a door labeled "Assertiveness Training Class." Below that sign is another message on the door: "Don't Bother to Knock, Barge Right In!" We hope to foster a less aggressive view of self-expression, and to correct the pushy image of assertiveness which is unfortunately widespread.

The process we advocate and teach in this book is NOT a magic formula for "getting your way." If you seek tools for manipulating others, you will have to look elsewhere. What you will find here is a systematic approach to more effective self-expression, based upon a balance between achieving your own goals and respecting the needs of others.

In helping thousands of persons learn to value themselves and to express themselves, we have found three particularly important barriers to self-assertion:

1. Many people do not believe that they have the *right* to be assertive;
2. Many people are highly *anxious* or *fearful* about being assertive;
3. Many people lack the *social skills* for effective self-expression.

In this book, we address these barriers to personal power and healthy relationships, and we present proven, effective tools to overcome them.

This is not a proposal for political, economic, or social revolution. We are concerned with power on a much more personal level — at home, on the job, at school, in stores and restaurants, in club meetings, wherever the sense of personal insignificance or frustration is encountered. Yet we also hope to empower persons to help build a society which is responsive to human needs.

Has anyone ever cut in front of you in a line? Do you have difficulty saying "no" to persuasive salespeople? Are you able to express warm, positive feelings to someone? Can you comfortably begin a conversation with strangers at a party? Have you ever regretted "stepping on" someone else in trying to gain your own objectives?

Many people find situations like these uncomfortable or irritating, and often seem at a loss for just the "right" action. In fact, there is no one "right way" to handle such events, but there are some basic principles which will help you to gain confidence and effectiveness in your relationships with others.

Let's start with a definition for the term we use to describe such self-enhancing action: *Assertive behavior enables a person to act in his or her own best interests, to stand up for herself or himself without undue anxiety, to express honest feelings comfortably, or to exercise personal rights without denying the rights of others.* (These dimensions of assertive behavior are examined in detail in Chapter 2).

The person who typically acts in a *non-assertive* manner is likely to think of an appropriate response after the opportunity has passed. On the other hand, an *aggressive* response is too vigorous, making a deep and negative impression for which one may later be sorry. This book will assist you in developing a more adequate repertoire of assertive behavior, so that you may choose appropriate and self-fulfilling responses in a variety of situations.

Research has shown that learning to make assertive responses will reduce the anxiety you may feel in dealing with others. By developing the ability to stand up for yourself and do things on your own initiative, you can cut down tenseness in key situations, and you can increase your sense of worth as a person — whether your present style is nonassertive or aggressive.

Every individual is equal and has the same fundamental human rights as the other person in a relationship, regardless of roles and titles. It is our goal to help you learn to exercise *your perfect rights* without infringing upon the rights of others. This concept of equality gained worldwide recognition with the adoption of The Universal Declaration of Human Rights by the

United Nations General Assembly in 1948.   We urge you to read through the Declaration (see Appendix A), and let its principles encourage you to support the rights of the individual — including *yourself!*

Such a broad view of individual human rights has much meaning for each of us as citizens of a shrinking planet. This view could go far in helping us to counteract the influence of those forces which pit us against one another in the steadily escalating conflict of nations. We are all human beings after all!

Unfortunately, our society often evaluates human beings on scales which make some people "better" than others. Consider the following assumptions:

adults are better than children
bosses are better than employees
men are better than women
whites are better than blacks
physicians are better than plumbers
teachers are better than students
politicians are better than voters
generals are better than privates
winners are better than losers
Americans are better than "foreigners"

and so on, *ad infinitum.* Our social structures perpetuate these and similar myths, and allow individual human beings in these roles to be treated as if they were of lesser value *as human beings.*

If you go through life inhibited, giving in to the wishes of others, holding your own desires inside yourself, or conversely, destroying others in order to have your way, your feeling of personal worth will be low. Even such physical complaints as headaches, general fatigue, stomach disturbances, rashes, and asthma are often related to a failure to develop assertive behavior. The person who is assertive avoids such symptoms, for the most part, and remains healthy, fully in charge of self in interpersonal relationships, confident and capable without cockiness or hostility, spontaneous in the expression of feelings and emotions. Such persons are generally admired by others, as well.

Commonly, people mistake aggression for assertion, but assertive behavior does not malign others, deny their rights, or run roughshod over people. Assertiveness is open and flexible, genuinely concerned with the rights of both persons in an encounter.

We have tried to avoid gimmicks on "how to manipulate others" or "gamesmanship" in this book. We know that many popular books on "assertiveness" present techniques for "getting your way." This is not our goal. We are concerned with helping to bring about enduring, positive behavior patterns, and loving, equal relationships.

In later chapters, the concepts of aggressive, assertive and nonassertive behavior are defined and illustrated to help you make positive changes in your own behavior. Specific instructions to help you achieve greater assertiveness are provided in clear, nontechnical terms. A concluding section discusses issues of concern in the use of assertiveness. We have included many different illustrations of assertive situations which are useful for anyone seriously interested in a course of self-improvement. Part Two of the book expands the theoretical and technical aspects of assertive behavior, and is designed as a brief guide for professionals who are engaged in facilitating personal growth in their clients.

Whether your goals are personal or job-related or both, you will find a careful *reading-and-practice* approach to the ideas and procedures presented in the following chapters will help you to develop more effective self-expression and healthier relationships. Give some thought now to your own goals as you read this material, and look for ways to regularly practice what you learn! We will discuss specific goals for growth in more detail in later chapters.

Society Often Discourages Assertiveness

The family, educational and business worlds frequently squelch assertive behavior. Teachings of religious organizations often discourage straightforward expression in interpersonal situations.

Women, children, and members of ethnic minorities in the United States have discovered that assertive behavior is usually viewed by society as the province of the white adult male. Indeed, such attitudes run deep and die hard in our culture. It is extremely difficult for the *haves* to acknowledge the human rights of the *have nots*. The gains resulting from the civil rights movement of the 1950s and 1960s were slow, painful, and tragically costly. One wonders even now if the changes are any more than slight. Lyndon Baines Johnson and Martin Luther King Jr. agreed that the Civil Rights Acts of 1964 and 1965 were "the best bills we could get" from a Congress powerfully influenced by individuals who had dedicated their lives to the preservation of the *status quo ante*. (Johnson later commented similarly about the 1968 Act.)

In the 1970s and 80s, women have encountered similar resistance to their new efforts of self-assertion. Their husbands, their employers, their legislators, their President — all have demonstrated reluctance ranging from foot-dragging to open hostility and political battles. The phenomenal resistance to ratification of the Equal Rights Amendment is a powerful example.

But women are making overdue gains in recognition of their individual rights. The widespread offering of assertiveness training for women, including a tremendous number of specialized workshops for women in management and other fields, is one hopeful sign. Women of all social viewpoints, ethnic and socio-economic backgrounds, educational and professional involvements, homemakers, hard hats, and high ranking executives have made phenomenal gains in becoming more adequately assertive.

At the same time, a smaller but equally committed number of men acknowledge a great gap in their own preparation for inter-personal relationships. Limited to only two options: the powerful, dominating aggressor or the "97-pound weakling" with sand in his face, most have found neither to be particularly satisfying. Assertiveness has offered them an effective alternative.

The 1970s saw much public recognition in our society of the inadequacy of a social "ideal" which identifies women as characteristically "passive, sweet, submissive, accepting, warm, loving, nurturing, empathetic" and the counterpart male (as if by "nature") as "strong, active, decisive, dominant, cool, rational." We have, at long last, begun to value the *assertive* woman and the *assertive* man.

In their excellent book *The Assertive Woman* (which is good reading for men, too), Stanlee Phelps and Nancy Austin present the behavioral styles of four "women we all know." Their characterizations of *Doris Doormat, Agatha Aggressive, Iris Indirect,* and *April Assertive* are self-explanatory by the names alone. Yet, in describing the patterns of each, Phelps and Austin help us to gain a clearer picture of the social mores which have *devalued* assertiveness in women. Agatha gets her way, though she hasn't many friends. Iris, the sly one, also gains most of what she wants, and sometimes her "victims" never even know it. Doris, although denied her own wishes much of the time, is highly praised by men and by the power structure as "a good woman." April's honesty and forthrightness have often led her into trouble (at least until recently) at home, at school, on the job, and even with other women.

A long overdue balance is now emerging: Women are people, have rights, deserve equal recognition/status/pay, are not inherently "weaker", do not (except when they freely so choose) "belong in the home." Thus the *assertive* woman — albeit slowly and not without considerable effort — is becoming a person valued by society, by men, by other women. She is capable of choosing her own lifestyle, free of dictates of tradition, government, husband, children, social groups, bosses. She may *elect* to be a homemaker and not fear intimidation by her "liberated" sisters. She may elect to pursue a male-dominated profession and enjoy confidence in her rights and abilities.

In her sexual relationships, she can be comfortable taking initiative, asking for what *she* wants (and thereby freeing her partner from the "automatic" role of making the first move). She can also say "no" with firmness and can make it stick.

As a consumer, she can make the marketplace respond to her needs by refusing to accept shoddy merchandise, service, or marketing techniques, which often assume "she doesn't know any better."

In short, the assertive *woman* is an assertive *person* who exhibits the qualities we espouse throughout this book; and she likes herself — and is liked — better for it!

As this fourth edition is written, only a few months remain for ratification of the Equal Rights Amendment to the Constitution of the United States. How sad it will be for all of us if we turn our backs on this unique opportunity to demonstrate our commitment to the equality our nation stands for in the world.

Imagine the following scene: John's day has been exhausting: he has washed windows, mopped floors, completed three loads of wash, and continuously picked up and cleaned up after the children. He is now working hurriedly in the kitchen preparing for dinner. The children are running in and out of the house banging the door, screaming, throwing toys.

In the midst of this chaos, Mary arrives home from an equally trying day at her office. She offers a cursory "I'm home!" as she passes the kitchen on her way to the family room. Dropping her briefcase and kicking off her shoes, she flops in her favorite chair in front of the television set, calling out, "John, bring me a beer! I've had a helluva day!"

This scene is humorous partly because it seems highly unusual. After all, shouldn't *John* be the breadwinner, working at an office rather than at home? Isn't a man's *place* to go out and conquer the world on behalf of his family? To demonstrate his *man*hood, his *macho*, his strength and courage?

Unfortunately, we have for too long accepted as proper the stereotype of the male as "mighty hunter" who must protect and provide for his family. Indeed, from earliest childhood, the "accepted" male roles have encouraged assertive and often aggressive behavior in pursuit of this "ideal." Competitiveness, achievement, striving to be "the best" are integral components of male child-rearing and formal schooling — much more so than for their sisters.

There are encouraging signs. Increasing numbers of men have begun to reject the aggressive, climbing, "success" stereotype in favor of a more balanced role and lifestyle. Psychological concepts of "masculinity" have changed to acknowledge the caring, nurturing side of men as well. And perhaps most significantly, men have recognized that they can accomplish their own life goals in *assertive* — not aggressive — ways. Professional advancement in all but the most stubbornly competitive (and often dehumanizing) fields is available for the competent, confident, *assertive* man.

Similarly, the assertive man is held in greater esteem in personal relationships. Family and friends are closer and have greater respect for the man who is comfortable enough with himself that he needn't put others down in order to put himself up. The honesty of assertiveness is an incalculable asset in close personal relationships, and assertive men are coming to value such closeness much more than the fleeting rewards of a competitive economic system.

Gail Sheehy's enormously successful book *Passages* (1976) records the recognition, by men who have lived the aggressive style in their 20s and 30s, that those achievements mean little in their later years: The values of personal intimacy, family closeness, and trusted friendships — all fostered by assertiveness, openness, honesty — are the lasting and *important* ones. The assertive man is finding himself too!

Despite these important gains, our society's support of appropriate assertive behavior has been and is inadequate. We must begin to value and reward the assertions of each individual, acknowledging the right of self-expression without fear or guilt, valuing the right to an opinion, and recognizing the unique contribution of each person. We must emphasize the difference between such appropriate *assertion* and the destructive *aggression* with which it is often confused.

In the family, the individual who decides to speak up for his or her rights is often promptly censored: "Don't you dare talk to your mother (father) that way!" "Children are to be seen, not heard." "Never let me hear you say that word again!" Obviously, these common parental commands are not conducive to a child's assertion of self!

Teachers are guilty of anti-assertive behavior in basically the same manner as parents. Quiet, well-behaved children who do not question the system of the school are rewarded, whereas those who "buck the system" in some way are dealt with sternly.

Educators acknowledge that the child's natural spontaneity in learning is conditioned out no later than the fourth or fifth grade, replaced by conformity to the school's approach.

The residue of such upbringing affects our functioning in occupations and daily lives. In the workplace, employees are aware that typically one must not do or say anything that will "rock the boat." The boss is "above," and others who are "below" feel obliged to go along with what is expected of them even if they consider the expectations completely inappropriate. Early work experiences often teach that those who "speak up" are not likely to obtain raises or recognition, and may even lose their jobs. You quickly learn to be a "company person," to keep things running smoothly, to have few ideas of your own, to be careful how you act lest it "get back to the boss." The lesson is clear once again: be nonassertive in your work!

The teachings of many churches seem to indicate that to be assertive is not the "religious" way of life, either. Such qualities as humility, self-denial, and self-sacrifice are usually fostered, to the exclusion of standing up for oneself. There is a mistaken notion that religious ideals of brotherhood/sisterhood must, in some mystical way, be incompatible with feeling good about oneself and with being calm and confident in relationships with others. We believe that being assertive in life is *very* compatible with the teachings of the major religious groups. Your escape from freedom-restricting behavior *allows* you to be of more service to others as well as to yourself. What could be irreligious about that?

Political institutions, while not so likely as the home, school and church to influence early development of assertive behavior, do little to encourage its expression. Political decision-making has come only a short distance from the days of "star chambers," and remains largely inaccessible to the average citizen. Nevertheless, it is still true that the "squeaking wheel gets greased," and when individuals do become expressive enough, governments usually respond. It is our hope that more adequately assertive expression will preclude the necessity of aggressiveness among the activist politically alienated. The growth and successes of such assertive citizen lobbies as Common Cause are powerful evidence: assertion does work!

We contend that *each person has the right to be and to express himself or herself, and to feel good (not guilty) about doing so, as long as he or she does not hurt others in the process.* It is common for a person who has been aggressive to feel some guilt as a result of this behavior. Even the person who acts assertively may experience such guilt, produced by childhood conditioning. The institutions of society have so carefully taught us not to express even reasonable rights, that we may feel bad simply for having stood up for ourselves.

It is not healthy to suffer guilt feelings for being yourself. Yet families, schools, businesses, churches, and governments tend to discourage individual self-assertion; and the anti-assertive influence of these social systems has resulted in a "built-in" set of limits on people's self-fulfilling actions.

Many individuals whose lives were constricted by an inability to be adequately assertive have achieved self-fulfillment by following the assertiveness training program in this book. We believe you can discover similar help in these pages!

Who Will Read This Book?

This book is for all who wish to develop a more enhancing life for themselves, and for those who will facilitate the personal growth of others. Thus, the material is designed for both those who seek to develop their own assertiveness *and* for such "people-helping" professionals as teachers, counselors, and personnel workers in schools and colleges, speech therapists, psychiatrists, psychologists, medical doctors, marriage and family counselors, pastors, social workers, and rehabilitation and employment counselors. Many therapists recommend the book as helpful reading for their clients. For some professionals, this book provides a brief review and an organized approach to methods they already employ in varying degrees, and may serve to increase their effectiveness.

Human resources development and training officers as well as line managers in large industrial or government organizations find ready applications for these concepts and techniques, as do a variety of individuals engaged in community and youth organizations. A more detailed discussion of professional applications of assertiveness training in these and other settings will be found in Part Two.

We wrote with practical application in mind, and the book is organized to facilitate its usefulness in practice. We urge you to become familiar with the concept of assertiveness, recognize its validity in your own experience, and apply its principles in your personal life.

Make the most of what we offer here to help yourself and others, and let us hear from you. Reader feedback and reports of both lay and professional work employing assertiveness training have helped us to refine and update this work through four editions. Well-written, brief reports are also invited for possible publication in *ASSERT*, the bi-monthly "Newsletter of Assertive Behavior and Personal Development." (A sample copy is available at no charge from Impact Publishers Inc., Post Office Box 1094, San Luis Obispo, Calif. 93406).

2

What Is Assertive Behavior?

...There are three possible broad approaches to the conduct of interpersonal relations. The first is to consider one's self only and ride roughshod over others...The second...is always to put others before one's self...The third approach is the golden mean... The individual places himself first, but takes others into account.

—Joseph Wolpe, M.D.

You're beginning to see that assertiveness is not a simple characteristic. Indeed, some have suggested that there is no generalized characteristic of "assertiveness" and that the concept is so complex and has such diverse meaning as to be undefinable! Despite these complexities, we know from the experience of thousands of people that training in assertiveness can be valuable, if training procedures are carefully matched to individual needs.

In this chapter, we will examine several approaches to the concept of "assertiveness." Our brief definition in Chapter 1 offers a starting point:

Assertive behavior enables a person to act in his or her own best interests, to stand up for herself or himself without undue anxiety, to express honest feelings comfortably, or to exercise personal rights without denying the rights of others.

Let's examine the elements of that complex sentence in greater detail:

To act in one's own best interests refers to the ability to make life decisions (career, relationships, life style, time schedule), to take initiative (start conversations, organize activities), to trust one's

13

own judgment, to set goals and work to achieve them, to ask help from others, to participate socially.

To stand up for oneself includes such behaviors as saying "no," setting limits on time and energy, responding to criticism or put-downs or anger, expressing or supporting or defending an opinion.

To express honest feelings comfortably means the ability to disagree, to show anger, to show affection or friendship, to admit fear or anxiety, to express agreement or support, to be spontaneous — all without painful anxiety.

To exercise personal rights relates to competency (as a citizen, as a consumer, as a member of an organization or school or work group, as a participant in public events) to express opinions, to work for change, to respond to violations of one's own rights or those of others.

To not deny the rights of others is to accomplish the above personal expressions without unfair criticism of others, without hurtful behavior toward others, without name-calling, without intimidation, without manipulation, without controlling others.

Thus, assertive behavior is a positive self-affirmation which also values the other people in your life. It contributes both to your personal life satisfaction and to the quality of your relationships with others.

Assertive, Nonassertive, and Aggressive Behavior

Our way of life gives mixed messages about behavior in many areas. A typical example is found in the common attitudes and teachings about human sexuality. Sexual restraint is the norm of the middle-class family, school and church. The popular media, however, bombard audiences with a different view of sexuality. On one hand, girls are expected to be sweet and innocently non-assertive; whereas on the other they are rewarded for being sultry, vampish, and sensual. Sexual aggressiveness, especially in the male, is highly valued: the "lover" is glorified in print and on the screen, and is admired by his peers. Paradoxically, he is cautioned to date "respectable" girls and warned that sexual intercourse is guiltless only after marriage.

Examples of such conflicts between *recommended* and *rewarded* behavior are evident in other areas as well. Even though it is typically understood that one should respect the rights of others, all too often we observe that parents, teachers, and churches contradict these values by their own actions. Tact, diplomacy, politeness, refined manners, modesty, and self-denial are generally praised; yet to "get ahead" it is often acceptable to "step on" others.

The male child is carefully coached to be strong, brave, and dominant. His aggressiveness is condoned and accepted — as in the pride felt by a father whose son gets in trouble for socking the neighborhood bully in the nose. Ironically (and a source of much confusion for the child), the same father will likely encourage his son to "have respect for his elders," "let others go first," and "be polite."

Although it is seldom openly admitted, the athlete who participates in competitive sports knows when he or she has been aggressive or perhaps "bent" the rules a little. That is O.K. because "It's not important how you play the game; it's just important that you win." (Those who would argue with this statement are invited to contrast the rewards for winning coaches with those for losing coaches who "build character.") Woody Hayes, much acclaimed football coach at Ohio State University, is quoted as saying, "Show me a good loser, and I'll show you a loser."

We believe that you should be able to *choose for yourself* how to act in a given circumstance. If your "polite restraint" response is too well developed, you may be unable to make the choice to act as you would like. If your aggressive response is overdeveloped, you may be unable to achieve goals without hurting others. Freedom of choice and self-control are made possible by developing assertive responses for situations which have previously produced nonassertive or aggressive behavior.

Contrasting assertiveness with nonassertive and aggressive actions will help to clarify these concepts. The pattern which appears in Figure 2-A is also demonstrated in each of the examples presented in Chapter 4. The chart displays several feelings and consequences typical for the person (sender) whose actions are

FIGURE 2A

Non-Assertive Behavior	Aggressive Behavior	Assertive Behavior
As Sender	**As Sender**	**As Sender**
Self-denying	Self-enhancing at expense of another	Self-enhancing
Inhibited		Expressive
Hurt, anxious	Expressive	Feels good about self
Allows others to choose	Chooses for others	Chooses for self
Does not achieve desired goal	Achieves desired goal by hurting others	May achieve desired goal
As Receiver	**As Receiver**	**As Receiver**
Guilty or angry	Self-denying	Self-enhancing
Depreciates sender	Hurt, defensive humiliated	Expressive
Achieves desired goal at sender's expense	Does not achieve desired goal	May achieve desired goal

nonassertive, assertive, or aggressive. Also shown, for each of these actions, are the likely consequences for the person toward whom the action is directed (receiver).

As seen in Figure 2-A, a *nonassertive* response means that the sender is typically denying self and is inhibited from expressing actual feelings. People who behave nonassertively often feel hurt and anxious since they allowed others to choose for them. They seldom achieve their own desired goals.

The person who carries a desire for self-expression to the extreme of *aggressive* behavior accomplishes goals at the expense of others. Although frequently self-enhancing and expressive of feelings in the situation, aggressive behavior hurts other people in the process by making choices for them and by minimizing their worth.

Aggressive behavior commonly results in a *putdown* of the receiver. Rights denied, the receiver feels hurt, defensive, and humiliated. His or her goals in the situation, of course, are not achieved. Aggressive behavior may achieve the sender's goals, but may also generate bitterness and frustration which may later return as vengeance.

In contrast, appropriately *assertive* behavior in the same situation would be self-enhancing for the sender, and an honest expression of feelings. Usually, the sender achieves his or her goals. Having *chosen* for oneself how to act, a good feeling typically (not *always*) accompanies the assertive response (even when one's goals are *not* achieved).

Similarly, when the consequences of these three contrasting behaviors are viewed from the perspective of the *receiver* (i.e., the individual toward whom the behavior is directed), a parallel pattern emerges. Nonassertive behavior often produces feelings ranging from sympathy to outright contempt for the sender. Also, the receiver may feel guilt or anger at having achieved goals at the sender's expense. In contrast, assertion enhances feelings of self-worth and permits full expression of oneself. In addition, while the sender achieves his or her goals, the goals of the receiver may also be achieved.

In summary, then, it is clear that the sender is hurt by self-denial in nonassertive behavior; the receiver may be hurt by aggressive behavior. In the case of assertion, neither person is hurt, and it is likely that both will succeed.

It is important to note that assertive behavior is *person-and-situation-specific,* not universal. Although we believe the definitions and examples presented in this book are realistic and appropriate for *most* people and circumstances, individual differences must be considered. Cultural or ethnic background, for example, may create an entirely different set of personal circumstances which would change the nature of "appropriateness" in assertive behavior. In the following section, we'll continue our look at the differences in assertive, nonassertive, and aggressive behavior.

Classifying Behavior

"I told my father-in-law not to smoke his cigar in my house! Was that assertive or aggressive?"

In AT (assertiveness training) groups and workshops, we are often asked to classify a particular act as "assertive" or "aggressive." What criteria *do* make the importance difference?

A good deal of controversy exists over the relative definitions of these concepts. We have suggested that assertive and aggressive behavior differ principally in that the latter involves hurting or stepping on others in the course of expressing oneself. Albert Bandura (1973) notes that aggression is defined by both the *behavior* and the *social labels* applied to it.

Practitioners and writers with a psychoanalytic orientation have proposed that *intent* must be considered. That is, did you intend to *hurt* your father-in-law (aggressive) or to *inform* him of your wishes (assertive)?

In his extensive research on AT, Richard McFall (1978) has followed the assumption that behavior must be measurable according to its *effects*. Thus, if your father gets the assertive message and *responds* accordingly (i.e., by agreeing not to smoke), your behavior may be classified as assertive. If he pouts in a corner, or shouts, "Who do you think you are?", your statement may have been aggressive, as described by this criterion.

Finally, Donald Cheek (1976) has pointed out that the *social-cultural context* must be taken into account in classifying behavior as assertive or aggressive or nonassertive. A culture, for example, which regards honoring one's elders as one of its ultimate values may view the request as clearly out of line and aggressive: regardless of the behavior, response, or intent.

It is clear that there are no absolutes in this area, and that some criteria may be in conflict. A particular act may be at once assertive in *behavior* and *intent* (you wanted to and did express your feelings), aggressive in *response* (the other person could not handle your assertion), and nonassertive in the social *context* (your subculture expects a powerful, put-down style). It may not be possible to reconcile such mutually exclusive classifications.

It should be noted that a specific situation may vary considerably from the "usual case" shown here. In any event, the question "Is it assertive or aggressive?" is not one which may be answered simply!

The issues are complex, and each situation must be evaluated individually. Indeed, the labels "nonassertive," "assertive," and "aggressive" themselves carry no magic, but they may be useful in assessing the *appropriateness* of a particular action. Our concern is not with the *labels*, but with helping you to *choose for yourself* how you will act, and with helping you know that you have the tools you need to succeed.

Ten Key Points About Assertive Behavior

We can synthesize a working definition which includes what *we* believe to be the most important elements. To us, *assertive behavior* is:

1. self-expressive;
2. honest;
3. direct and firm;
4. self-enhancing and relationship-enhancing;
5. respectful of the rights of others;
6. partially composed of the *content* of the message (feelings, rights, facts, opinions, requests, limits);
7. partially composed of the *nonverbal style* of the message (eye contact, voice, posture, facial expression, gestures, distance, timing, fluency, listening);
8. appropriate for the person and the situation, rather than universal;
9. socially responsible;
10. a combination of learned skills, not an inborn trait.

Now you have a better idea of what it means to be "assertive," and you are probably ready to begin taking steps toward increasing your own assertiveness.

The following chapter examines elements 6 and 7 — the "components" of an assertive act — in detail. This is where we begin to look at how behavior can be changed.

3

"I Couldn't Think of What To Say!"

> *It takes two to speak truth—one to speak and another to hear.*
>
> —*Henry David Thoreau*

Many people view assertiveness as a *verbal* behavior, believing that they must have just the right words to handle a situation effectively. It is our experience that the *manner* in which you express an assertive message is a good deal more important than the exact *words* you use. Although popular with many assertiveness trainers, it has never been our style to offer scripts of "what to say when..." We are primarily concerned with encouraging honesty and directness, and much of that message is communicated *nonverbally*.

People in our groups and workshops have enjoyed watching us role-play a scene which makes this point clear: Bob is a dissatisfied customer who wishes to return a defective copy of *Everything You Always Wanted to Know About Assertiveness, But Were Too Timid To Ask* to the bookstore; Mike is the clerk. Using essentially the same words, "I bought this book here last week, and discovered that 20 pages are missing. I'd like a good copy or my money back," Bob approaches Mike in three different ways:

1. Bob walks slowly and hesitatingly to the counter. His eyes are downcast at the floor, he speaks just above a whisper, his face looks as though it belongs on the cover of the book. He has a tight grip on the book, and a "tail-between-the-legs" posture.

2. Bob swaggers toward the counter, glares at Mike, addresses him in a voice heard all over the store. Bob's posture and fist-like gesture are an obvious attempt to intimidate the clerk.

3. Bob walks up to the counter facing Mike. He stands relaxed and erect, smiles, and looks directly at Mike with a friendly expression. In a conversational volume and tone of voice, he states the message, gesturing to point out the flaw.

The three styles are over-exaggerated in our demonstration, of course, but the point is clear. The nonassertive, self-defeating style says to Mike that this customer is a pushover, and the slightest resistance will cause him to give up and go away. The second approach may achieve the goal of refund or exchange, but the aggressive Bob will leave with Mike's hostility directed at his back! With the assertive approach, Bob gets what he came for, and Mike feels good about having helped solve a problem for an appreciative customer.

The Components of Assertive Behavior

Systematic observations of assertive behavior have led behavioral scientists to conclude that there are several important components which contribute to an assertive act. Our thinking in this area was significantly influenced by the late Michael Serber, M.D. (1972). Let us examine the key components of assertive behavior in detail:

Eye Contact: One of the most obvious aspects of behavior when talking to another person is where you look. If you look directly at the person as you speak, it helps to communicate your sincerity and to increase the directness of your message. If you look down or away much of the time, you present a lack of confidence, or a quality of deference to the other person. If you stare too intently, the other person may feel an uncomfortable "invasion."

We do not advocate that you *maximize* eye contact. Continuously looking at someone can make the other person uncomfortable, is inappropriate and unnecessary, and may appear to be a "game." Moreover, eye contact is a cultural variable; many cultural groups limit the amount of eye contact which is acceptable, particularly between age groups or members of the opposite sex. Nevertheless, the importance of eye contact is obvious. A relaxed and steady gaze at the other, looking away occasionally as it is comfortable, helps to make conversation more personal, to show interest in and respect for the other person, and to enhance the directness of your messages.

As is true with other behaviors, eye contact may be improved by conscious effort, in small steps. Be aware of your eyes as you talk with others, and attempt to gradually optimize your eye attention in conversation.

Body Posture. As you watch other people talking with each other, carefully observe how each is standing or sitting. You may be as amazed as we have been by the number of people who talk with someone while their bodies are turned away from that person! Often while sitting side by side (e.g., on an airplane, bus, or train, or on a couch, in a classroom, or at dinner), one may turn only the head toward the other while talking. Next time you are in that situation, notice how much more personal the conversation becomes with a slight turn of the torso — say 30 degrees — toward the other person!

Relative "power" in an encounter may be emphasized by standing or sitting. A particularly evident power imbalance may be seen in the relationship between a tall adult and a small child; the adult who is thoughtful enough to bend or crouch to the child's height will find an observable difference in the quality of communication (and usually a much more responsive child!).

In a situation in which you are called upon to stand up for yourself, it may be useful to do just that — stand up. An active and erect posture, facing the other person directly, lends additional assertiveness to your message. A slumped, passive stance gives the other person an immediate advantage, as does any tendency on your part to lean back or move away.

Distance/Physical Contact: An interesting aspect of cross-cultural research into nonverbal communication is that of distance vs. closeness between people in conversation. As a rough guide, it may be said that, among European peoples, the farther North one goes, the farther apart are found individuals engaged in conversation. In the United States, as in Europe, closeness seems to increase with average annual temperature; but there are important exceptions, notably among ethnic subcultures which value closeness and contact differently.

Closeness is, of course, not universally a function of temperature. Cultural and social customs are products of very complex historical factors. It is fascinating, for example, to contrast the almost obligatory, polite distance present in the queue for a London bus, with the pushing, shoving body contact which is part of the cloakroom scramble at a winter play in Moscow!

In any case, distance from another person does have a considerable effect upon communication. Standing or sitting very closely, or touching, suggests a quality of intimacy in a relationship, unless the people happen to be in a crowd or very cramped quarters. The typical discomfort of elevator passengers is a classic example of the difficulty we have in dealing with closeness! "Coming too close" may offend the other person, make him/her defensive, or open the door to greater intimacy. It is often worthwhile to check out verbally how the other person feels about your closeness or distance (depending, of course, upon your investment in the relationship!).

Gestures: Accentuating your message with appropriate gestures can add emphasis, openness, and warmth. Bob Alberti "traces" his use of gestures in conversation to his Italian heritage. While enthusiastic gesturing is indeed a somewhat culturally-related behavior, a relaxed use of gestures can add depth or power to your messages. Uninhibited movement can also suggest openness, self-confidence (unless the gesturing is erratic and nervous), and spontaneity on the part of the speaker.

Facial Expression: Ever see someone trying to express anger while smiling or laughing? It just doesn't come across. Effective assertions require an expression that agrees with the message. An angry message is clearest when delivered with a straight, non-smiling countenance. A friendly communication should not be delivered with a dark frown. Let your face say the same thing your words are saying!

If you will look at yourself in the mirror, you can learn a great deal about what your face says on your behalf. First, relax all the muscles of your face as much as you can. Let go of your expression, relax the muscles around your mouth, let your jaw go loose, let your cheeks soften, along with the wrinkles of your forehead and around your eyes. Pay careful attention to the relaxed, soft feelings. Now smile, bringing your mouth up as widely as you can. Feel the tightness in your cheeks, around your eyes, all the way up to your ears. Hold that smile, look at the expression in the mirror, and concentrate on the feelings of tightness. Now relax your face completely again. Notice the difference between the relaxed feelings and those of the tight smile, and the difference between the expressions you see in the mirror.

With greater awareness of the feelings in your face, and of how you look when you smile and when you are relaxed, you can begin to more consciously control your facial expression to be congruent with what you are thinking, feeling, or saying. And you may develop a more natural, less "plastic" smile for those times when you really want your happiness to show!

Voice Tone, Inflection, Volume: The way we use our voices is a vital element in our communications. The same words spoken through clenched teeth in anger offer an entirely different message than when they are shouted with joy or whispered in fear.

A level, well modulated, conversational statement is convincing without being intimidating. A whispered monotone will seldom convince another person that you mean business, while a shouted epithet will bring defenses into the path of communication.

Voice is one of the easiest of the components of behavior on which to gain accurate feedback these days. Most everyone has easy access to a small cassette recorder which can be used to "try out" different styles of your voice. You may wish to experiment with a conversational tone, an angry shouted blast, a supportive, caring message, persuasive argument. You may be surprised at how quiet your "shouts" are, or at how loud your "conversational tone" is.

Consider at least three dimensions of your voice: *tone* (is it raspy, whiny, seductively soft, angry?); *inflection* (do you emphasize certain syllables, as in a question, or speak in a monotone, or with "sing-song" effect?); *volume* (do you try to gain attention with a whisper or to overpower others with loudness, or is it very difficult for you to shout even when you want to?).

If you can control and use your voice effectively, you have acquired a powerful tool in your self-expression. Practice with a recorder, trying out different styles until you achieve a style you like. Allow time for changes to come, and use the recorder regularly to check your progress.

Fluency: Mike Serber employed an exercise he called "sell me something," in which he asked the client to talk for thirty seconds persuasively about an object, such as a watch. For many people, it is very difficult to put together a string of words lasting thirty seconds.

A smooth flow of speech is a valuable asset to get your point across in any type of conversation. It is not necessary to talk rapidly for a long period; but if your speech is interrupted with long periods of hesitation, your listeners may get bored, and will probably recognize you are very unsure of yourself. Clear and slow comments are more easily understood and more powerful than rapid speech which is erratic and filled with long pauses and stammering.

Once again, the tape recorder is a valuable tool. Use the machine to practice by talking on a familiar subject for thirty seconds. Then listen to yourself, noticing pauses of three seconds or more and space fillers such as "uhhh..." and "you know..." Repeat the same exercise, more slowly if necessary, trying to eliminate any significant pauses. Gradually increase the difficulty of the task by dealing with less familiar topics, trying to be persuasive, pretending to respond in an argument, or working with a friend to keep a genuine dialog going.

Timing: In general, we advocate spontaneity of expression as a goal. Hesitation may diminish the effectiveness of your assertion, but "he/she who hesitates" is *not* lost! Nevertheless, spontaneous assertion will help keep your life clear, and will help you to focus accurately on the feelings you have at the time.

At times it may be important to *choose an occasion* to discuss a strong feeling. It is not a good idea to confront someone in front of a group, for example, because extra defenses are sure to be present under those conditions. Remember, too, that it is *never too late* to be assertive! Even though the "ideal" moment has passed, you will find it worthwhile to go to the person at a later time and express your feelings. Indeed it is so important that we express feelings constructively that psychologists have developed special techniques to help individuals to work through strong feelings toward those (e.g., parents) who may have died before the feelings could be expressed. More on "too late" assertions in Chapter 14.

Listening: This component is perhaps the most difficult both to describe and to change, yet it may well be the most important of all. Assertive listening involves an active commitment to the other person. It requires your full attention, yet calls for no overt act on your part (although eye contact and certain gestures—such as nodding— can be appropriate elements of listening.) It demonstrates your respect for the other person. It requires that you avoid expressing *yourself* for a time, yet is *not* a nonassertive act. Effective listening may involve the act of giving feedback to the other person, so that it is clear that you understand what was said. Listening is not simply the physical response of hearing sounds— indeed, deaf persons may be excellent "listeners." Rather, assertive listening involves *tuning in* to the other person, *attending* to his/her message, and actively attempting to *understand* it before responding.

We are not yet sure of the full implications of the listening component for the concept of assertiveness. We do know, however, that if we are to be faithful to our commitment that assertiveness includes respect for the rights and feelings of others, our concept must include assertive *receiving*—sensitivity to others—as well as assertive *sending*!

As with the other components of assertive behavior, listening may be trained and developed. It is hard work, takes patience, and requires other people willing to "send" to you. If you truly work at it, you might enjoy yourself so much that you neglect other components! Don't get *that* good at listening, but strengthen your capacity. It will make all of your assertions more effective, and will contribute much to the quality of your relationships!

Thoughts. Another component of assertiveness which escapes direct observation is the thinking process. Although it has long been intuitively understood that attitudes influence behavior, only recently has psychological research been sophisticated enough to deal directly with the link. Because thinking is not directly observable, behavioral psychologists tended to ignore its influence. Albert Ellis (1979, 1980) and Donald Meichenbaum (1977) have been particularly influential in changing our outlook.

Ellis has reduced the process to a simple A-B-C: (A) an event takes place; (b) a person sees and interprets it internally; (C) the person reacts in some way. Part "B" — the perception and thought process — is what we have tended to ignore in the past. More recent developments in the field of "cognitive behavior therapy" have produced specific procedures for developing *assertive* thinking. Thus you can now work on your thoughts as well as your eye contact, posture, etc.

Thinking, of course, is probably the most complex thing we humans do. As you might imagine, procedures for changing our thoughts and attitudes are very complex also. We will discuss this area more in Chapter 7, but for now, consider two aspects of your assertive thinking: your attitudes about whether it is a good idea *in general* for people to be assertive, and your thoughts about *yourself* when you are in a situation which calls for assertive action. Some people, for instance, think it is not a good idea for *anybody* to express themselves. Others say that's okay for *others*, but *I* don't count. If either of these beliefs rings a bell with you, we want you to pay particular attention to Chapter 7 and work on *thinking assertively!*

Content: We save this obvious dimension of assertiveness for last to emphasize that, although *what* you say is clearly important, it is often *less* important than most of us generally believe. We encourage honesty and spontaneity of expression in interpersonal communication. In our view, that means saying forcefully, "I'm damn mad about what you just did!" rather than, "You're an S.O.B.!" People who have for years hesitated because they "didn't know *what* to say" have found the practice of saying *something* to express their feelings *at the time* to be a valuable step toward greater spontaneous assertiveness.

We encourage you to express your own feelings—and to *accept responsibility for them.* Note the difference in the above example between "I'm mad" and "You're an S.O.B." It is not necessary to put the other person down (aggressive) in order to express *your* feeling (assertive).

Your imagination can carry you to a wide variety of situations which demonstrate the importance of the *manner* in which you express your assertions. The time you spend *thinking about* "just the right words" would be better spent *making* those assertions! The ultimate goal is expressing *yourself*, honestly and spontaneously, in a manner "right" for you.

A definition of assertive content is proposed in a paper by Cooley and Hollandsworth (1977). They offer a "components" model for assertive statements, made up of seven elements which are grouped into three general categories. They suggest that *saying "no" or taking a stand* includes stating your position, explaining your reason, and expressing understanding. *Asking favors or asserting rights* may be expressed by stating the problem, making a request, and getting clarification. Finally, *expressing feelings* is accomplished by a statement of your emotions in a situation.

Assertiveness does not depend upon being highly verbal, but if you have difficulty finding the "right words," the Cooley and Hollandsworth model may help you to construct your messages. We have resisted advocating particular formulas or scripts for assertive expression, preferring to encourage you to use your own language, and to recognize that the *style* of your delivery is more important than the words anyway. We recognize that words are not *unimportant* and that many people do stumble over vocabulary. Often, however, we are impressed with how clearly clients tell *us* how they feel about a particular situation, and then ask, "What shall I say to the person?" Our answer is quite direct: "Tell that person what you just told me!"

One further word about content: Donald Cheek (1976) has pointed out the need to adapt assertiveness to the cultural setting in which you find yourself. Particularly for minorities who may find themselves in "survival" situations, he suggests that *what* you say must take into consideration *to whom* you are saying it! Language which would be interpreted as assertive within one's own subculture, for example, could easily be interpreted as aggressive by "outsiders." The experimental work of Richard McFall, noted in Chapter 2, confirms this view, and reinforces the importance of dealing with each person and situation as unique.

We do not advocate that you change yourself to adapt to whatever the situation seems to call for. Nevertheless, all of us *do* deal with individuals differently, depending upon our respective roles and the perceived "power" of others over us. We hope you can be yourself. *Honest expression of yourself* is the best overall guide.

In our experience, it is not usually the content that hangs people up. It is the anxiety, or the lack of confidence, or the belief that "I have no right..." In the next few chapters, we will give you some examples, help you to assess your own assertive strengths and weaknesses, and suggest ways to overcome obstacles to expressing yourself more effectively.

4

Examples of Assertive, Nonassertive
and Aggressive Behavior

*Between people, as among nations, respect of each
other's rights insures the peace.*

—*Benito Juarez*

A look at some everyday situations will improve your understanding of the behavioral styles we've discussed. As you read the
examples in this chapter, you may wish to pause and think about
your own response before reading the alternative responses we
have presented. These examples are oversimplified, of course, so
we can demonstrate the ideas more clearly.

Dining Out

Mr. and Mrs. A are at dinner in a moderately expensive
restaurant. Mr. A has ordered a rare steak; but when the steak is
served, Mr. A finds it to be very well-done. His action is:

Nonassertive: Mr. A grumbles to his wife about the "burned"
meat, and vows that he won't patronize this restaurant in the
future. He says nothing to the waitress, responding "Fine!" to her
inquiry "Is everything all right?" His dinner and evening are
highly unsatisfactory, and he feels guilty for having taken no
action. Mr. A's esimate of himself, and Mrs. A's estimate of him
are both deflated by the experience.

31

Aggressive: Mr. A angrily summons the waitress to his table. He berates her loudly and unfairly for not complying with his order. His actions ridicule the waitress and embarrass Mrs. A. He demands and receives another steak, this one more to his liking. He feels in control of the situation, but Mrs. A's embarrassment creates friction between them and spoils their evening. The waitress is humiliated and angry and loses her poise for the rest of the evening.

Assertive: Mr. A motions the waitress to his table. Noting that he had ordered a rare steak, he shows her the well-done meat. He asks politely but firmly that it be returned to the kitchen and replaced with the rare-cooked steak he originally requested. The waitress apologizes for the error, and shortly returns with a rare steak. The A's enjoy dinner, tip accordingly, and Mr. A feels satisfaction with himself. The waitress is pleased with a satisfied customer and an adequate tip.

Something Borrowed

Helen, an airline flight attendant, is bright, attractive, and a good worker liked by customers and peers. She lives in an apartment with two roommates, in a suite arrangement with six other women—all of whom date quite regularly. One evening, Helen's roommates are dressing for their dates, while Helen is planning a quiet evening preparing for a promotional exam. Roommate Mary says that she is going out with a "really special" young man, and she hopes to make a good impression. She asks Helen if she may borrow and wear a new and quite expensive necklace Helen has just received from her brother who is overseas in military service. Helen and her brother are very close and the necklace means a great deal to her. Her response is:

Nonassertive: She swallows her anxiety about loss or damage to the necklace. Although she feels that its special meaning makes it too personal to lend, she says "Sure!" She denies herself, reinforces Mary for making an unreasonable request, and worries all evening (which makes little contribution to her exam preparation).

Aggressive: Helen is outraged at her friend's request, tells her "Absolutely not!" and upbraids her severely for even daring to ask "such a stupid question." She humiliates Mary and makes a fool of herself too. Later she feels uncomfortable and guilty, which interferes with her work. Mary's hurt feelings show on her date, and she has a miserable time (which puzzles and dismays the young man). Thereafter, the relationship between Helen and Mary becomes very strained.

Assertive: She explains the significance of the necklace to her roommate. Politely but firmly, Helen observes that the request is an unreasonable one since this piece of jewelry is particularly personal. She later feels good for having asserted herself; and Mary, recognizing the validity of Helen's response, makes a big hit with the young man by being more honestly herself.

Have a Joint

Pam is a friendly, outgoing college junior who has been dating Paul, an attractive young man for whom she cares a great deal. One evening, he invites her to attend a small get-together with two other couples, both of whom are married. As everyone becomes acquainted at the party, Pam is enjoying herself. After an hour or so, one of the new friends brings out a small bag of marijuana, and a package of cigarette papers. He suggests that they all smoke, and everyone eagerly joins in except Pam. She does not wish to experiment with marijuana, and she is in conflict because Paul is smoking. As he offers her the "joint" she decides to be:

Nonassertive: She accepts the marijuana and pretends to have smoked it before. She carefully watches the others to see how they smoke. Inside, she dreads the possibility they may ask her to smoke more. As the others speak of getting "stoned," Pam is worried about what her friend is thinking about her. She has denied herself, been dishonest with Paul, and feels remorseful for giving in to something she did not wish to do.

Aggressive: Pam is visibly upset when offered the marijuana and blasts Paul for bringing her to a party of this "low type." She demands to be taken home right away. When the others at the party say that she does not have to smoke if she doesn't wish to, she is not appeased. As she continues to behave indignantly, Paul is humiliated, embarrassed before his friends, and disappointed in her. Although he remains cordial toward Pam as he takes her home, he does not ask her out again.

Assertive: Pam does not accept the cigarette, replying simply, "No, thank you. I don't care for it." She goes on to explain that she hasn't smoked pot before and doesn't wish to. She expresses her preference that the others not smoke, but acknowledges their right to make their own choices.

The Heavyweight

Mr. and Mrs. B, married nine years, have been having marital problems recently because he insists that she is overweight and needs to reduce. He brings the subject up continually, pointing out that she is no longer the woman he married (who had been 25 pounds lighter). He keeps telling her that such overweight is bad for her health, that she is a bad example for the children, and so on.

In addition, he teases her about being "chunky," looks longingly at thin women, while commenting how attractive they look, and makes reference to her figure in front of their friends. Mr. B has been acting this way for the past three months and Mrs. B is highly upset. She has been attempting to lose weight for those three months, but with little success. Following Mr. B's most recent rash of criticism, Mrs. B is:

Nonassertive: She apologizes for her overweight, makes feeble excuses, or simply doesn't reply to some of Mr. B's comments. Internally, she feels both hostile toward her husband for his nagging, and guilty about being overweight. Her feelings of anxiety make it even more difficult for her to lose weight and the battle continues.

Aggressive: Mrs. B goes into a long tirade about how her husband isn't any great bargain anymore, either! She brings up the fact that at night he falls asleep on the couch half the time, is a lousy sex partner, and doesn't pay enough attention to her. None of these comments are pertinent to the issue at hand, but Mrs. B continues. She complains that he humiliates her in front of the children and their close friends, and that he acts like a "lecherous old man" by the way he eyes the sexy women. In her anger, she succeeds only in wounding Mr. B and driving a wedge between them by "defending" herself with a counterattack on him.

Assertive: Approaching her husband when they are alone and will not be interrupted, Mrs. B says that she feels that Mr. B is right about her need to lose weight, but she does not like the way he keeps after her about the problem. She points out that she is doing her best and is having a difficult time losing the weight and maintaining the loss. He admits that his harping is ineffective, and together they work out a plan in which he will systematically reinforce her for her efforts to lose weight.

The Neighbor Kid

Mr. and Mrs. E have a two-year-old boy and a baby girl, two months old. Over the last several nights, their neighbor's son, who is 17, has been sitting in his own driveway in his car with his stereo tape player blaring loudly. He begins just about the time the E's two young children go to bed on the side of the house where the boy plays the music. The E's have found it impossible to get the children to bed until the music stops. Mr. and Mrs. E are both disturbed and decide to be:

Nonassertive: Mr. and Mrs. E move the children into their own bedroom on the other side of the house, wait until the music stops (around 1 a.m.), then transfer the children back to their own rooms. Then they go to bed much past their own usual bedtime. They continue to quietly curse the teenager and soon become alienated from their neighbors.

Aggressive: Mr. and Mrs. E call the police and protest that "one of those wild teenagers" next-door is creating a disturbance. They demand that the police "do their duty" and stop the noise at once. The police do talk with the boy and his parents, who become very angry as a result of their embarrassment about the police visit. They denounce the E's for reporting to the police without speaking to them first, and resolve to have nothing further to do with them.

Assertive: Mr. and Mrs. E go over to the boy's house and tell him that his stereo is keeping the children awake at night. They ask what arrangement they could work out concerning the music so that it would not disturb their children's sleep. The boy reluctantly agrees to set a lower volume during the late hours, but he appreciates the E's cooperative attitude. Both parties feel good about the outcome, and agree to follow up a week later to be sure it is working as agreed.

The Loser

Russell is a 22-year-old college dropout who works in a plastics factory. He lives alone in a small one-room, walk-up apartment. Russell has had no dates for the past fourteen months. He left college after a series of depressing events—academic failures, a "Dear John" letter, and some painful harassment by other students in his residence hall. He has been in jail overnight for drunkenness on two recent occasions. Yesterday, he received a letter from his mother inquiring about his well-being, but primarily devoted to a discussion of his brother's recent successes. Today, his supervisor berated him harshly and somewhat unjustly for a mistake which was actually the supervisor's own fault. A secretary at the plant turned down his invitation to dinner.When he arrived at his apartment that evening, feeling particularly depressed and overwrought, his landlord met him at the door with a tirade about "drunken bums" and a demand (one week early) that this month's rent be paid on time. Russell's response is:

Nonassertive: He takes on himself the burden of the landlord's attack, feeling added guilt and even greater depression. A sense of helplessness overcomes him. He wonders how his brother can be so successful while he considers himself so worthless. The secretary's rejection and the boss' criticism strengthen his conviction that he is "no damn good." Deciding the world would be a better place without him, he finds the small revolver he has been hiding in his room, and begins loading it for the purpose of committing suicide.

Aggressive: The landlord has added the final straw to Russell's burden. He becomes extremely angry and pushes the landlord out of the way in order to get into his room. Once alone, he resolves to "get" the people who have been making his life so miserable recently: the supervisor, the secretary, the landlord, and possibly others as well. He finds his revolver and begins loading it with the intent of going out after dark to hurt the people who have hurt him.

Assertive: Russell responds firmly to the landlord, noting that he has paid his rent regularly, and that it is not due for another week. He reminds the landlord of a broken rail on the stairway and the plumbing repairs which were to have been accomplished weeks earlier. The following morning, after giving his life situation a great deal of thought, Russell calls the local mental health clinic to ask for help. At work, he approaches the supervisor calmly and explains the circumstances surrounding the mistake. Though somewhat defensive, the supervisor acknowledges her error and apologizes for her aggressive behavior.

Recognizing Your Own Nonassertive and Aggressive Behavior

The examples given in this chapter help to point out what "assertiveness" means in everyday events. Perhaps some of the situations "rang a bell" in your own life. Take a few minutes to honestly listen to yourself describe your relationships with others who are important to you. Carefully examine your contacts with parents, peers, co-workers, classmates, spouse, children, bosses, employees, teachers, salespeople, neighbors, relatives. Who is dominant in these relationships? Are you easily taken advantage of in dealings with others? Do you express your feelings and ideas openly in most circumstances? Do you take advantage of others or hurt others frequently?

Your responses to such questions provide hints which may lead you to explore in greater depth your assertive, nonassertive or aggressive behavior. We think you will find such self-examination rewarding, and a very important step on your journey toward increased interpersonal effectiveness.

Chapter 5 offers a systematic procedure for determining your own strengths and shortcomings in assertiveness, and will help you to plan your own course of action.

Measuring Your Assertiveness

*Never play another person's game. Play your
own.*

—*Andrew Salter*

What do you know about your own assertiveness? Certainly
you have observed reactions that give clues: Aunt Jane says,
"You're sassy!"; the boss indicates you should be more forceful
with customers. Or perhaps the children believe you need to "tell
off" the mechanic. Maybe you have tried to speak up to the clerk
and he or she looked hurt.

While everyday comments and reactions such as these are
helpful indications of your progress in assertiveness, it is
important to be more thorough and systematic in observing
yourself.

Take a few minutes right now to respond to the
"Assertiveness Inventory" given on the next two pages. Be honest
with yourself! After you complete the Inventory, read on for the
discussion of results and some specific steps to follow to make the
results practical. The Inventory is not a "psychological test," so
just relax and enjoy this brief exploration of your ability to express
yourself appropriately.

The Assertiveness Inventory

The following questions will be helpful in assessing your assertiveness. Be honest in your responses. All you have to do is draw a circle around the number that describes you best. For some questions the assertive end of the scale is at 0, for others at 4. Key: 0 means **no** or **never;** 1 means **somewhat** or **sometimes;** 2 means **average;** 3 means **usually** or **a good deal;** and 4 means **practically always** or **entirely.**

1. When a person is highly unfair, do you call it to attention? 0   1   2   3   4
2. Do you find it difficult to make decisions? 0   1   2   3   4
3. Are you openly critical of others ideas, opinions, behavior? 0   1   2   3   4
4. Do you speak out in protest when someone takes your place in line? 0   1   2   3   4
5. Do you often avoid people or situations for fear of embarassment? 0   1   2   3   4
6. Do you usually have confidence in your own judgment? 0   1   2   3   4
7. Do you insist that your spouse or roommate take on a fair share of household chores? 0   1   2   3   4
8. Are you prone to "fly off the handle?" 0   1   2   3   4
9. When a salesman makes an effort, do you find it hard to say "No" even though the merchandise is not really what you want? 0   1   2   3   4
10. When a latecomer is waited on before you are, do you call attention to the situation? 0   1   2   3   4
11. Are you reluctant to speak up in a discussion or debate? 0   1   2   3   4
12. If a person has borrowed money (or a book, garment, thing of value) and is overdue in returning it, do you mention it? 0   1   2   3   4
13. Do you continue to pursue an argument after the other person has had enough? 0   1   2   3   4
14. Do you generally express what you feel? 0   1   2   3   4
15. Are you disturbed if someone watches you at work? 0   1   2   3   4

We find most readers and assertiveness trainees have some common reactions when they complete the Inventory. Typical comments include:

"I hate tests!"

"The questions are easy to figure out, I could have cheated."

"I didn't feel well when I took it."

Unfortunately, you can't talk to the questions: "What does that mean?"; "It depends on the situation"; "Some days I feel moody

16. If someone keeps kicking or bumping your chair in a
    movie or a lecture, do you ask the person to stop?.........0 1 2 3 4
17. Do you find it difficult to keep eye contact when
    talking to another person?.............................0 1 2 3 4
18. In a good restaurant, when your meal is improperly
    prepared or served, do you ask the waiter/waitress
    to correct the situation?...............................0 1 2 3 4
19. When you discover merchandise is faulty, do you
    return it for an adjustment?............................0 1 2 3 4
20. Do you show your anger by name-calling or
    obscenities?...0 1 2 3 4
21. Do you try to be a wallflower or a piece of the furniture
    in social situations?..................................0 1 2 3 4
22. Do you insist that your property manager (mechanic,
    repairman, etc.) make repairs, adjustments or
    replacements which are his/her responsibility?.............0 1 2 3 4
23. Do you often step in and make decisions for others?.......0 1 2 3 4
24. Are you able openly to express love and affection?........0 1 2 3 4
25. Are you able to ask your friends for small favors or
    help?...0 1 2 3 4
26. Do you think you always have the right answer?...........0 1 2 3 4
27. When you differ with a person you respect, are you able
    to speak up for your own viewpoint?.....................0 1 2 3 4
28. Are you able to refuse unreasonable requests made
    by friends?...0 1 2 3 4
29. Do you have difficulty complimenting or praising
    others?...0 1 2 3 4
30. If you are disturbed by someone smoking near you,
    can you say so?.......................................0 1 2 3 4
31. Do you shout or use bullying tactics to get others to
    do as you wish?.......................................0 1 2 3 4
32. Do you finish other people's sentences for them?.........0 1 2 3 4
33. Do you get into physical fights with others, especially
    with strangers?.......................................0 1 2 3 4
34. At family meals, do you control the conversation?.........0 1 2 3 4
35. When you meet a stranger, are you the first to introduce
    yourself and begin a conversation?.....................0 1 2 3 4

and find it hard to be assertive." Also, such an inventory is necessarily general. You may have found that some items don't apply to your life. Nevertheless, if you took the time to answer relevant questions honestly, the Inventory can be a great help to your growth in assertiveness.

There are two primary ways to analyze your results. First, you could add up your total score. *Don't!* It really has no meaning. Instead, take the second approach: Examine the response you gave to *each individual question.*

Because the Inventory is not a standardized psychological

test (not enough studies have been conducted to evaluated it thoroughly), a "total score" approach is not appropriate. A question-by-question analysis is quite valuable.

An even more important reason we discourage a "total assertiveness score" approach is that there really is no such thing as a *general* quality of assertiveness. As you will recall from earlier chapters, and as you have no doubt experienced in your own life, assertiveness is *person-and-situation specific*. Look at individual events in your life, involving particular people or groups, and consider your strengths and shortcomings accordingly.

Here are some suggestions for further analysis:

Step 1. Look at your responses to questions 1, 2, 4, 5, 6, 7, 9, 10, 11, 12, 14, 15, 16, 17, 18, 19, 21, 22, 24, 25, 27, 28, 30, and 35. These questions are oriented toward *nonassertive* behavior. Do your answers to many of these items tell you that you are rarely speaking up for yourself? Or are there perhaps some specific situations which give you trouble?

Step 2. Look at your responses to questions 3, 8, 13, 20, 23, 26, 29, 31, 32, 33, and 34. These questions are oriented toward *aggressive* behavior. Do your answers to many of these questions suggest you are pushing others around more than you realized?

Step 3. You may examine your *assertive* responses by noting how often you answered 3 or 4 to Step 1 questions and 0 or 1 to Step 2 questions. In short, it is assertive to "usually" take the action described in Step 1 items, and to rarely do those things described in Step 2 items.

What most people find out from completing the first three steps is that assertiveness is *situational.* No one is nonassertive *all* the time, aggressive *all* the time, assertive *all* the time! Each person behaves in each of the three ways at various times, depending upon the situation. It is possible that you have a *characteristic style* that leans heavily in one direction. You may discover your "Achilles Heel," and by so doing, begin the necessary change process. The next step will add further clarification.

Step 4. Re-read each question on the Inventory and write out a statement which exands on your feelings about the item. An example:

Question 1. When a person is highly unfair, do you call it to attention?

> (a) My response - 0

> (b) Statement - I'm afraid that if I said anything the person would become very upset.

Step 5. Go over all of the information you have generated from Steps 1 through 4 and begin drawing several conclusions.

Look closely at four aspects of the information:

...What *situations* give you trouble? And which can you handle easily?

...What are your *attitudes* about expressing yourself? Does it generally feel "right" to you?

...What *obstacles* are in the way of your assertions? Are you frightened of the consequences? Do other people in your life make it especially difficult?

...Are your *behavior skills* up to the job? Can you be expressive when you need to?

A careful examination of these four areas may help you to see where to begin your assertiveness training program.

6

Your Assertiveness Log

*A man who trims himself to suit everybody will
soon whittle himself away.*

—*Charles M. Schwab*

As a nautical device, a log is used as a daily record of a
ship's speed and progress. Much the same could be said for the
components of an assertiveness log! Although we are not overly
concerned with the speed of your change, we are definitely
interested in your progress.

The Assertiveness Inventory you have just completed gives a
good picture of where you are *now*. A log will add a *future
dimension*. A daily record of your assertiveness helps you judge
your progress over time, and provides a wealth of information
about your ongoing assertiveness.

We urge you to obtain a special notebook in which to record
your progress. Your log entries can include a systematic examination of yourself on four separate dimensions: *situations,
attitudes, behaviors,* and *obstacles.*

A sample page of your log might look like this:

ASSERTIVENESS LOG FOR   19

Situations

Attitudes

Behaviors

Obstacles

Progress/Problems/Comments

Used in this way, your log can become a very important tool for your growth program—helping your self-assessment, recording your progress, and serving as a "motivator" to continue working on your personal development.

Here are some ideas which may help you to be thorough in your self-assessment:

Situation assessment may be conducted by referring to the Assertiveness Inventory, determining those situations and persons which you can handle effectively and those which are troublesome. Write down the results in the log. Pay particular attention to any *patterns* which may appear. Are you more adequate with strangers than with intimates, for example (or perhaps vice versa)? Can you readily stand up for your rights, but fall down on expressing affection? Do such factors as age, sex, or roles of the other person make a difference?

Attitude assessment has plagued behavioral scientists for decades. It is very difficult to accurately measure *any* attitudes, and particularly difficult to be "objective" about one's own. Nevertheless, we encourage you to approach this task by simply writing down in your log how you feel about *your right* to behave assertively. Look at the various situations and people noted in each of the five categories of the definition of assertive behavior (Chapter 2), and in the situations described in the Assertiveness Inventory. Determine how you feel about whether it's even *okay*, for example, to respond to criticism.

Behavior assessment is not so difficult, but may take longer. In Chapter 3, we described in detail several "components" of behavior which are key to any assertive act. If you monitor your own behavior carefully for a time (a week or more is a good idea), and record your observations regularly in your log, you will have a good idea of your own effectiveness with eye contact, body posture, and the other components noted there. It will probably help if you make it a point to watch some other people whom you consider effectively assertive, and to note in your log some of their behavioral qualities as well.

Obstacle assessment may be the easiest area for you to complete. We know that most people *want* to act assertively. However, for many, there are barriers which seem to make assertion difficult. Common obstacles: *anxiety* (fear of the possible consequences: maybe the other person won't like me, or will hit me, or will think I'm crazy, or maybe I'll make a fool of myself, or maybe I'll fail to get what I want, or maybe I can't put my finger on it, but I just feel anxious!); *lack of skills* (I don't know how to meet girls. What do I do to express a political opinion? I never learned how to show affection.); and *other people in your life* (parents, friends, lovers, roommates, and others have an interest in making it difficult for you to change, even if they *believe* they want you to be more assertive). Record in your log those obstacles which you think are making assertiveness more difficult for you.

If you will take the time and effort to proceed carefully and thoroughly with your self-assessment, you will find that the results will pinpoint quite specifically what you will need to do to increase your assertiveness. At every point, of course, you have the choice of whether to carry this personal growth project further, and of what direction you will take. And *choice* is the key element in your assertiveness anyway!

After you have kept your log or journal for a week, carefully examine the four entries: situations, attitudes, behaviors, obstacles. Look for patterns. Assess your particular strengths as well as your weaknesses.

If you have complex and severe shortcomings in the four dimensions you have evaluated, it is possible that you will need professional assistance in reaching your goal. Particularly for those individuals with very high levels of anxiety about being assertive, we suggest contact with a qualified counselor, psychologist, psychiatrist, or other therapist. Your local community mental health center and/or college/university counseling center can assist you in finding someone to help. Also, Appendix B identifies standards which will help you to evaluate a professional therapist.

The first week or two of entries in your journal should give you a pretty good picture of how you are doing now, and provide a basis for setting goals for yourself.

Your results, for example, might indicate that you have difficulty with people in authority—that you do not believe you have a right to speak up to them, that you cannot maintain good eye contact with them, and that you are very anxious around such people. Each of these items is something you can work on individually and overcome through the process of assertiveness training described in this book.

As you proceed, *keep using your log* to keep a careful record of how you're doing. It will provide a series of "bench marks" so you can watch yourself grow. It will help motivate you to work at your progress. It will allow you to be more systematic about your work on assertiveness. And that can make all the difference!

7

Don't Let Your Thoughts Stop You!

> *If a person continues to see only giants, it means he is still looking at the world through the eyes of a child.*
>
> *—Anais Nin*

"O.K.," you say, "maybe I'm not as assertive as I'd like to be. You can't teach an old dog new tricks. That's just the way I am. I can't change it."

We don't agree. Thousands of people have found that becoming more assertive is a *learning* process, and that it *was* possible for them to change. Sometimes it takes longer for an "old dog." But, the rewards are great, and the process not really that difficult.

Right *thinking* about assertiveness is crucial. Inner thoughts, beliefs, attitudes, feelings—these set the stage for outward behavior. Your mind needs to be uncluttered and free to respond to each new assertive situation. Old entrenched faulty attitudes, feelings, beliefs, and thoughts hold you back, stop your natural flow. "You are what you think" supercedes "you are what you eat" in importance! Your mind will be a great powerhouse and help generate assertiveness if you will work to rid yourself of counterproductive thinking!

In this chapter, you will find some "pep talks" about ways to look at your thinking process in relation to assertiveness. Consider what is said here carefully. We want to challenge some of your closely held beliefs about how you operate in life.

Your Attitude Toward Assertive Growing

Assertive growing only takes place when you are willing to start. Worrying about life does no good. You must begin by taking an *action* step. Decide where you wish to start, and proceed.

You may be able to "see yourself" in one of the descriptions of other people we have given earlier, or those which appear later in this book. Your Assertiveness Inventory and Log results may be motivating you to change.

One implication of assertion recurs time and again: self-denying behavior subtly reinforces another's bad or unwanted behavior. Two examples help to make this point clear.

Diane, a married woman of 35, had a husband who wanted sexual intercourse every evening. At times, she would clearly be tired from the day's activities. However, whenever she refused him, her husband would begin to pout and feel hurt, carrying on until she finally "felt sorry" for him and gave in. This sequence was a consistent pattern in their marriage—the more Diane would not give in, the more he would pout until she did so. Of course, by eventually giving in, she promptly reinforced all of his pouting, not to mention the reinforcement value of his sexual gratification! Diane was thus *teaching* her husband that he could have what he wanted if he would pout.

A college student, Wendy, age 20, was living off-campus in a cheap habitat with two roommates. By living together, they cut expenses and saved a good deal of money. Wendy and her roommates had a reputation for being "anti-establishment." Word of her behavior and living conditions got back to her parents, who then confronted her with a long tirade about the younger generation, respect for authority, her mother's health, being disgraceful, and so on. This happened on several occasions. Each time Wendy would eventually get upset and either ask what she could do to help ease things or simply give in to some of their demands.

Here again, by getting upset and giving in, Wendy *taught them* how to have these tirades against her.

Although it may be more difficult to admit the negative consequences of aggressive actions, it is not hard to see how others react to a denial of their rights. The aggressor feels the pain of alienation which this behavior brings about. If you are seeking help, you may admit to yourself your concern and guilt for the hurt you cause others, and you may acknowledge that you simply do not know how to gain your goals nonaggressively. At this point, you could be an excellent candidate for assertiveness training.

One individual of this type was "reached" in a therapy group setting. After considerable time had been spent listening to Jerry's loud dominance over the group, several members took him to task. Although he was a large, rugged man, Jerry soon reacted to this *caring but confronting* response from the others and began to cry. He confessed that he had developed this facade of bravado to protect himself from the closeness which he feared. He really considered himself to be quite an inadequate person, and had used the "strong man" mask to keep others at a distance. The group responded to Jerry's need for others to care for him and later helped him to learn appropriate assertive responses to replace his previously gruff behavior.

Members of our assertive behavior groups have observed how much *attitudes* can change as a result of taking part in the group. The group provides support for acting assertively, expressing oneself and standing up for rights. For some group members, the group's support and encourgement of assertiveness are as important as the opportunity for practice which the group also affords. Throughout life, many of them have experienced people in authority (parents, teachers, even peers) saying, "You have *no right...*" Now, a group of people, including some psychologists, are saying, "You have a *perfect right....*" Thus, a key part of our message to you is that it is *good*, it is *right*, it is *okay* to assert yourself!

Your Attitude Toward Yourself

Take a look at your *good* feelings toward yourself. Can you

A Behavioral Model for Personal Growth

Dr. Carl Rogers, in his 1961 book **On Becoming A Person,** has identified three characteristics of personal growth. These lend themselves to use as models in the process of developing personal growth. The checklist has been developed by Dr. Alberti, based upon Rogerian phrases:

"An Increasing Openness to Experience"

How recently have you
- participated in a new sport or game?
- changed your views on an important (political, personal, professional) issue?
- tried a new hobby or craft?
- taken a course in a new field?
- studied a new language or culture?
- spent fifteen minutes or more paying attention to your body feelings, senses (relaxation, tension, sensuality)?
- listened for fifteen minutes or more to a religious, political, professional, or personal viewpoint with which you disagreed?
- tasted a new food, smelled a new odor, listened to a new sound?
- allowed yourself to cry? or to say "I care about you"? or to laugh until you cried? or to scream at the top of your lung capacity? or to admit you were afraid?
- watched the sun (or moon) rise or set? or a bird soar on the wind's currents? or a flower open to the sun?
- traveled to a place you had never been before?
- made a new friend? or cultivated an old friendship?
- spent an hour or more really communicating (actively listening and responding honestly) with a person of a different cultural or racial background?
- taken a "fantasy trip"—allowing your imagination to run freely for ten minutes to an hour or more?

"Increasingly Existential Living"

How recently have you
- done something you felt like doing at that moment, without regard for the consequences?
- stopped to "listen" to what was going on inside you?
- spontaneously expressed a feeling—anger, joy, fear, sadness, caring—without "thinking about it"?
- done what you wanted to, instead of what you thought you "should" do?
- allowed yourself to spend time or money on an immediate "payoff" rather than saving for tomorrow?
- bought something you wanted "on impulse"?
- done something no one (including you) expected you to do?

"An Increasing Trust in One's Organism"

How recently have you
- done what felt right to you, against the advice of others?
- allowed yourself to experiment creatively with new approaches to old problems?
- expressed an unpopular opinion assertively in the face of majority opposition?
- used your own intellectual reasoning ability to work out a solution to a difficult problem?
- made a decision and acted upon it right away?
- acknowledged by your actions that you can direct your own life?
- cared enough about yourself to get a physical exam (within a year)?
- told others of your religious faith, or philosophy of life?
- assumed a position of leadership in your profession, or an organization, or your community?
- asserted your feelings when you were treated unfairly?
- risked sharing your personal feelings with another person?
- designed and/or built something on your own?
- admitted you were wrong?

give expression to the feeling of elation which accompanies the achievement of a highly valued personal goal? Do you allow yourself the pleasure of feeling satisfied with a job well done? Of making someone else happy? Of congratulating yourself?

Read over "A Behavioral Model for Personal Growth." How are you treating yourself? Can you honestly answer those questions and say you are behaving in a caring, loving way toward yourself? Care enough for yourself to *believe* you can, then *do it.* In therapy, we temporarily overcome a lack of self-love by *authorizing* the assertive behavior. The result of the "authorized" action is an enhanced concept of self-worth, which is the beginning of a positive turn in the attitude-behavior-feedback-attitude cycle. Encouragement from a professional therapist enables a person to begin acting more assertively. *You* can achieve the same results on your own or with a minimum of help by following the procedures we have described.

Are Some More Equal Than Others?

One of our most important goals for this book is to help you feel *equal* to others on a personal level. True, there will always be someone more talented, more assertive, more beautiful. But you are just as good as anyone else *as a human being.* You have rights *just because you are a person*!

No one has a right to take advantage of another on a human-to-human level. For instance, an employer has no right to take advantage of an employee's rights to courtesy and respect as a human being. A doctor does not have the right to be discourteous or unfair in dealing with a patient or nurse. A lawyer should not feel she or he can "talk down" to a laborer. Each person has a perfect right to express opinions even though he or she may "only have a grade school education" or be "from the wrong side of the tracks" or be "just a secretary."

All people are indeed created equal on a human-to-human plane and deserve the privilege of expressing their inborn rights. There is so much more to be gained from life by being free and able to stand up for oneself, and from honoring the same right for others! By being assertive, one is actually learning to give and take more equally with others, and to be of more service to self and others.

Try to avoid the viewpoint of "one-down" or "one-up." Approach others with respect, treat them with dignity.

Avoid the extreme of behaving too politely, sweetly, agreeably. Let the other person share mutually in the interaction. No one is *above* you on the person-to-person level.

The person you approach assertively is not the enemy! There is no need to be a crusader, no need to "set others straight." Some use "assertiveness" as a weapon, assuming the "right" to teach others a lesson. There is no such right. Deal with the issue at hand while treating each person with respect. No one is *below* you on the person-to-person level.

Difficult, isn't it? Being *just equal* is the hardest part of all because that attitude sets the stage for our interactions.

We can hear you say, "As Rodney Dangerfield says, 'I don't get no respect!' " Others react to you depending upon the way you "come across." Respond assertively, with self-respect, and you will be treated that way in return. *Almost* always.

An excellent way to foster equality is to begin translating your thoughts into assertive verbal messages. Reading someone else's mind generally leads to trouble. *Assuming* that others know how you feel often leads to disappointment. Make your nonverbal messages or ideas into verbal ones. Facial expressions are fine, but more likely to be understood when accompanied with words. Yawning, twiddling your thumbs, placing hands on hips are all effective gestures, but they communicate clearly only if you *speak out* at the same time.

Complaining to yourself is a sure sign that you have not spoken up enough about your feelings. Most of us don't want others to use guesswork or to harbor unkind thoughts. It is best to use words. Unwillingness to be verbal hurts both parties. There are limits, of course, and time to let it go. But if it matters enough to upset you for more than a moment, you'd better speak up!

The goal of assertiveness is to foster mutual communication if at all possible. If your feelings are still not "clear" after dealing with someone verbally, but you are satisfied that you have done all you can, stop. Keep your mind free and clear—let go. There is no use letting your thoughts continue to put the other person down.

Larry thought he had a quick answer to that: "Yes, but I'll bet I could get him to respond by saying something to shock the devil out of him!" Obviously, this tactic can work; Larry would probably get a response! However, we believe that you lose more than you gain that way. We do not advocate manipulation, gamesmanship, or one-upmanship. These styles of behavior violate the ideals of assertiveness. If no resolution can be reached, perhaps the best course is to keep quiet externally, and work out your own feelings within yourself, perhaps with the help of a friend or therapist.

Helpful Aids for Handling Thoughts

Three excellent "cognitive-behavioral" methods have been developed for dealing with your thinking patterns: stress inoculation, thought-stopping, and positive self-statements.

Stress Inoculation: This type of "inoculation" not only minimizes expected stress, it can also be used on the spot to deal with stress. (Donald Meichenbaum [1977] gets credit for this one.)

Assume you have a situation coming up which you know will be stressful, such as a job performance evaluation interview. Your supervisor tends to be a fast talker and not a good listener. In the past, you have become very uptight and upset.

To inoculate yourself this time, start by writing yourself a message about the situation beforehand. Speak to yourself as a wise counselor would. Here is a sample message:

"When you have your performance evaluation, relax. Don't let yourself be thrown off. It does no good to get upset. Remember your supervisor's style, and be ready for it. When your supervisor says something you question, be firm but polite in asking about it. Ask for time to consider further. Speak up about information the supervisor is forgetting. You can handle it. Take a deep breath once in a while. You'll be fine. If surprises come, just roll with them. This is only one small event in your total life."

Once you have a tailor-made message, read it aloud several

times before the actual situation arises. Read it especially when you start worrying excessively or when you feel undue anxiety.

Remember the essence of the message so you can repeat key portions silently during the actual event (e.g., interview). If you find yourself slipping back in confidence, listen within yourself for the key parts.

One of our clients used this method successfully with her estranged husband. They were to meet in court and she knew she would "fall apart" and perhaps ruin her chances for a fair settlement. She developed her stress inoculation message and practiced it often. Upon entering the courtroom, her husband came up and said "Hi." She immediately broke into tears and ran to the bathroom! While there, she re-read her message aloud several times, gained her confidence and "sailed through " both talking to him again and the subsequent proceedings. Afterwards, she was amazed that it worked! In the past, she would have continued to be upset and cry. Her stress inoculation helped pull her through.

Thought Stopping: Have you ever had an annoying tune or thought continually "run through your head?" Nothing you do seems to work to stop it. Such a case is the time to try "thought stopping," another method developed by Joseph Wolpe. Close your eyes right now and conjure up some recurring thought that bothers you. When it comes in clearly, yell "STOP!" out loud. (Make sure no one is nearby or they may think you a bit weird!) Your thoughts *will* actually stop. When they do, shift immediately to a pleasant thought to replace the unwanted one. The unwanted thought will typically return in short order, but if you will persistently repeat the procedure, it will be longer and longer before the offender sneaks back in. Soon, the unwanted thought will give up. No, you don't have to run around yelling "STOP!" continually! The technique works just as effectively when done silently in your head. Of course, you may still want to yell it out loud once in a while because it is so much fun!

One warning: Be careful that the unwanted thoughts are not actually carrying constructive messages that you're not catching on to. You need to pay attention to *some* unpleasant thoughts and act upon them! With practice and trial and error, however, the difference between good and not-so-good thoughts will become apparent.

Positive Self-Statements: "The hardest step for most people I know," commented high school counselor Gail Wainwright at an AT group meeting, "is to *be assertive with yourself:* to convince *yourself* to go ahead and take the action you know is needed!" If your thoughts are filled with self-denying "rules" and "attitudes," your behavior will in all likelihood be similar. You may think in negative statements: "I'm not important." "My opinions don't count." "No one will be interested in what I have to say." "I'll probably make a fool of myself if I say anything." "I'm really not sure." "I have no right to say that." If so, chances are very good you will act accordingly—that is, you'll keep quiet and let others control the situation!

Try, for a short period of time, to allow yourself to say the *positive* form of those statements: "I am important." "My opinions count." "Someone will be interested in what I have to say." "I have a right to say that." You needn't *act* on any of these at this point, just "get the feel" of saying positive things to yourself. The "positive self-statements" procedure simply consists of developing complimentary statements about yourself that you memorize and repeat regularly. The purpose is to build self-confidence. Examples:

I am respected and admired by my friends.
I am a kind and loving person.
I have a job.
I handle anger well.
I got through school successfully.
I am firm when the situation calls for it.

Some of the statements you choose may not be totally true of you, but we want you to "fudge" a little at first. Then proceed "as if" they were true. Place these statements on the refrigerator, on the bathroom wall, in your purse or wallet. Regularly remind yourself that you are a positive and valuable person.

Positive self-statements can be used as replacement thoughts in conjunction with thought stopping. Or, they can be part of your stress inoculation message.

After you have practiced the positive thoughts for a while, you may wish to begin—still in your own thoughts—to consider the ways you would act in those situations if you followed through on the thoughts. Perhaps, for example, you were thinking, "Someone will be interested in what I have to say," in regard to joining in on a group discussion. If you were to imagine *acting* on that thought, you might see yourself asking a question of one of the more out-spoken participants. Or, maybe you could just start out by saying, "I agree." Think about ways you could *act* like a person who *thinks* positively!

Stop Imagining the Worst!

Too often people do not respond assertively because they have conjured up dire consequences: "If I do this, she'll be mad;" "I could never say that because he'd fire me;" "I'll feel guilty;" "She'll divorce me;" "My mother always cries;" "I'd hurt him too much." On and on go the imagined disasters. A part of the mind often works overtime in stifling assertiveness.

Psychologist Albert Ellis has done a remarkable job of helping us figure out how irrational beliefs hurt our chances of responding satisfactorily to situations. In *A New Guide To Rational Living*, he and Robert Harper suggest that our thoughts always come before our emotional reactions to situations. Ellis and Harper describe some of the irrational ideas and beliefs about how life "ought to be" that lead to upsetting emotions, thus blocking adequate responses. These beliefs relate to such life events as rejection, fear, being treated unfairly. Read their book, and stop inhibiting your assertiveness by believing (irrationally) that the world should somehow be perfect!

A Few Words About Your Goals

Assertiveness training evolved out of the idea that people live better lives if they can express what they want, if they can let others know how they would like to be treated. Some folks, however, find it hard to really know *what* they want from life. If you have spent most of your life doing for others, and believing that what YOU want is not important, it can be quite a chore to get a handle on just what is important to you!

Some people do seem to know exactly how they feel and what they want. If the neighbor's dog is noisy, the feeling may be annoyance or anger or fear, but such people are able to translate the feeling, get to the key issues at hand and make the needed assertions, if any.

Others find it difficult to know what their feelings are and what they want to accomplish in an encounter. They often hesitate to be assertive, lamenting *"Assert what? I don't know what I want!"* If you have such trouble you may find it valuable to try to *label* your feelings. Anger, anxiety, boredom, discomfort, and fear are common feelings. Among others you will experience are happiness, irritation, love, relaxation, sadness.

Labelling for some will require only a few moments reflection to reveal what is being felt inside. Others may need a more active first step. It often helps to *say something* to the people involved: "I'm upset, but I'm not sure why." Or perhaps, "I'm feeling depressed." "Something feels wrong, but I can't put my finger on it." Such a statement will start you on an active search for the feeling you have, and will help begin to clarify your goals.

Perhaps it is a fear of some sort which is preventing you from recognizing your feelings — a type of protective mechanism. Or you may just be so far "out of touch" with your feelings that you have virtually forgotten what they mean. Don't bog down at this stage. Go ahead and try to express yourself. You will probably become aware of your goal even as you proceed. Indeed, maybe all you *wanted* was to express something! If you do begin to recognize the "underlying" feeling and decide to change directions in midstream ("I started out angry, but realized that what I really wanted was attention!"), that is a constructive step!

You can go a long way toward clarifying your feelings in a specific situation by identifying your general life goals. Assertiveness does need direction; while it seems like a good idea in general, it is of little value for its own sake!

You will find at times that goals will be in conflict. You may wish, for example, to keep a friendly relationship with your next door neighbor, but *also* wish to quiet his noisy dog. If you confront him about the dog, you may risk the good relationship. At such a point, clarification of your own goals will be invaluable in deciding what to do, and how to do it.

You may wish to pursue the process of personal goal setting even further. "Values Clarification" is a process which offers many systematic aids (see Simon, et al., 1972 and Goodman, 1978, 1979).

When You Are Ready to Begin

First, make certain that you understand thoroughly the basic principles of assertion. Realizing differences between assertive and aggressive behavior is important to your understanding and success. Re-read Chapters 1-4 if you need to.

Second, decide whether you are ready to begin trying self-assertive behavior on your own. If you have chronic patterns of nonassertion or aggression *or* if you are highly anxious, more caution needs to be taken. We recommend slow and careful practice and work with another person, preferably a trained therapist, as a facilitator. This recommendation is particularly strong for those who feel *very* anxious about beginning (more on this in Chapter 8).

Third, your initial attempts at being assertive should be chosen for their high potential of success, so as to provide reinforcement. This point is important with all beginning asserters. The more successfully you assert yourself at first, the more likely you are to be successful from then on!

Begin with small assertions that are likely to be rewarding, and from there proceed to more difficult assertions. You may wish to explore each step with a friend or trained facilitator until you are capable of being fully in control in most situations. You should proceed with care when taking it upon your own initiative to attempt a difficult assertion without special preparation. And be especially careful not to instigate an assertion where you are likely to fail miserably, thus inhibiting further attempts at assertiveness.

If you do suffer a setback, which very well may happen, take time carefully to analyze the situation and regain your confidence, getting help from a friend or facilitator if necessary. Especially in the early stages of assertion, it is not unusual to experience such difficulties as inadequate technique or overzealousness to the point of aggression. Either miscue could cause negative returns, particularly if the other individual becomes hostile and highly aggressive. Don't let such an occurrence stop you. Consider your goal again, and remember that although successful assertiveness requires practice, the rewards are great.

"If At First You Don't Succeed . . ."

There will be some failures with your assertions. These procedures will not turn you into a 100 percent success in all your relationships! There are no instant or magic answers to life's problems. Assertiveness does not always work—for *us* either! Sometimes, your goals will be incompatible with the other person's. When two people head for the same parking space, someone has to give! (Letting the other person go first can be an assertive act, too!) At times, others may be unreasonable or unyielding, and your best assertions (or *ours!*) will be to no avail.

Also, because you're human, you'll blow it sometimes—as we all do. Allow yourself to make mistakes! You'll be uncomfortable, disappointed, down, discouraged. Allow yourself to be human, then pick yourself up and try again. You'll find that every home run king was also a strikeout king! If you are going to hit the ball, you've got to keep swinging the bat!

If you feel your assertions are failing a bit too often, take a close look at what's going on. Are you setting your goals too high? Take small steps to ensure succes! Are you overdoing it and becoming aggressive? Monitor your behavior carefully — refer to Chapter 2 and check yourself. (Some aggression is to be expected at first. The pendulum will balance in a short time.)

We all want our assertions to work, and to achieve our goals. Nevertheless, the greatest value of self-assertion is the good feeling that comes from having expressed yourself. To know that you have a *perfect right* to self-expression, to feel free to say what you're feeling, and to *do* it are the best benefits of all.

Usually, you'll find assertiveness *will* make things happen. But whether it works or not, remember how good it felt to speak up for yourself! You did what you could, even if the outcome wasn't what you hoped for. If you *have* genuinely tried and done all you can, that's all you can ask of yourself!

One final caution: Nothing turns people off faster than a self-righteous attitude. Avoid the trap some new assertiveness trainees fall into—feeling you *must* assert yourself in all situations, at all costs. Let moderation, consideration for others, and *common sense* prevail!

We have covered a great deal of ground in this chapter. You can see just how important your *brain activity*—thoughts, feelings, attitudes, beliefs — is to your *emotional and physical behavior*. If you begin to follow the suggestions of this chapter toward "changing your mind," you'll see rapid changes in your assertive action as well!

8

"But I'm Really Afraid!"

An appeaser is one who feeds a crocodile—hoping it will eat him last.

—*Sir Winston Churchill*

Many readers of *Your Perfect Right*—perhaps you, too—find *anxiety* to be the most significant obstacle to greater assertiveness. "Sure," you say, "I know *how* to express myself! I just get really uptight about doing it. The risks seem too great. I want people to like me...."

Moreover, you may not even be aware of the source of such fears. Often, they result from childhood experiences—for example, well-meaning parents may have taught you that "children are to be seen and not heard."

Perhaps you find yourself perspiring heavily, your heart racing, your hands icy, as you walk into a job interview. Or maybe you have avoided asking your boss for a raise because you fear the words will catch in your throat. Do you take the long way home so you don't have to confront the neighbor who is always asking favors which you're afraid to refuse? You may even be among the surprisingly large proportion of the population known as *agoraphobics*, whose fears of social contact are so pervasive that they elect to remain at home virtually all the time.

Although learning to be assertive will help to reduce such fears, when the level of anxiety is very high it may be necessary to deal more directly with the anxiety itself.

To overcome fear, nervousness, anxiety and stress about assertiveness, it is necessary to determine what *causes* the reaction. Once you know what you are dealing with, you can learn methods to eliminate the fear.

We suggest you begin by *tracing* your fear. Narrow down exactly what causes you to feel afraid in the process of assertiveness. Use your log to systematically record reactions. Learn to collect evidence about what is causing your anxiety level to rise. There are also formal tests that help measure fears. It may be helpful for you to see a mental health professional to take them.

Finding Your Fears: The SUDS Scale

A useful aid in assessing your own anxiety level is the "SUDS scale." "SUDS" is an acronym for Subjective Units of Disturbance—simply rating your own physical feelings of anxiety on a scale of 0-100. Because anxiety, by definition, has physical elements, you can become aware of your degree of discomfort in a situation by "tuning in" to your body's indicators: heart rate (pulse), breathing rate, coldness in hands and feet, perspiration (particularly in hands), and muscle tension. (There are others, but we usually are not aware of them; biofeedback training is allowing many people to learn when they are relaxed or anxious by monitoring physical indicators.)

Try this: get yourself as relaxed as you can right now—lie flat on the couch or floor or relax in your chair, breathe deeply, relax all the muscles in your body, and imagine a very relaxing scene (lying on the beach, floating on a cloud, etc.). Allow yourself to relax in this way for *at least* five minutes, paying attention to your heartbeat, breathing, hand temperature and dryness, muscle relaxation. Those relaxed feelings can be given a SUDS scale value of 0, to represent near-total relaxation. If you did not do the relaxation exercise, but are reading this alone, relatively quietly and comfortably, you may consider yourself somewhere around 20 on the SUDS scale.

At the opposite end of the scale, visualize the most frightening scene you can imagine. With your eyes closed, picture yourself narrowly escaping an accident, or being near the center of an earthquake or flood. Pay attention to the same body signals: heart rate/pulse, breathing, hand temperature/moisture, muscle relaxation. These fearful feelings can be given a SUDS scale value of 100—almost *totally* anxious.

Now you have a roughly calibrated comfort/discomfort scale which you can use to help yourself evaluate just how anxious you are in any given situation. Each 10 points on the scale represents a "just noticeable difference" up or down from the units above and below. Thus, 70 is slightly more anxious than 60, and by the same amount more comfortable than 80. (The SUDS scale is too subjective to be able to define more closely than 10 units.)

Most of us function normally in the range of 20-50 SUDS. A few life situations will raise anxiety above 50 for short periods, and on rare occasions (rare for most of us, anyway!) one can relax below 20.

You can easily see how such a "measure" of anxiety can help to identify those life situations which are most troublesome. Once again, being systematic in your observations of yourself can pay big dividends! The procedure described below shows a way to use the SUDS scale to develop a "plan of attack" against your fears.

List/Group/Label

A method developed by Patsy Tanabe-Endsley in the field of creative writing will be helpful. In her book, *Project Write,* she tells how to *list, group* and *label* ideas. We can use her system by substituting "fears or anxieties" for "ideas."

Start by recording or *listing* life situations when you feel fear or anxiety. Use some space in your Log to list *all* your reactions that hinder your assertiveness, including the situation or event involved, people, circumstances, other factors which contributed to your reaction. Assign a SUDS value, as described in the previous section, to each of the items on your list.

Next, find the reactions on your list which are similar, those that seem to have a common theme, and *group* them together. Now see if you can *label* your groups, applying appropriate names to each grouping of anxiety-producing factors. Among your groups may be such common phobias as fears of snakes or spiders or heights or enclosed places. *Interpersonal* fears are more likely to be the problem in assertiveness. Fears of *criticism, rejection, anger* or *aggression,* or *hurting the feelings of others* greatly hinder your assertive response.

You may find a grouping which centers around one or more of the situations given in the Assertiveness Inventory in Chapter 5. Instead of a classic fear like rejection, you may simply experience a good deal of anxiety when standing in line or when facing salespersons. Perhaps people in authority scare you. Obviously, your assertiveness will not be optimum if your anxiety is already working against you beforehand!

Now, one more step in this analysis of your fears. In each labeled group, relist the items in order, according to the SUDS scores you have assigned. Now you have a rough agenda, in priority order, for dealing with your anxieties! Usually, it is best to start working to reduce or overcome those which are most disturbing *before* (or at least concurrently with) your attempt to develop your assertive skills further.

Overcoming Anxiety

Now that you have carefully identified the anxieties which are inhibiting your assertiveness, you will want to begin a program to overcome them. There are a number of effective approaches. Since this topic is a book in itself, let us briefly describe one popular approach, and then refer you to other excellent resources for further information.

AT pioneer Dr. Joseph Wolpe (1969) developed an immeasurably valuable procedure: *systematic desensitization.* Like AT, systematic desensitization is based on learning principles; you *learned* to be anxious about expressing yourself, and you can *unlearn* it! *No one* was *born* fearful! The process of desensitization simply involves repeated association of an anxiety-producing situation (an item from your list, for example) with a feeling of deep relaxation throughout your body. Gradually, you learn to "automatically" associate relaxation, instead of anxiety, as a response to that scene. Practically speaking, it is not possible to be relaxed and anxious at the same time. The intricacies of the procedure are somewhat more complex, but that is the essence of desensitization. It has been proven effective for a wide range of fears, including phobic reactions to heights, public speaking, animals, flying, test taking, and social contact.

If you are very concerned about your anxiety, you may wish to do some further reading. Two good books on the topic are *BT* (*Behavior Therapy*) by Spencer Rathus (1978) and *Stress Relief* by Michele Haney and Ed Boenisch (1982). Both books explore self-help procedures for anxiety and describe further resources available.

Expect to invest some time — probably several weeks — practicing the methods of anxiety relief described here and in the resources noted. It took time for you to learn to be anxious; it will take time to learn to overcome it.

Finally, if your best self-help efforts do not accomplish sufficient anxiety reduction, consult a competent therapist. Your goal is to eliminate obstacles to effective self-expression. If your anxiety is still at high levels after your own best attempts, obtain professional help!

This discussion of anxiety about assertiveness is not meant to discourage you. On the contrary, most readers will find themselves able to handle their mild discomfort about self-expression without major difficulty. There are some of us, however, who *do* need some extra help in overcoming obstacles. *Don't be embarrassed or hesitant about asking for help,* just as you would seek competent medical aid for a physical problem. Then, when you've cleared up the anxiety obstacle, turn back to the procedures outlined in this book for developing your assertiveness.

9

One Step At A Time:
Developing Assertive Behavior

He that respects himself is safe from others; he wears a coat of mail that none can pierce.
—*Henry Wadsworth Longfellow*

Perhaps you have heard it said that "when two engineers (lawyers, housekeepers, plumbers, nurses) are talking together and a psychologist walks up and joins the conversation, there are now two engineers and a psychologist, but when two psychologists are talking and an engineer (substitute your own favorite) walks up and joins them, there are now three psychologists!" Everyone believes she/he is a psychologist in some sense. Indeed, we all have some practical, first-hand knowledge of human behavior, beginning with ourselves.

Changing Behavior and Attitudes

Popular wisdom often suggests that to improve yourself you need to "change your attitude." For many years, until quite recently, behavioral psychologists argued that it was more important to change *behavior*; that attitude change would follow.

A great deal of recent research in a field of psychology called *cognitive behavior therapy* has shown that, for many people at least, *thoughts are as important as actions* in bringing about life changes.

In the first three editions of this book, we advocated the position of traditional behavior therapy, that it was easier and more effective to change behavior first, then attitude change will slowly follow. While we still consider attitude change the "tougher nut to crack," we have learned that one's thinking processes can be modified by procedures such as those we described in Chapter 7, and that such changes will powerfully affect one's behavior.

Positive self-statements provide a good example. By consciously telling yourself "I have the ability to succeed in this situation," you greatly enhance your *chances* of success, even without any other changes. *We view and interpret life events through our own unique attitudes and beliefs about ourselves and the world, and we act according to those interpretations.* If I go about believing that "I am no damn good," I will approach life situations with an outlook of failure — and thus increase my *chance* of failure. Conversely, if I tell myself I am capable of succeeding, my actions will be more likely to follow a pattern of success.

For a time, as usually happens when a new idea emerges from psychological research, the "cognitive folks" seemed to have everyone convinced that such *changed thinking* was all-important. Very recently, the "pendulum" has begun to swing back toward a more moderate position, and that is the view we hold: *Both thinking and behavior are vital elements in the process of bringing about personal growth.* Some people respond more readily to cognitive (thinking) interventions, others to behavioral (action) interventions. In any comprehensive program for growth, therefore, *both* areas must be dealt with. Put most of your energy into whichever is most helpful for *you!* (Funny how *common sense* seems to emerge from psychological research, if we allow enough time to pass!)

As you begin the process of becoming more assertive, we won't ask you to wake up some morning and say, "Today, I'm a new, assertive person!" You will find here instead a systematic, step-by-step guide to change. The key to developing assertiveness is *practice.*

A cycle of nonassertive or aggressive behavior tends to perpetuate itself until a decisive intervention occurs. A person who has acted nonassertively or aggressively in relationships for a long time usually has a poor self-image. His or her behavior towards others — whether self-denying or abusive — is responded to with scorn, disdain, avoidance. Observing the response, this person says, "See, I knew I was no damn good!" Confirmed in this low self-evaluation, the inadequate behavior patterns are continued. Thus the cycle is repeated: inadequate behavior, negative feedback, attitude of self-depreciation, inadequate behavior.

The cycle can be reversed, becoming a positive sequence: more adequately assertive behavior gains more positive responses from others; positive feedback leds to an enhanced evaluation of self-worth ("Wow, people are treating me like a worthwhile person!"); and improved thoughts and feelings about oneself result in further assertiveness.

Or, the cycle may be entered at the cognitive point: by saying positive things to oneself and beginning to *think* as if one were a valuable person, one begins to *act* more effectively, thereby producing more positive *responses* from others and the resulting confirmation of the original thought ("Maybe I *am* a good person, after all!").

Harold had been convinced for years that he was truly worthless. He was totally dependent upon his wife for emotional support and, despite a rather handsome appearance and ability to express himself well, had literally no friends. Imagine his utter despair when his wife left him! Fortunately, Harold was already in therapy at the time, and was willing to try to make contact with other people. When his first attempts at assertiveness with eligible young women were successful beyond his wildest hopes, the reinforcing value of such responses to his assertions was very high! Harold's entire outlook toward himself changed rapidly, and he became much more assertive in a variety of situations.

Not everyone, to be sure, will experience such an immediate "payoff" for his/her assertions; and not all assertions are fully successful. Success usually requires a great deal of patience, and a gradual process of handling more and more difficult situations.

A general rule we have found is that *assertiveness tends to be self-rewarding.* It feels good to have others begin to respond more attentively, to achieve one's goals in relationships, to find situations going one's way more often. *And you can make these changes happen!* Remember, begin with assertions where you are somewhat certain of success before proceeding to more difficult ones requiring greater confidence and skill. It is often quite helpful and reassuring to obtain support and guidance from another person, perhaps a friend, teacher, or professional therapist.

Keep in mind that changed *behavior* leads to changed attitudes about oneself and one's impact upon people and situations. Moreover, changed *thinking* leads to changed *behavior.* The balance of this chapter presents the steps involved in bringing about these changes. Read *all* the material here carefully *before* you begin. Then return to this point and begin to follow the steps in your own life. You'll like the difference in you!

The Step-by-Step Process

Step 1. Observe your own behavior. Are you asserting yourself adequately? Are you satisfied with your effectiveness in interpersonal relationships? Look over the discussion in Chapters 1-5 again, and assess how *you* feel about yourself and your behavior.

Step 2. Keep track of your assertiveness. Keep your log very carefully for a week. Each day, record those situations in which you found yourself responding assertively, those in which you "blew it," and those you avoided altogether so you would not have to face the need to act assertively. Be honest with yourself, and systematic, following the guidelines for self-assessment described in Chapter 5.

Step 3: Set realistic goals for yourself. Your self-assessment will help you select specific targets for your growth in assertiveness. Pick out situations, or people, toward which you want to become more effective. Be sure to start with a small, low-risk step to maximize your chances of success. (See "a Few Words About Your Goals" in Chapter 7.)

Step 4. Concentrate on a particular situation. Spend a few moments with your eyes closed, imagining how you handle a specific incident (being short-changed at the supermarket, having a friend "talk your ear off" on the telephone when you had too much to do, letting the boss make you feel like 2 cents" over a small mistake). Imagine vividly the actual details, including your specific feelings at the time and afterward.

Step 5. Review your responses. Write down your behavior in Step 4 relating to the components of assertiveness noted in Chapter 3 (eye contact, body posture, gestures, facial expression, voice, message content, etc.) Look carefully at the components of your behavior in the recalled incident, including your thoughts. Note your strengths. Be aware of those components which represent nonassertive or aggressive behavior. If a major element of your response involves anxiety, refer to the discussion in Chapter 8, "But I'm Really Afraid!" Do not attempt to force yourself into very painful situations. On the other hand, do not avoid new growth if it is only moderately uncomfortable!

Step 6. Observe an effective model. At this point it would be very helpful to watch someone who handles the same situation very well. Watch for the components discussed in Chapter 3, particularly the *style* — the words are less important. If the model is a friend, discuss his/her approach, and its consequences.

Step 7: Consider alternative responses. What are other possible ways the incident could be handled? Could you deal with it more to your own advantage? Less offensively? Refer to Figure 2A, and differentiate between nonassertive, aggressive, and assertive responses.

Step 8. Imagine yourself handling the situation. Close your eyes and visualize yourself dealing effectively with a situation. You may act similarly to the "model" in Step 6, or in a very different way. Be assertive, but be as much your "natural" self as you can. Repeat this step as often as necessary until you can imagine a comfortable style for yourself which succeeds in handling the situation well.

Step 9. Practice positive thoughts. Spend some time going over the material in Chapter 7. Develop a list of several brief positive statements about yourself which are related to this situation (e.g., "I've had job interviews before, and have done alright.") Practice saying those statements to yourself several times. Remember, this is *not* a "script" for what to say to *someone else*, it is a "prompter" for what you say to *yourself.*

Step 10. Get help if you need it. As we have noted several times, the process of becoming more assertive may require you to stretch yourself considerably. If you feel unable on your own to deal with the situations you have visualized, seek help from a qualified professional (see Appendix B).

Step 11: Try it out. Having examined your own behavior, considered alternatives, observed a model of more adaptive action, and practiced some positive thoughts about yourself, you are now prepared to begin trying out for yourself new ways of dealing with the problem situation. A repeat of Steps 6, 7, 8 and 9 may be needed until you are ready to proceed. It is important to select an alternative, more effective way of behaving in the problem situation. You may wish to follow your model and enact the same approach taken by him or her in Step 6. Such a choice is appropriate, but should reflect an awareness that you are a unique person. You may not find the model's approach one which you could feel good about adopting for yourself. After selecting a more effective alternative behavior, you now should role-play the situation with a friend, teacher, or therapist, attempting to act in accord with the new response pattern you have selected. As in Steps 2, 4, and 5, make careful observation of your behavior, using available mechanical recording aids whenever possible. Don't worry about not having your goals absolutely clear. As you try out new behavioral skills, you'll become more aware of what you want in the situation.

Step 12. Get feedback. This step essentially repeats Step 5 with emphasis on the positive aspects of your behavior. Note particularly the strengths of your performance, and work positively on your weaker areas.

Step 13. Behavior shaping. Steps 8, 9, 11 and 12 should be repeated as often as necessary to "shape" your behavior — by this process of successive approximations of your goal — to a point wherein you feel comfortable dealing in a self-enhancing manner with the previously threatening situation.

Step 14. The real test. You are now ready to give your new response pattern a real test. Up to this point your preparation has taken place in a relatively secure environment. Nevertheless, careful training and repeated practice have prepared you to react almost "automatically" to the situation. You should thus be encouraged to proceed with an *in vivo* trial. If you are unwilling to do so, further rehearsals or help may be needed. (Repeat steps 8-12). Again, remember that *doing*, honestly and spontaneously, is the most important step of all.

Step 15. Further training. You are encouraged to repeat procedures that help you develop your desired behavior pattern for other specific situations in which you wish to develop more useful responses. Look over Chapters 4 and 10 for examples which may be helpful in planning your own program for change.

Step 16. Social reinforcement. As a final step in establishing an independent behavior pattern, it is very important that you understand the need for on-going self-reinforcement. In order to maintain your newly-developed assertive behavior, you should achieve a system of reinforcements in your own social environment. For example, you now know the good feeling that comes from a successful assertion and you can rest assured that this good response will continue. Admiration from others will be another continuing positive response to your growth. You may wish to develop a checklist of specific reinforcements which are unique to your own environment.

Although we emphasize the importance of this systematic learning process, we are not recommending a lock-step forced pattern that does not consider your personal needs and objectives. You are encouraged to provide a learning environment which will help *you* grow in assertiveness. No one system is "right" for everyone. We encourage you to be systematic, but to follow a program which will meet your own unique individual needs. There is, of course, no substitute for the *active practice* of assertive thoughts and behavior in your own life, when *you* choose to, as a means of developing greater assertiveness and enjoying its accompanying rewards.

Because a number of approaches to assertiveness training have proved valuable, we are providing in the following section a brief commentary on each of several important contributions to AT practice. Most of these are available in book form, so you should have a minimum of difficulty in locating those of interest to you.

Other Approaches to Assertiveness Training

Andrew Salter, truly the pioneer in developing a therapeutic approach to increasing personal effectiveness, describes *excitation* (a behavioral style he later agrees is like assertion) as "a matter of emotional freedom." In his classic book *Conditioned Reflex Therapy* (1949), Salter says excitatory responses must be honest, direct, outward, energetic, unaffected, and free of anxiety. Salter teaches six major elements of excitatory (assertive) behavior: *feeling talk, facial talk, contradiction and attack, deliberate use of "I," agreement with praise,* and *improvisation* (spontaneity). That's a pretty good description of what we are calling *assertiveness!*

Another key figure in the development of assertiveness training is psychiatrist Joseph Wolpe. Wolpe's definition (1969, 1973) is broad and direct: *"Assertive behavior is defined as the proper expression of any emotion other than anxiety towards another person."* His approach to training, from which we have drawn heavily, emphasizes desensitization and behavior rehearsal.

As assertiveness training has grown in popularity, trainers and researchers have looked at the concept of assertiveness in greater detail, much as we are doing in this chapter. Patricia Jakubowski was the first to present a systematic approach to AT for women (1973). Later, in her books with Arthur Lange, *Responsible Assertive Behavior* (1976), and *The Assertive Option* (1978), several types of assertive behaviors are proposed: *Basic assertion* (standing up for personal rights); *Empathetic assertion* (communicating understanding and empathy); *Escalating assertion* (gradually increasing firmness); *Confrontive assertion* (pointing out mistakes, giving directions); *I-language assertion* (expressing negative feelings phrased in the "how I feel" language).

The Assertive Woman (1975), by Stanlee Phelps and Nancy Austin, is the first AT book specifically devoted to the concerns of women. Phelps and Austin have integrated AT procedures with consciousness raising, and include helpful material on such topics as manipulation, put-downs, sexuality, children, and social change. Their book includes many exercises and self-assessment surveys.

A different book with a similar title, *The New Assertive Woman* (1975), by Lynn Bloom, Karen Coburn, and Joan Pearlman, presents material related to women's rights, irrational beliefs, and games women play in avoiding self-assertion. AT procedures similar to *Your Perfect Right* are included.

Don't Say Yes When You Want to Say No (1975), by Herbert Fensterheim and Jean Baer, is a presentation of AT within the context of behavior therapy, and includes assignments and exercises, as well as material on weight control, sex therapy, and relaxation training.

In her own book, *How to Be an Assertive [not Aggressive] Woman* (1976), Jean Baer draws much from the Fensterheim/Baer volume, applying it to women. She describes many "blocks" to assertiveness, and discusses the differences between "therapy" and "education."

I Can If I Want To (1975), by Arnold Lazarus and Allen Fay, although not an AT book *per se*, is a brief series of self-affirmation exercises based on AT and humanistic-behavioral principles. Lazarus was a pioneer in developing the AT model in the 1960s with Joseph Wolpe, although their views have diverged markedly in recent years, with Lazarus adopting a style he calls "broad spectrum behavior therapy."

Among other major contributors to the AT field whose works we consider worthy of your attention are John and Merna Galassi (1976), Donald Meichenbaum (1977), Eileen Gambrill and Cheryl Richey (1976), Iris Fodor and Janet Wolfe (1975), Robert Liberman and associates (1976), and Spencer Rathus (1975, 1977). We consider the work of all of the professionals mentioned thus far to be positive and constructive. (Others whose work is primarily directed toward AT professionals are discussed in Part Two.)

It is our opinion that such styles as those in the books of Manuel Smith (1975) and Robert Ringer (1976), although often popularly identified with AT, are more oriented toward *manipu-lating* others in pursuit of one's goals (and are thereby aggressive rather than assertive as we define it). Thus we cannot support the approaches advocated in their work.

There is a considerable range and variety of approaches to assertiveness training. Although highly structured techniques and "scripts" can be useful in learning assertiveness, our preference is to offer the general set of steps presented in this chapter. We do not wish to tell you what to say, or even to give a "formula" for what to say, in a given situation. Rather, we encourage your indi-viduality, and hope that you will develop your own assertive style, following guidelines of *honesty, directness, respect for the rights of others,* and *your own freedom of choice* in your self-assertion. Examine other approaches, and select a method which will be of maximum value to *you!*

A Gentle Shove

Now that you know what is involved in the process of devel-oping assertive behavior, don't allow yourself to remain a passive observer. If you are interested enough to read this far, you are either thinking seriously about improving your own assertiveness or considering how you can help others to become more assertive. In either case, *do something about it!* You cannot change solely by sitting there reading this book. If we don't move you to action in your own life, we have served only as a diversion and we are disap-pointed. If, on the other hand, you go out now and handle *one* interpersonal situation more in your own best interests, we are pleased to have had a part in your growth.

10

Assertiveness Takes Practice

> *If people would dare to speak to one another*
> *unreservedly, there would be a good deal less*
> *sorrow in the world a hundred years hence.*
>
> *—Samuel Butler*

The following are everyday life situations which call for assertive behavior, but which cause difficulty for many people. Each situation is presented with alternatives from which you may choose a response. Each alternative response may be categorized in the "nonassertive-aggressive-assertive" framework we have described.

The situations are designed for your practice according to the step-by-step process described in Chapter 9. Select situations appropriate to your needs (one at a time!). As you read the situation description, fill in from your own imagination any details as may be desired.

Follow steps 4 to 7 of Chapter 9, utilizing the alternative responses suggested here for the situation, and any others you may think of. For each situation you choose, enact the role-playing and feedback exercises described in Steps 8, 9, 11 and 12, then continue with remaining steps of the step-by-step process.

The examples are grouped according to several characteristic types of situations: family, consumer, employment, school and community, and social. In each case, only a few situations are suggested although the number of categories and examples is as infinite as life itself. In addition to this series of representative illustrations, you may—on your own initiative—apply assertive behavior to examples from your own life.

Family Situations

Slumber Party. Your 12-year-old daughter is having a slumber party with five other girls. It is past 2 a.m.; the girls should have settled down to sleep by now, but are still quite noisy.

Alternative Responses:

(a)   You toss and turn in bed, wishing your spouse would get up and say something to the girls. You do a slow burn, but just lie there trying to block out the sounds.

(b)   Jumping out of bed, you thoroughly scold and berate the girls, especially your daughter, for their unladylike conduct.

(c)   Talking to the girls in a tone which they will recognize as meaning business, you tell them that they have had enough fun for tonight. You point out that you need to get up early tomorrow, and that everyone needs to get to sleep.

Late for Dinner. Your wife was supposed to be home for dinner right after work. Instead, she returns hours later explaining she was out with the girls for a few drinks. She is obviously drunk.

Alternative Responses:

(a)   You say nothing about how discourteous she has been, but simply start preparing something for her to eat.

(b)   Screaming, yelling and crying, you tell her that she is a drunken fool, doesn't care about your feelings, is a poor example for the children. You ask about what the neighbors will think. You demand that she get her own dinner.

(c)   You calmly and steadfastly let her know that she should have informed you beforehand that she was going out for a few drinks and would likely be late. Telling her that her cold dinner is in the kitchen, you add that you expect to discuss her behavior further tomorrow.

Visiting Relative. Aunt Margaret, with whom you prefer not to spend much time, is on the telephone. She has just told you of her plans to spend three weeks visiting you, beginning next week.
Alternative Responses:
(a) You think, "Oh, no!" but say, "We'd love to have you come and stay as long as you like!"
(b) You tell her the children have just come down with bad colds, and the spare bed has a broken spring and you'll be going to Cousin Bill's weekend after next—none of which is true.
(c) You say, "We'll be glad to have you come for the weekend, but we simply can't invite you for longer. A short visit is happier for everyone, and we'll want to see each other again sooner. We have many school and community activities which take much of our time and energy."

"Past Midnight." Your teenage son has just returned from a school party. It is 3 o'clock in the morning, and you have been frantic, concerned primarily for his well-being, since you had expected him home before midnight.
Alternative Responses:
(a) You turn over and go to sleep.
(b) You shout, "Where the hell have you been? Do you have any idea what time it is? You've kept me up all night! You thoughtless, inconsiderate, selfish, no-good bum—I ought to make you sleep in the street!"
(c) You say, "I've been very worried about you, son. You said you'd be home before midnight, and I've been frantic for hours. Are you alright? I wish you'd called me! Tomorrow we'll discuss your arrangements for staying out late."

Consumer Situations

Haircut. At the barber shop, the barber has just finished cutting your hair and turns the chair toward the mirror so you can inspect. You feel that you would like the sides trimmed more.
Alternative Responses:
(a) You nod your head and say, "That's ok."

(b) Abruptly you demand that he do a more thorough job, saying sarcastically, "You sure didn't take much off the sides, did you?"

(c) You say that you would like to have the sides trimmed more.

Short-changed   As you are leaving a store after a small purchase, you discover that you have been short-changed by 70 cents.

Alternative Responses:

(a) Pausing for a moment, you try to decide if 70 cents is worth the effort. After a few moments, you decide it is not and go on your way.

(b) You hurry back into the store and loudly demand your 70 cents, making a derogatory comment about "cashiers who can't add."

(c) Re-entering the store, you catch the attention of the clerk, saying that you were short-changed by 70 cents. In the process of explaining, you display the change you received back.

Waiting in Line.   You are standing near a cash register waiting to pay for your purchase and have it wrapped. Others, who have come after you, are being waited on first. You are getting tired of waiting.

Alternative Responses:

(a) You give up and decide not to buy the article.

(b) Shouting, "You sure get poor service in this store!" you slam the intended purchase down on the counter and walk out.

(c) In a voice loud enough to be heard, you tell the clerk you were ahead of people who have already been served. You ask to be waited on now.

Employment Situations

Working Late. You and your spouse have an engagement this evening which has been planned for several weeks. You plan to leave immediately after work. During the day, however, your supervisor asks you to stay late this evening to work on a special assignment.

Alternative Responses:

(a) You say nothing about your important plans and simply agree to stay until the work is finished.

(b) In a nervous, abrupt voice you say, "No, I will not work late tonight!" Adding a brief criticism of the boss for not planning the work schedule better, you then turn back to your work.

(c) In a firm, pleasant voice, you explain your important plans and say you will not be able to stay this evening to work on the special assignment, but perhaps you can help find an alternative solution.

Job Error. You have made a mistake on the job. Your supervisor discovers it and is letting you know rather harshly that you should not have been so careless.

Alternative Responses:

(a) Overapologizing, you say, "I'm sorry. I was stupid. How silly of me. I'll never let it happen again!"

(b) You bristle up and say, "You have no business whatsoever criticizing my work. Leave me alone, and don't bother me in the future. I'm capable of handling my own work!"

(c) You agree that you made the mistake, saying, "I'm sorry and will be more careful next time. However, I feel you are being somewhat harsh and I see no need for that."

Late to Work. One of your subordinates has been coming in late consistently for the last three or four days.

Alternative Responses:

(a) You grumble to yourself or to others about the situation, but say nothing to the person, hoping he will start coming in early.

(b) You tell the worker off, indicating that he has no right to take advantage of you and that he had better get to work on time or else you will see that he is fired.

(c) You point out to the worker that you have observed him coming in late recently and wonder, "Is there an explanation I should know about? It will be necessary for you to start coming to work on time. You should have come to me and explained the situation, rather than saying nothing at all, and leaving me up in the air."

School and Community Situations

Quiet Prof. In a physics lecture with 300 students, the professor speaks softly and you know that many others are having trouble hearing him, as you are.

Alternative Responses:

(a) You continue to strain to hear, eventually move closer to the front of the room, but say nothing about his too-soft voice.

(b) You yell out, "Speak up!"

(c) You raise your hand, get the profesor's attention and ask if he would mind speaking louder.

Clarification. At a Lion's Club meeting, the President is discussing the procedures for the annual high school speech contest. You are puzzled by several of his statements and believe he has misstated an important aspect.

Alternative Responses:

(a) You say nothing, but continue to puzzle over the question, looking up your notes from last year's contest later in the day

(b) You interrupt, telling him he is wrong, pointing out the mistake and correcting him from your own knowledge of the contest. Your tone is derisive, and your choice of words makes him obviously ill-at-ease.

(c) You ask the President to further explain the procedures, expressing your confusion and noting the source of your conflicting information.

Morals. You are one of eleven people in a discussion group on human sexuality. The concepts being supported by three or four of the more verbal students are contrary to your personal moral code.

Alternative Responses:

(a) You listen quietly, not disagreeing openly with the other members or describing your own views.

(b) You loudly denounce the views which have been expressed. Your defense of your own belief is strong, and you urge others to accept your point of view as the only correct one.

(c) You speak up in support of your own beliefs, identifying yourself with an apparently unpopular position, but not disparaging the beliefs of others in the group.

"Know It All." As a member of the community beautification committee, you are dismayed by the continued dominance of group discussion by Mr. Brown, an opinionated member who has "the answer" to every question. He has begun another tirade. As usual, no one has said anything about it after several minutes.

Alternative Responses:

(a) Your irritation increases, but you remain silent.

(b) You explode verbally, curse Mr. Brown for "not giving anyone else a chance," and declare his ideas out-of-date and worthless.

(c) You interrupt, saying, "Excuse me, Mr. Brown." When recognized, you express your personal irritation about Mr. Brown's monopoly on the group's time. Speaking to Mr. Brown as well as the other group members, you suggest a discussion procedure which will permit all members an opportunity to take part, and will minimize domination by a single individual.

Social Situations

Breaking the Ice. At a party where you don't know anyone except the host, you want to circulate and get to know others. You walk up to three people talking.

Alternative Responses:

(a) You stand close to them and smile but say nothing, waiting for them to notice you.

(b) You listen to the subject they are talking about, then break in and state you disagree with someone's viewpoint.

(c) You break in while they are talking and introduce yourself.

(d) You wait for a pause in the conversation, then introduce yourself and ask if you may join in.

Making a Date. You are interested in a date with a person you have met and talked with three or four times recently.

Alternative Responses:

(a) You sit around the telephone going over in your mind what you will say and how your friend will respond. Several times you lift the phone and are almost finished dialing, then hang up.

(b) You phone and as soon as your friend answers, you respond by saying, "Hi, baby, we're going out together this weekend!" Seemingly taken aback, your friend asks who is calling.

(c) You call, and when your friend answers, you say who is calling and ask how school (job, etc.) is going. The reply is, "Fine, except I am worried about a test I will be taking soon." Following the lead, you talk for a few minutes about the test. Then you say that you would like it if the two of you would go together to a show downtown this Friday evening.

Smoke Gets in Your Lungs. You are at a public meeting in a large room. A man enters the room and sits down next to you, puffing enthusiastically on a large cigar. The smoke is very offensive to you.

Alternative Responses:

(a) You suffer the offensive smoke in silence, deciding it is the right of the other person to smoke if he wishes.

(b) You become very angry, demand that he move or put out the cigar and loudly assail the evils and health hazards of the smoking habit.

(c) You firmly but politely ask him to refrain from smoking because it is offensive to you.

(d) You ask him to sit in another seat if he prefers to continue smoking, since you were there first.

11

Assertion Builds Equal Relationships

> *Is not the expression of affection toward other people also assertion?*
>
> —*Michael Serber*

"Stand up for yourself" is the slogan often equated with assertive behavior. The first edition of *Your Perfect Right* was devoted almost exclusively to fostering that type of behavior. In a critical review of that first edition, published in *Behavior Therapy,* a professional journal, the late psychiatrist Michael Serber noted our oversight. A colleague who had substantial influence on our work, Serber wrote in that early review (1971):

> *Certainly, behavioral skills necessary to stand up to the multiple personal, social, and business situations confronting the majority of people are imperative to master. But what of other just as necessary skills, such as being able to give and take tenderness and affection? Is not the expression of affection toward other people also assertion? There are many behavior modifiers who are completely "turned off" to sensitivity-training groups...Nevertheless, the content of sensitivity training, the ability to express warmth and affection, to be able to give and take feelings, including anger, badly needs the special attention behavior modifiers can bring to it. Sensitivity training can become a unique area in which humanistic goals and behavioral techniques can yield both meaningful and concrete new behaviors.*

We have found that *positive, caring feelings* are often more difficult to express for nonassertive and aggressive persons than "standing up" behavior. The "soft" assertions are especially important for relationships. How much more easily and quickly friendships grow when people are openly warm! And even the "cold, cruel world" of business can be made human and warm by a simple show of friendliness!

Expressions of warmth are often inhibited, particularly for adults. Embarrassment, fear of rejection, or ridicule, the "superiority of reason over emotion" — all are excuses given to explain the suppression of spontaneous expressions of warmth, caring, and love.

Freedom of such expression has not been encouraged in our culture. As we discussed in Chapter 1, "polite restraint" is in the accepted order of things. Nevertheless, the new lifestyles and youth subcultures, which have been potent forces for change, encourage greater spontaneity. We heartily endorse greater openness in the communication of genuine positive feeling toward other persons.

It is encouraging to note the freedom in expression of caring, joy, and warm feelings among young people, blacks, and Latinos. Each of these groups is becoming more influential in shaping our social order. Perhaps future generations will find emotional freedom more natural!

Sadly, for some people even "thank you" is difficult. An acquaintance of ours, president of a multimillion dollar giant organization, is noted for rarely expressing appreciation to the people on his staff. A job well done is seldom openly rewarded, recognized, or even acknowledged. Because the chief executive is apparently afraid to act in warm and positive ways (perhaps he might appear "soft" or others might come to *expect* rewards?), the morale of staff members in that organization is not very high.

To be a caring person, and to openly express that, seems to be a "high-risk" style in our society. How sad for all of us that we make it so difficult for warmth to be expressed openly!

Psychologist Eric Fromm has differentiated five types of love in his excellent book *The Art of Loving* (1956): fraternal, maternal, erotic, love of God, and self-love. We hope you can view love in this broader context, and allow yourself to love *you* and *others* more openly. Fraternal love — caring for other members of the human family — has few of the qualities we popularly associate with the romantic idea of "love." Nevertheless, it is a vital and critically important aspect of our lives. However independent we may become, we are fundamentally interdependent and social creatures!

Relationships: The Bottom Line

Alas, assertiveness training is often identified with the "me" decade of the 1970s. Truth to tell, much AT *has* been presented as if its major purpose were to help trainees "get their way" in life. Careless, poorly trained and sometimes downright unethical trainers have sold their clients a "quick and easy" cure to dissatisfaction with their lives, through manipulation of others.

The result of such programs has been a black eye for AT in the minds of many persons. "Oh yeah, that's where you learn to push other people around, isn't it?" Some popular books associated with assertiveness have also taught a manipulative, "me first" style, unfortunately.

The assertiveness we advocate is aimed toward building positive, equal relationships between people — the most valuable assets any human being can have. And straightforward openness which respects other people is the best method we know to acquire those assets!

All of us live on a continuum of human interrelatedness which begins with ourselves as individuals, touches family and friends closest to us, and includes neighbors, membership groups, community, region, nation, hemisphere, world (even the universe?). In the early 1980s we are witnessing a resurgence of nationalism throughout the world; it may be hoped that we do not lose sight of our *world citizenship* in the process. The earth is small; we can ill afford the arrogance and ethnocentricity of separation by political boundaries. Relationships with others begin at home, on the block and down in town; but they must extend to our fellow human beings all over this tiny globe — at risk is the continued existence of the species.

More on far-reaching human relationships later in the chapter. First, let us get more personal.

Reaching Out

Expressing your warm feelings for another person is a highly assertive act. And, as with other assertions we have noted, the act itself — that is, *doing it* — is more important by far than the words you use or your own style of communication. This is even more true for expressions of caring. Nothing represents a more personal, individual expression than that which says, "You mean a great deal to me at this moment."

Consider some ways of communicating that message:

A warm, firm, and extended handshake (ever notice the duration and feeling of a "brotherhood" hand clasp — e.g., Black Power, fraternity members?)

A hug, the squeeze of an arm, an arm around the shoulders, an affectionate pat on the back, the squeeze of a hand held affectionately.

"Thank you."

"You're great!"

"I really understand what you mean."

"I like what you did."

A warm smile.

Extended eye contact.

"I'm here."

A gift of love (made by the giver, or uniquely special to the recipient).

"I believe you."

"I trust you" (better yet an *act* of trust).

"I love you."

"I believe in you."

"I'm glad to see you."

"You've been on my mind."

Probably none of these messages is a new thought to you. Yet you may find it difficult to allow yourself to say or do them. It is too easy to be hung up on embarrassment, or to assume: "She knows how I feel," or "He doesn't care to hear that." But *who* doesn't care to hear that? All of us need to know we are cared about and admired and needed. If those around us are *too* subtle in their expressions of positive regard, we can too easily begin to doubt, and perhaps look elsewhere for what the Transactional Analysis people call our "strokes" — positive feedback from others.

In very *intimate relationships,* between lovers for example, it is often assumed that each partner "knows" the feelings of the other. Such assumptions often lead to the marriage counselor's office with complaints such as, "I never know how he feels," "She never tells me she loves me," "We just don't communicate any more." Frequently it is necessary only to re-establish a communication pattern in which each partner is expressing *openly* his/her feelings — particularly those of caring. The expression of caring is seldom a panacea for all the ills of an ailing marriage, but can "shore up the foundation" by helping each partner remember what was good about the relationship in the first place!

Not long ago, we asked a group of university students to tell what makes each of them feel especially good. Some of their favorite experiences are in the following list (notice how many involve someone else caring!):

Acceptance of an invitation	Giving a compliment
Achievement	Good grades
Affection	Greeting someone else
Approval	Having a friend
Assurance	Having someone say "hello"
Compliments from the opposite sex	Helping others
	Implementation of ideas
Encouragement	Independence
Expressed interest of other	Jobs completed
Friendliness	Keeping my plants alive
Getting an A on an exam	Laughter

Making new friends	Recognition when speaking
My boyfriend's/girlfriend's	Request to repeat a job
actions of love toward me	previously done
Personal satisfaction with myself	Satisfaction
Positive comment	Security
Praise	Singing
Receiving a compliment	Spoken affirmation
Recognition	Touch

We all need to *hear* positive feedback from others. Therapists encounter many, many clients who are unhappy precisely *because* they are not getting such "strokes" in their lives.

Compliments are a frequent source of discomfort for non-assertive and aggressive persons. To praise someone as a person or something someone has done may be a difficult thing for you. Again, we encourage *practice* of that which causes some anxiety. Go out of your way to praise others — not dishonestly or insincerely — but whenever a genuine opportunity presents itself. Don't concern yourself with waiting for the "right words" either. Your thoughtfulness — the honest expression of what you are feeling — will convey itself with almost any vehicle *if you act!* Try simply, "I like what you did" or "Great!" or a big smile.

Accepting compliments — to hear someone else direct a very supportive statement to you, or about you to a third person — is perhaps an even more challenging task, particularly difficult if you are not feeling good about yourself. Nevertheless, it is an assertive act — a mutually enhancing response — to accept praise from another person.

First of all, you really have no right to deny that person his/her perception of you. If you say, "Oh, you just caught me on a good day!" or "It wasn't anything special" or "It was an accident that it turned out well," you have in effect told the complimentor that he or she has poor judgment. It is as if you said to that person, "You're wrong!" Try to allow everyone the right to feelings, and if they are positive toward you, do others — and yourself — the service of accepting.

You need not go about praising yourself, or accepting credit for achievements which are not your own. However, when another person sincerely wishes to convey a positive comment about you, allow the expression without rejection or qualification. Try saying at the least, "It's hard for me to accept that, but thank you," or better yet is simply, "That feels good" or "I like to hear that."

Imagine the following scenes:
While you are wandering alone at a large gathering, a stranger walks up to you and starts a conversation, and you no longer feel anxious and lost.

Three days after you arrive in a new neighborhood, the couple next door come to welcome you with a pot of coffee and a freshly baked cake.

During your visit in another country, you are looking in vain for a street sign. A native appears and asks, "May I help you find something?"

Thoughtful acts like these are not only "strokes" for the receiver, they produce warm feelings for the person who reached out assertively. People often hesitate to initiate contact in these ways for fear of rejection — a common response for avoiding assertions! Such initiative involves concern for the other person, and some courage of your own. Yet, realistically, who could reject such a kindness?

Often actions like these are easier than you might suppose. As you enter a classroom, meeting, bus, airplane, think how easy it would be to simply approach a vacant seat and ask the person in the seat, "Is anyone sitting here?" Not only have you found a place to sit — assuming the seat *is* available — *you have begun a conversation!* Having thus opened contact, you may easily proceed to find out more about the other person ("Where are you headed?" "Have you heard this lecturer before?" "My name is Mary Doe/John Doe").

Don't wait for others to take the initiative. Take the risk of reaching out! It's a key means to caring about yourself and about others, and an important step toward greater assertiveness (and more fun!).

Parents and Children in the Assertive Family

How long has it been since you were on a seesaw ("teeter-totter")? Remember how you could affect the ride of the person on the other end by shifting your weight forward or back? If you moved forward quickly, your friend would likely drop with a solid bump! By leaning way back, you could keep the other suspended in mid-air.

Families and other interpersonal systems have a balance system not unlike that of the seesaw. A change in one member of the family will generally "upset" the balance of the total system, affecting everyone. Often families are strong "resistors" of change because of the delicate balance, even though it may be a painful or even destructive system.

Becoming more assertive is clearly a change which may upset the family balance. A formerly passive mother, for example, may severely strain family relationships as she begins to express a new assertiveness. Children who were able to easily manipulate her must find new and more direct avenues to achieve their goals. Her perhaps "pampered" husband may soon be ironing his own shirts and sharing in household chores. Such changes present a difficult adjustment for everyone, and offer a considerable obstacle to the woman (for example) who wishes to become more assertive. Similar problem potential exists for the newly assertive father, of course. For the children, a whole new set of difficulties are introduced into the path of their growing assertiveness.

It has been said that "the last frontier of human rights is that of the rights of children." Despite the history of apparent dedication to individual rights in the United States, and even despite the recent gains in rights for minorities, women, and others who have been denied and oppressed, we have made few changes in our basic notions that children are indeed second-class citizens. The veneration of "youth" in popular media, dress styles, music, literature has not carried over into a comparable respect for the rights of those who *are* young.

Without debating the relative concerns of innocence and inexperience *vs.* age and wisdom, let us simply suggest that *assertive* children, like assertive adults, are likely to be healthier and happier, more honest, less manipulative, feeling better about themselves, and headed toward more self-actualized adulthood. We favor a conscious effort in families, schools, churches, and public agencies to foster assertiveness in young people — and to create conditions which will facilitate their "natural" spontaneity of expression and which will value the honesty and openness which typically characterizes the young before fearful parents and schools destroy it.

Let us be clear — we do not advocate totally "permissive" child-rearing. The "real world" places limits upon us all, and children need to learn that fact early if they are to develop adequate life s-u-r-v-i-v-a-l skills. However, we do consider it vital that families, schools, and other child rearing social systems view children as human beings worthy of respect, honor their basic human rights, and teach them 1) that honest self-expression is a valued behavior and 2) the skills to act accordingly.

Most of the principles and procedures advocated elsewhere in this book apply to the development of assertiveness in children, so we will not present here any specialized material. Interested readers may wish to consult the approach presented directly to younger children by Pat Palmer (1977).

It is worth mentioning here that parents — and we don't mean just those who may be physically or emotionally *abusing* their children — often have difficulty discriminating between assertion and aggression when disciplining or otherwise dealing firmly with their youngsters. We believe that the same general rules we have discussed earlier for defining assertiveness apply in the case of parent-child relationships. Although each situation is unique in terms of its context, response, intent, and behavior, the key to defining assertiveness in family interactions is the notion of *mutual respect*. Notwithstanding the unique nature of the parent-child relationship, both persons are individual human beings, deserving of all the respect due any other person, child or adult.

A few words about teen-age and adult "children" are in order. Independence from our parents may be the single most important life issue we all face, certainly it is the core around which "growing up" revolves. Some rebelliousness is normal and healthy for teenagers, and facilitates their developing independence. Parental dominance and teenage inhibition may slow down that process, and delay the necessary steps toward independent adulthood. Unresolved ties with parents sometimes restrict independence in the lives of adults of all ages. In our experience, an assertive approach by the "child" can clear the air, make the situation clear to the parent, and allow needed expression of feelings on both sides.

Such a confrontation is almost inevitably painful, and it is a considerable risk for both parent and child to open up old wounds. Despite this considerable obstacle, we believe continued silence exacts much too high a price. Adults who avoid dealing with their parents or adult children as they would any other adult (with whom they feel a special closeness) can suffer unmeasured guilt, self-denial, inhibition, repressed anger, and often depression. Our colleagues in New York City, Drs. Janet Wolfe and Iris Fodor, have done excellent work with the relationship of adult mothers and daughters (1977), and their model of assertiveness in the mother-daughter relationship is useful for anyone who is dealing with this issue.

Summing up this discussion of assertiveness in the family:

1) Assertive behavior enhances both individuals and relationships.

2) Honest, open and nonhurtful assertive communication is desirable and highly valuable in families.

3) Children as well as adults should learn to be assertive within the family and beyond it.

4) The principles and procedures for defining and learning assertiveness, which are described in this book, are applicable to adults and to children (i.e., modelling, rehearsal, feedback, practice, reinforcement, mutual respect, and individual rights).

Changing family systems is more difficult, more time and energy consuming, and potentially more risky (families can and do break up) than is changing individual behavior. We encourage you to carefully evaluate, to proceed slowly, to involve everyone openly, to avoid coercion, to tolerate failure, and to remember that nobody and no approach is perfect! Notwithstanding these cautions, we also encourage you to work toward the development of an "assertive family." It can be a tremendously exciting and growth enhancing environment in which to live!

Friendship

"Nancy has seen me at my worst, watched me make stupid mistakes, felt the sting of my unjustified anger, and been there when I was coming apart at the seams. It's amazing; she's still my friend!"

There is no relationship quite like that of friendship. Not so irrational as love; yet far more intense than acquaintance, friendship is perhaps the least understood of human interactions.

Most relationship research involves strangers or lovers, and our actual *knowledge* of friendship continues to be sketchy at best. Yet some popular wisdom is useful in examining the bond between friends:

...friends have some interests in common;

...friends share an on-going relationship, with periodic (although not necessarily regular) contact;

...friends trust one another, at least to some degree, with information, money, safety, other relationships;

...friends can say "no" to each other and still remain friends;

...friends can see the worst in each other and still remain friends;

...friends rarely feel they "owe" each other anything; give and take is without obligation between them (perhaps with some limits!);

...friendship is also characterized by understanding, communication, acceptance, lack of embarrassment, trust.

Friends may go a long time without seeing one another. It is not uncommon to see tearful reunions at airports, parties, and homecomings between friends who have not seen each other for years. Friendships often survive no more contact than an annual ritual holiday card! What keeps them going? Can such a relationship really be called a "friendship"?

Friendship is held within us, an attitude toward another person much like love, anger, or prejudice. It requires no overt expression over extended periods. It requires merely a *feeling of commitment* to the relationship. Often such a feeling is supported by the *belief* that the other person cares about one's well-being, that the other values the relationship as well. If we believe that we are important to each other — important enough that we think of each other warmly now and again — we will likely remain friends, even if we don't see each other for years.

Friends usually share warm memories of pleasant times past. Some such "pleasant times" may include traumatic experiences, such as having been in an accident or natural disaster together. To have survived, perhaps through mutual cooperative effort, creates a lasting bond which requires little attention to maintain its strength for a very long time.

But what has this to do with assertiveness? How does assertive action contribute to friendship, or vice versa?

Let us pose an unproven theory for your consideration: *If you act assertively most of the time, you are more likely to have satisfying relationships than if you act in nonassertive or aggressive ways.* We cannot prove that idea. In fact, we have not even dreamed up a research study which would allow us to test it (if you do, we would love to hear from you!). But our observation of assertive people over many years leads us to conclude that it is a pretty good bet!

Acting on that hypothesis, then, and assuming that you would like to have satisfying relationships, we invite you to apply the assertive skills you are learning to the development of friendship: ...Take the risks necessary to build an acquaintance into a friend. ...Allow yourself to be seen "as you are" by that person...Share something of yourself you would not ordinarily tell someone else. ...Be more spontaneous with your new friend, suggest an activity on the spur of the moment, really listen to what is important in your friend's life, give a gift for no special occasion...Ask your friend's advice with problem or help with a project (remembering that an assertive friend can say "no" and still like you!)... Simply tell the person you like him/her...Get things "up front" between you, seeking understanding and openness; don't allow assumptions to define your relationship...Clear the air between you; if you are annoyed or suspect that your friend may be, bring it up...Get *honest*; if the relationship can't handle it, it probably would not have lasted anyway; if it can, you'll be miles ahead! As adults, friendship helps to define who we are, much as family does when we are children. (The absence of friends also says a great deal about us.) Assertive action on your part can make all the difference in nurturing friendships. Maybe you've put it off long enough?

Membership in the Human Community

Thornton Wilder, in his popular play, *Our Town*, addressed one of his key characters thus: "Jane Crofeet, the Crofeet Farm, Grover's Corners, Sutton County, New Hampshire, United States of America, Continent of North America, the Earth, the Solar System, the Universe, the Mind of God." Wilder showed a remarkable sense of citizenship in the world; few of us have so thoughtfully considered our relationships to the entire human community.

Indeed, is it even possible to deal with that virtually unreachable concept? In what sense *am* I a world citizen? I can talk with and see my neighbors in the local community. I can visit, with minimal difficulty, people in nearby states, or even across the country. I can share government agencies; vote in local, state and national elections; share a historical and cultural heritage with other citizens of the United States. What have I in common with the people of Nepal, or Luxembourg, or Sri Lanka? Do I really think of them as my brothers and sisters in humankind?

No individual can exist alone. None of us has the necessary knowledge, skills, or personal resources necessary to function with total independence in the world. We are interdependent, and our assertiveness must take into account and respect the needs of our neighbors as well as our own.

Even without the dramatic evidence offered from space, we may easily recognize the fragility of world order in any day's headlines. We note the continuing efforts by governments of many nations to maintain world peace and some balance of order on the planet. And we see how easily aggression and the quest for power disturb that balance.

So many international issues remain unresolved, awaiting assertive action by those courageous enough to transcend nationalistic limits and assume leadership in *solving problems*, rather than displaying power. Hunger, extreme poverty, sanitation, disposal of nuclear and other hazardous wastes...the list goes on.

The principles of assertive action which we have discussed throughout this book apply to these concerns as well. Perhaps you have found assertiveness training helpful in your own life and relationships. We urge you to demonstrate your appreciation for that help by taking assertive action as a world citizen. Write letters supporting public officials who take courageous action. Contact your elected representatives to express your views on important issues.

Work to replace aggression with assertion wherever you can. You may choose to support tighter controls on handguns, for instance, or reduced television violence. Some will demonstrate against nuclear power plants or weapons proliferation. Perhaps you advocate free-enterprise replacement of government bureaucracies which fail to provide necessary services. The ERA may be your major cause (as this is written, just six months remain available for ratification). Support is always needed for local programs of rape crisis intervention, and training for parents to help them protect their children.

The principle of assertive action is well established in Western culture, and a vital element in the U.S. Constitution. The spirit of civil disobedience, when other attempts to change intolerable situations have failed, has a proud heritage. Henry David Thoreau is the "patron saint" of civil disobedience, but one need look no further than the U.S. Declaration of Independence or such famous historic events as the Boston Tea Party for other well known and highly respected foundations. A vital principle of any such action, of course, is the individual's willingness to accept responsibility for the consequences thereof. Twentieth century examples of such personally responsible, public assertiveness are Mahatma Ghandi and Martin Luther King. Whatever our personal views of the substantive issues in their actions, we must stand in awe of those who have made their deepest beliefs public by living accordingly, caring more for the welfare of humankind than for their individual comfort and safety.

Ultimately, those acts which are in the best interest of our fellow humans are in our own best interests as well. If I act assertively to right a social wrong, I act to the benefit of all who are members of the society, including myself. Thus assertive action, in the best sense, is at once in my own self-interest *and* unselfish!

There are a thousand causes worthy of your energies. If your assertiveness ends when your steak is served the way you like it, or when you get correct change, your life may be more pleasant temporarily, but will not count for much.

Oliver Wendell Holmes said it beautifully (if you can forgive his sexist language):

"A man must share in the action and passion of his times, at the risk of being judged not to have lived."

12

Anger is Not Aggression

Peace cannot be kept by force. It can only be achieved by understanding.

—*Albert Einstein*

The common confusion of angry *feelings* with aggressive *behavior* creates a tremendous barrier to expression of the natural, healthy, universal, and useful human emotion we call anger.

Nonassertive people often say, "I never get angry." We don't believe it! Everyone *gets* angry. Some people have so controlled themselves that they do not openly *show* anger. Typically, such a controlled individual suffers from migraine headaches, asthma, ulcers, or skin problems.

We are convinced that expression of anger is a healthy thing, and that it can be done constructively. People who develop spontaneous assertiveness can release anger effectively in nondestructive ways, and thus make aggressive actions unnecessary.

An important part of nondestructive expression of anger is to accept responsibility for your own feelings. It is *you* who feels the anger, and that doesn't make the other person "stupid," "an S.O.B.," or the cause of your feeling.

A physical expression of a strong feeling can be a useful means for "venting" hostility. Banging the table, stomping the floor, crying, striking at the air, hitting a pillow — all can be good devices for releasing strong feeling without aggression toward another person. However, they are *not* adequate alone, as will be discussed later in this chapter.

Preventing the buildup of hostility over time, by spontaneous expression when you feel angry, is the healthiest way we know to deal with anger. Some of the verbal expressions others have found useful include:

"I'm very angry."
"I'm becoming very mad."
"I strongly disagree with you."
"I get damn mad when you say that."
"I'm very disturbed by this whole thing."
"It bothers me."
"Stop bothering me."
"That's not fair."
"Don't do that to me."
"That really pisses me off."
"You have no right to do that."
"I really don't like that."
"I'm mad as hell, and I'm not going to take this anymore!"

All too often, we have observed people who express anger, frustration, or disappointment with another person by cowardly, indirect, and unnecessarily hurtful methods. Moreover, if the desired goal is to change the behavior of the intended target, these approaches are rarely successful.

A "classic" example is the case of the newlyweds, Martha and John. In the first few weeks of their marriage, Martha had discovered at least a dozen of John's habits which she found objectionable. Unfortunately for both, she was unable — or unwilling — to find the courage to confront John openly with her concerns. Martha instead chose the "safe" way to express her dislike of John's behavior; she confided in her mother. Worse yet, not content with almost daily telephone conversations with mother about John's shortcomings, she also used family get-togethers as occasions to berate John before the rest of the family.

This "see-how-bad-he is" style — telling a third person (or persons) about one's dislikes of another — may have disastrous effects upon a relationship. John feels hurt, embarrassed, and hostile about Martha's attacks upon him. He wishes she had chosen the privacy of their own relationship to tell him of her annoyances. Instead of being motivated to change his habits, he responded to her aggressive approach with bitterness and a resolve to strike back by intensifying the very behaviors she would have him change. Had Martha chosen courageously to assert herself directly by telling John of her feelings, she would have created a good foundation for a cooperative effort in modifying John's behavior.

Another example will help clarify our point of view concerning the expression of anger:

Adam took his car to a large repair shop for several hours of work. Maintenance in this shop is done on a first-come, first-served basis, and Adam arrived at 8 a.m. He told the manager he would pick the car up around 4:30 p.m. When he came back, the following conversation took place:

Adam: "Hi, my name is Adam Z., and I'm here to pick up my car."

Manager (looking through his worksheets): "I'm sorry, sir, we haven't gotten to your car yet."

Adam: "Damn! That really makes me mad! This is supposed to be first-come, first-served, and I was here at 8 a.m. What happened?"

Manager: "It was our mistake, we put it in the back and got busy and overlooked it."

Adam: "Well, hell, that doesn't do me any good. It's an inconvenience for me to get my car in and leave it all day."

Manager: "I know that and I apologize. I promise to get it done first thing in the morning if you want to bring it back."

At this point, the customer must decide what his options are and choose accordingly. Adam could try to get the manager to have someone fix his car by working overtime; he could decide to take his car elsewhere; he could return the next day for the repair work; he could demand a loan car; he could become aggressive.

Notice Adam expressed his anger without being aggressive toward the manager. He was rightfully mad and told the manager so without downgrading him as a person. He might have responded aggressively: "You can take that repair job and shove it," and stormed out, or said, "You damn S.O.B.s never do anything right around here. I demand that you fix my car right now!" Either of these statements would likely inflame the manager and not accomplish much.

It is possible and desirable to express angry feelings without hurting someone (physically or emotionally) in the process. Honest and spontaneous expression will help to prevent inappropriate and destructive anger. It will often achieve your goals at the outset. Even when assertion doesn't gain what you're after, however, it still defuses the anger you might direct toward yourself if you had done nothing.

Despite its advocacy by some popular psychological theorists, the current fad of *venting* aggression (by hitting other people with foam bats or by shouting obscenities) is *not* psychologically healthy. By "releasing" angry feelings through aggressive acts (however "benign" they may *appear*), one simply learns to handle anger aggressively. The discussion later in this chapter of "The Myth of Instinctive Aggression" will help to clarify our thoughts on this controversy.

Facts, Theories, and Myths About Anger

We keep looking for the easy answers.

We elect a President who offers glib solutions to the incredibly complex issues of the day, as if the good guys and the bad guys could still be identified by the color of their hats. We try to identify straight-line relationships between apparent "causes" and their "effects" — as if questions about "why I behave that way" are satisfied by a simple "because you were toilet trained too early." And we search for effortless equations which "explain" the mysteries of human behavior.

Anger is one of those phenomena which is an easy target for such simplistic shots. It is variously characterized as "sinful" (and therefore to be avoided at all costs), "freeing" (and therefore to be expressed at all costs), and all of the options in between.

Part of the reason for the lack of adequate explanations and

Anger: Facts, Theories, and Myths

FACTS	THEORIES	MYTHS
Anger is a feeling, with physiological components.	Shy people, depressed people, and suicides are expressing anger at themselves.	Venting (by yelling, pounding pillows, hitting with foam bats) "releases" anger and therefore "deals with" it.
Anger is not a mode of behavior.	Anger should always be expressed spontaneously/immediately.	Women are less angry than men.
Anger is universal among human beings.		Some people never get angry.
Nonexpression of anger leads to increased risk of coronary heart disease in both men and women.	Anger should always be contained until it can be expressed in a calm, rational manner.	Anger always results from frustration.
What really matters is resolving the issue. Thus, the method of anger expression is important.	Verbal expression of anger is always desirable.	Anger is always a "secondary" emotion, with another "real" feeling behind it.
Venting of anger — "catharsis" — is of lasting value only insofar as it sets the stage for resolution.	Men in our culture are able to express anger more easily than women.	Aggressive behavior is a sure sign of an "angry person."
Aggressive expression leads to further aggressive expression, not resolution.	Women are generally inhibited in anger expression by their social conditioning in our culture.	TV violence, active sports and/or competitive work "releases" anger.
Anger is not a "steam kettle" phenomenon; it does not build up and finally explode.		Aggressive behavior is instinctive in humans.
Most anger is directed toward those close to us, not strangers.		Anger is a destructive, sinful, undesirable emotion.

methods for dealing with anger is that anger research has been limited and not very clear, at least until very recently. Nevertheless, a fairly consistent pattern of data is now emerging which could move us a giant step toward a theoretically sound and usable working model of anger. Bob Alberti has developed a scheme for examining some current notions about anger, classified under three headings: *facts* — findings which are clearly demonstrated by careful research, or are self-evident; *theories* — ideas which contain some demonstrable fact, but which lack clear evidence of validity, and sometimes lead us astray; and *myths* — ideas which, despite their "seniority" in many cases, have proven inaccurate, or which contradict the evidence, or which may appear on the surface to be accurate but contain false assumptions. The chart on page 107 is a summary of what we "know" about anger. Consult the References for further information   (Averill, J., 1981; Berkowitz, L., 1978; Biaggio, M.K., 1980; Bohart, A.C., 1980; Hoffman, R.A. et al., 1979; Hokanson, J.E. et al., 1968; Van Egeren, L.F., 1978).

The Myth of "Instinctive Aggression"

"Look at the history of humankind," you say, "wars, violence, inhumanity, street fights, child abuse, senseless killings. I *must* believe that we are *naturally* aggressive beings" And after all, our social systems tend to give a great deal of reinforcement for "aggression" even in its less violent forms: the "aggressive" salesperson, the "highly competitive" athlete, the "hard-nosed" manager, the "strong-willed" politician — all tend to be esteemed.

Popular views of the "aggression-is-natural" viewpoint include those of such heavyweights as psychoanalyst Sigmund Freud, ethologist Konrad Lorenz, and psychotherapist George Bach. They offer persuasive arguments:

Freud: "The tendency to aggression is an innate, independent, instinctual disposition in man." (*Civilization and Its Discontents,* Chapter 6).

Lorenz: "We find that aggression...is really an essential part of the life-preserving organization of instincts." (*On Aggression*, page 44).

Bach: "The healthy fusion of aggression with developmental process is crucial to the child's eventual mastery of the environment and his struggle for survival in a difficult, competitive culture." (*Creative Aggression*, page 45).

Can we dismiss our disagreement with these views as merely an honest difference of opinion? No. We submit that the most enlightened evidence supports a view of aggression as a *potential, but not universal* form of behavior. It would be foolish to deny the widespread existence of human aggression, but good cross-cultural studies show that it is not a universal form of human expression.

It is worth special mention here that *aggression* is not the same thing as *anger*! Anger is a perfectly natural, healthy human emotion which may be expressed in a number of ways, including aggressively, nonassertively, assertively, or not at all. Anger is a *feeling*, an emotion we all feel at times. Aggression is a *behavioral style* of expression.

We have come a long way since 1970 when in the first edition of *Your Perfect Right*, we cited Lorenz' *On Aggression* as a helpful resource in understanding aggressive behavior. Our own understanding of the research literature, and the general level of knowledge of aggression and assertion have increased tremendously.

Simplistic, "instinctive" theories of aggression are no longer viable, if indeed they ever were. Ethologists like Lorenz, aided by popular writers such as Robert Ardrey (1966), presented a view of instinctive human aggressive behavior which, like the animal cousins we were said to emulate, appeared whenever we were called upon to defend honor, life, or territory. Lorenz further advocated the regular release of our aggressive energy, lest it "build up" and come out spontaneously in uncontrolled, potentially destructive ways.

Paralleling the work of Lorenz, an entire school of psycho-therapy grew up around the notion of "letting it out," integrating Freudian concepts of the innate need to express energy with Gestalt notions of the oneness of mind and body and existential philosophy of living each moment "in the here-and-now." Therapists Fritz Perls, George Bach and a host of their followers got clients up off the couch, shouting at each other in groups, flailing each other with foam bats and epithets, confronting feelings loudly, and expressing aggression "creatively."

There is no doubt some value in such "venting" of strong feelings. However, the clear evidence from more recent, careful experimental studies is that *aggression produces aggression.* Thus, if you learn — as a young child under your parents' tutelage, or as an adult taught by a therapist — to express strong feelings aggressively (hurtfully), you will adopt an aggressive style.

Psychologist Leonard Berkowitz (1965, 1969), for example, has reported experimental studies which confirm our contention that there are nonviolent methods of emotional release which contain the benefits but not the harmful effects of direct aggression. He suggests that a direct aggressive attack provokes additional aggression, both in the attacker and in the subject.

In one study, for instance, women who were insulted were permitted two styles of response. Group one was allowed to describe their angry feelings to the insulter (e.g., "That really makes me mad"). Group two women were given freedom to strike back and attack the insulter. After the experiment, the women who described their feelings (group one) maintained less hostile feelings toward their insulter than did the women in group two, who were permitted to attack directly.

Berkowitz concludes, from the results of many such studies, that although persons may "feel better" after venting hostility aggressively, such reinforcement of destructive acts leads to further hurtful behavior. We agree heartily.

Assertive responses, on the other hand, can both effectively express your strong feelings *and* give the other person a chance to respond nondefensively — perhaps even to change that behavior toward you which angered you in the first place!

As research and more sophisticated analyses of human behavior have evolved, the position of *social learning theory* most adequately explains the nature of aggressive — and other — behavior. Albert Bandura, leading theorist of the social learning viewpoint states it succinctly (1973):

> The social learning theory of human aggression adopts the position that man is endowed with neurophysiological mechanisms that enable him to behave aggressively, but the activation of these mechanisms depends upon appropriate stimulation and is subject to cortical control. Therefore, the specific forms that aggressive behavior takes, the frequency with which it is expressed, the situations in which it is displayed, and the specific targets elected for attack are largely determined by social experience. (pp. 29-30)

Thus, in a refinement of the "instinct" notion, contemporary theorists of the social learning and socio-biology schools agree that humans have the genetic *potential* which makes aggression *possible* — but not automatic or universal. *Social and cultural learning* determines how a person will respond under particular circumstances, and governs one's personal standards for the appropriateness of particular actions.

You have the power of conscious choice as to whether, when, and how to express your anger. We urge you to choose the assertive alternative!

"I'm Afraid of My Buried Anger!"

Anger is a powerful influence on our capacity to understand and express feelings, and on our mental health in general. Psychotherapist Andrew Salter observes that, "Whenever I'm feeling depressed, it's because I've forgotten to be nasty to somebody!" We are acquainted with the delightfully spontaneous Mr. Salter (who is responsible for the fundamental concepts of assertiveness training), and believe that he uses the word "nasty" for effect; it may also be read "direct," "firm," or "openly angry."

Yet, anger remains one of the most difficult emotions for many people to express. Our assertive behavior groups often lose members when "assertive expression of anger" becomes the topic. Many are simply *afraid* of their anger. Having "buried" it for years, they are terrified of the potential consequences should they suddenly "let it out." It is as if some evil and forbidding monster will escape from its cage.

In our experience, we've found the gradual freeing of anger expression can be frightening for some people. Often, they have not learned constructive, assertive approaches to expressing their anger. Finally, they assume that any anger brought into the open will be hurtful to the other person. "I'd sooner suffer in silence than to hurt anyone," is the common, unfortunate plea.

Unfortunate because so much agony in human relationships results from anger which is denied expression. Both persons suffer. There is evidence to suggest that buried anger comes out as resentment, envy, migraines, ulcers, or skin problems. (No clear proof, however, and the actual mechanisms are not yet known.) The other person doesn't hear of the unexpressed anger, continues to behave in ways which are upsetting, and wonders why the relationship is deteriorating.

However, an important distinction must be made here. Recent research has shown the popular concept of anger as a "steam kettle" to be false. Many people have believed that by *expressing* one's anger, the anger would go away and prevent the problems associated with "building up inside." We now know that anger expression is only the beginning.

It has been discovered recently that *emotional relief from anger comes only when expression is accompanied by some resolution of the problem which caused the anger.* Getting the feelings out — even in appropriately assertive ways — only "sets the stage." Working out the conflict with the other person, or sometimes within oneself, is the all-important, follow-up step which makes the difference.

The evidence also shows us that the lack of such coping or resolution action may actually increase anger whether it has been expressed or not. So, get your anger out, but follow up your (assertive) release of feelings with problem-solving actions which will help to resolve the issue. You may work toward assertive negotiation of solutions with the person with whom you have been angry, or you may sometimes find satisfaction within yourself (perhaps with the aid of a therapist or trusted friend). In either event, don't stop by saying, "I'm mad as hell!" Follow through with "...and here's what I think we can do about it..."

"So What Can I Do About My Anger?"

There *are* constructive ways to handle anger. Our view of a healthy approach to dealing with anger is this:

Before you get angry

(1) Recognize, and allow yourself to believe, that anger is a natural, healthy, non-evil human feeling. Everyone feels it, we just don't all *express* it. You needn't fear your anger.

(2) Remember that *you* are responsible for your own feelings. You got angry at what happened; the other person didn't "make" you angry.

(3) Remember that anger and aggression *are not the same thing!* Anger can be expressed assertively.

(4) Get to know yourself. Recognize those events and behaviors which trigger your anger. As some say, "Find your own buttons, so you'll know when they're pushed!

(5) Don't "set yourself up" to get angry! If your temperature rises when you must wait in a slow line (at the bank, in traffic), work at finding alternate ways to accomplish those tasks (bank by mail, find another route to work).

(6) Learn to relax. If you have developed the skill of relaxing yourself, learn to apply this response when your anger is triggered. You may wish to take this a step further by "desensitizing" yourself to certain anger-invoking situations (see Chapter 8).

(7) Develop several coping strategies for handling your anger, including relaxation, physical exertion, "stress inoculation" statements, working out resolution within yourself. Focus on relationship goals and assertive methods.

(8) Develop and practice assertive methods for expressing your anger, following the principles described in this book: be spontaneous; don't wait and let it built up resentment; state it directly; avoid sarcasm and innuendo; use honest, expressive language; avoid namecalling, putdowns, physical attacks, one-upmanship.

(9) Develop and practice assertive methods for resolution of your anger. Learn conflict management strategies. Learn how to listen nondefensively. Learn to identify exactly what triggered your anger in a situation, so you can be specific as you seek solutions.

When you get angry:

(10) Apply the coping strategies you developed in (7) above.

(11) Make some verbal expression of concern (assertively).

(12) Take a few moments to decide if this situation is one you wish to work out with the other person, or one you will resolve within yourself.

(13) "Schedule" time for working things out. If you are able to do so spontaneously, fine; if not, arrange a time (with the other person or with yourself) to deal with the issue later. [See also (18) below.].

(14) State your feelings directly, with appropriate nonverbal cues (if you are genuinely angry, a smile is inappropriate!).

(15) Accept responsibility for your feelings. [See (2) above].

(16) Stick to specifics and to the present situation. Avoid generalizing about the entire history of your relationship!

(17) Work toward *resolution*, not "victory."

(18) Keep your life clear! Deal with issues when they arise, when you feel the feelings — not after hours/days/weeks of "stewing" about it. When you can't deal with it immediately, arrange a specific time when you can and will!

Go ahead! Get angry! But develop a positive, assertive style for expressing it. You, and those around you, will appreciate it.

Constructive Conflict Resolution

As a footnote to this discussion of anger, let us take a brief look at a special application of what we have learned: How is it possible to improve the process of resolving conflicts between people or groups?

There are some useful guidelines for conflict resolution which have emerged out of the work of behavioral scientists working with marriage relationships and with organizational behavior. Most of these principles are parallel to the methods of assertiveness training presented throughout this book.

Conflict is more easily resolved when both parties...

...avoid a "win-lose position. The attitude that "I am going to win, and you are going to lose" will more likely result in *both* losing. By remaining flexible, both can win — at least in part.

...gain the same information about the situation. Because perceptions so often differ, it is good to make *everything* explicit!

...have goals which are *basically* compatible. If we both want to preserve the relationship more than to win, we have a better chance!

...act honestly and directly toward one another.

...clarify their individual actual needs in the situation. I probably don't *need* to win. I do need to gain some specific outcome (e.g., behavior change by you, more money) and to retain my self-respect.

...seek solutions rather than deciding who is to blame.

...accept responsibility for their own feelings ("I am angry!" NOT "You made me mad!").

...are willing to face the problem openly, rather than avoiding or hiding from it.

...agree upon some means of negotiation or exchange. I probably would agree to give on some points if you would give on some! (and vice versa).

When conflict involves strong angry feelings, many people fear bringing those feelings into the open. Many of us have been told since early childhood that anger is bad. Recognizing the *value* of anger and allowing that natural feeling to be expressed non-destructively will go a long way toward creating the conditions necessary for constructive conflict resolution.

13

Must We Put Up With Put Downs?

I am the inferior of any man whose rights I trample underfoot.

—Horace Greeley

Many questions we hear from workshop participants concern how to handle put-downs. Perhaps this is because there are so many reasons we humans find to put each other down: for the way we look or dress, for our cultural backgrounds, for our speech, for our mannerisms, for our work performance.

There is plenty to criticize in other people's behavior, of course. What's more, most people also engage in *self* put-downs. This chapter considers four types: the direct verbal put-down; the indirect verbal put-down; the nonverbal put-down; the self-put-down, and what you can do about them.

The Direct Verbal Put-Down. This type of behavior is obvious: another person is verbally "blasting" you for something. Let us say that you are coming out of an elevator, and accidentally brush someone as you pass by. That person responds immediately in a hostile manner: "Damn it! Why don't you watch where you're going! You fool, you could have hurt me!" The tirade may continue, but the person's intent is quite "up front," isn't it? How should you respond to such a caustic reaction, triggered by an innocent gesture on your part?

We suggest that your first action be to allow the person to vent the angry feelings until he or she slows down. When the outburst has subsided, you could say, "I apologize for brushing against you. I didn't do it intentionally. You're obviously upset, but I do not like to be called names or yelled at. I can get your point without that." It is important not to retaliate aggressively in return. Research tells us that aggression begets aggression, but we are asking you to "turn the other cheek" by remaining *assertive* in the face of an aggressive response.

Steps we have found valuable when confronted with a direct verbal put-down are: admit when you are wrong, even in the face of insult; acknowledge the other person's feelings; assert yourself about the way he or she is reacting; give a short statement to bring the encounter to an end.

Indirect Verbal Put-Downs. What should you say to a boss who states, "You did a nice job on that project you turned in yesterday. All the grammatical errors gave it a folksy quality." Or, what if your spouse says, "I love the way you look when you wear that outfit; old clothes become you." Do you do a double-take? Are you confused? What is the real meaning in statements of this kind?

Such indirect verbal put-downs are *indirect aggression.* In their book, *The Assertive Woman* (1975), Stanlee Phelps and Nancy Austin speak of indirect aggressive behavior in the following way: "...in order to achieve her goal, she may use trickery, seduction, or manipulation." They note further that the reactions this behavior causes in others are confusion, frustration, and feelings of being manipulated. Because indirect aggressive behavior comes out as a concealed attack, Phelps and Austin label the person who behaves in this manner a "mad dog in a lamb's suit."

Handle an indirect verbal put-down first by asking for more information. In either of the situations given above, one might reply with, "What are you saying?" or "What do you mean?" Such a response tends to help clarify the other person's true intent (You may have misunderstood!)

Your second response will depend upon the other person's

answer. Part of your goal in the interaction, however, is to teach the person a new way of behaving toward you. If the boss indicates on the second exchange that, "Oh, I think you did a good job," you might still want to say, "Well, thank you, but I was a little confused. If you're really concerned about my errors in grammar, I hope you can say so directly. I couldn't really tell if you thought the project was good or bad." The message you are trying to teach the boss is that you prefer that he or she be straightforward with you.

In marriage relationships, it is fun to have some good-natured teasing; too often, however, underlying hostilities come out in the guise of "teasing." Your spouse may have been kidding you all along, but there are more straightforward and less destructive ways to kid or tease people.

Nonverbal Put-Downs. "Sticks and stones may break my bones, but words will never hurt me" is a taunt children throughout the ages have used to rebuff name-callers. Unfortunately, no reply has yet been invented for our "adversaries" who put us down *without* words. What is the best way to respond to an obscene gesture or a dirty look? How should pouting and silly grins or smirks be dealt with when the person uses no words to help you verify his or her intention precisely? The nonverbal put-down is much harder to deal with because the person responding in this manner is not using words in the first place, and secondly, may not always be consciously aware of the put-down. Moreover, you cannot be certain you accurately "read" the nonverbal message.

If another person responds toward you with an obviously *aggressive* nonverbal put-down, attempt to get the person to use words instead of gestures. You might say, in an assertive manner, "Could you translate that look (gesture) into words for me? I have trouble knowing what you're feeling unless you tell me directly." Be prepared for a verbal put-down at this point and respond accordingly, as per the suggestions given above.

The *nonassertive* nonverbal put-down is the least direct of all. When someone aggressively shakes a fist in your face, it is difficult to misinterpret the meaning! If you are making a request of someone who begins to stare off into space or grins inappropriately, the intent is not so obvious. There is a good chance that the person who responds with an indirect nonverbal put-down is doing so automatically, out of habit. We all have mannerisms which take the place of words. Although our purpose is not to have people eliminate all nonverbal messages, we feel that it is good to accompany them with words if there is a chance they might be misinterpreted.

Imagine that you are about to pay for a purchase when the cashier looks at you, grimaces, and sighs in an anguished manner. You may wish to "write this off" as nothing personal, or merely assume the cashier is having a bad day. If you are bothered by the incident, however, we feel it is good to deal with the situation. Ask the person to explain further: "I didn't understand your expression," or, "I'm not sure what you mean by that," or, "Did I do something you didn't like?" This serves to place the nonverbal response out in the open, to clear the air. If you have done something that bothers the person, you deserve to know. Your next response will depend on what transpires, but we feel it is good at some point to explain to the person that it is difficult to interpret such nonverbal messages.

The Self-Put-Down. We all should be advocates for ourselves! Too much time is spent putting ourselves down verbally and through internal thoughts. The human machine works best when uncluttered by negative material. We should be fair judges or critics of our own behavior, but most of us go beyond the call of duty! Many engage in self-put-down behaviors which serve no constructive purpose. Start catching yourself when you engage in self-put-down behavior and replace those messages with good, self-confident ones. Be assertive with yourself; think and say self-fulfilling thoughts instead of self-deprecating ones!

"Assertive Aggression"

Although examples of physical aggression proliferate in the news media, its more common cousin, mental aggression, is much more of a problem in most of our lives. Physical aggression itself is seldom pure, because there is most often "a story" behind the violence. Mental aggression is usually the catalyst that triggers the physical outburst. The overt forms of mental aggression can be quite varied and unique, depending upon the inventiveness of the person engaging in the act. A threatening gesture, a firey look, a caustic remark, an aggressive body stance, sly innuendos — the parade of instigations and retaliations goes on.

The question is — are there any forms of nonphysical aggression which are justifiable? If an in-law writes you a nasty letter, do you have a right to be aggressive in return? If your boss calls you a foul name because you botched up a job, can you "give it right back?" If your spouse maligns you, is it ever acceptable to engage in the battle with full force? If you assert yourself with a line jumper and get told to "Go to hell!," are you then free to lambaste the offender? If you have been repeatedly assertive about a situation and there are still no changes forthcoming, do you then have a right to be aggressive?

When someone has done something which you feel is aggressive in nature, a first step should be to assertively *ask for clarification*. In other words, don't assume aggression was intended without checking it out. The next step is to assertively *deal with the act* of aggression rather than to take flight or to stay and fight. This is the true meaning of "turning the other cheek." It is not best to leave the situation; such an action at this point does not resolve anything. Neither does a fighting-back response. Many people mistakenly feel justified in retaliating against the aggressive person, feeling that someone who can dish out this type of response is not easily hurt, can take it, is hard-shelled. Our experience has been that the person who comes across aggressively, even chronically so, is often as personally insecure as those who behave nonassertively. It is a good idea to treat them with the same care most of us express with the overtly cowering nonassertive type: in an assertive, not aggressive, manner, even if you feel anger.

Regular assertive responses allow one to be slow to anger; but if those feelings arise, *express anger assertively*, not aggressively. Do not be afraid to use assertive anger if you have feelings of anger. You need not become aggressively angry in order for the other person to feel the intensity of your upset.

Finally, do not hesitate to *moralize with the individual* about his or her behavior toward you. Statements such as, "I feel what you're saying is really unfair," and "It seems to me you're being dishonest" may help the individual to settle down. Most will begin to de-escalate when met with an initial assertive retort; but if the individual "stays with" the aggression, assertive anger and moralizing may help bring the situation to an adequate resolution.

This leads us to the inevitable question: *Is it ever acceptable to be aggressive?* What if the individual doesn't respond to any of the above steps? What recourse do you have if the individual continually rebuffs your assertive attempts to ameliorate the conflict? The choice boils down to leaving the encounter or becoming aggressive in return. Your choice must necessarily focus on the "cruciality" of the issue at stake. You are probably ahead to leave the situation whenever the issues are not matters of moral or ethical importance, but only of "ego" importance. If the issue is a morally important one, however, the answer is "yes," we consider it acceptable to be verbally aggressive at times.

Even if one is forced to be aggressive, it should not be with an attitude of relish, but with an attitude of regret. If you find that there are times you "need" to be aggressive, be careful that you don't find yourself enjoying the chance to "pay the bastard back!"

Thus it seems to us that there are two types of aggression: "aggressive aggression" and "assertive aggression." The latter is an "appropriate" aggression born of righteous indignation, rather than hate or hostility.

14

Beyond Assertiveness

> *God, give us the serenity to accept what cannot be changed, the courage to change what should be changed, and the wisdom to distinguish the one from the other.*
>
> —*Reinhold Niebuhr*

Our theme throughout this book has been to emphasize *individual choice,* and the value of assertive behavior to people seeking self-direction. The perceptive reader will have recognized some of the potential shortcomings and hazards inherent in personal assertiveness. Sensitivity is required in taking into account some of these limitations and potentially negative consequences of asserting yourself.

Although assertive behavior will most often be its own reward, the consequences on occasion may deflate its value. Consider, for example, the young boy who assertively refuses the big bully's request to ride his new bike, and as a result finds himself nursing a black eye! His assertion was perfectly legitimate, but the *other person* was unwilling to accept the denial of *his* desire. Therefore, without suggesting that assertiveness be avoided if it appears hazardous, we do encourage you to consider the probable *consequences* of your assertive acts. Under certain circumstances, the value of an assertion will be outweighed by the value of avoiding the probable response to that assertion!

If you *can* act assertively, you are free to *choose* whether or not you will. If you are *unable* to act assertively, you have no choices; you will be governed by others, and your well-being will suffer. *Our most important goal is to enable YOU to make the choice!*

Potential Adverse Reactions

In our experience with helping others to learn assertiveness for more than a decade, we have found few negative results. Certain people do, however, respond in a disagreeable manner when they face assertion. Therefore, even if the assertion is handled properly — neither nonassertive nor aggressive to any degree — one may at times be faced with unpleasant reactions.

Here are a few examples:

1. *Backbiting.* After you have asserted yourself, the other person involved may be somewhat disgruntled, though perhaps not openly. For example, if you see someone jumping in line ahead of you and you assert yourself, the person may go to the end of the line, but grumble while passing you. You may hear such things as "Who do you think you are, anyway?" "Big deal!" "Big man!" and so forth. To our way of thinking, the best solution is simply to ignore the childish behavior. If you do retort in some manner, you are likely only to complicate the situation by reinforcing the fact that the words "got to you."

2. *Aggression.* At times the other party may become outwardly hostile toward you. Yelling or screaming could be involved, or physical reactions like bumping, shoving, or hitting. Again, the best approach is to avoid escalating the condition. You may choose to express regret that he or she is upset by your actions, but you must remain steadfast in your assertion. This is especially true if you will have further contacts. If you back down on your assertion, you will simply reinforce this negative reaction. After such reinforcement, the next time you assert yourself with this person, the probability will be high that you will receive another aggressive reaction.

3. *Temper Tantrums.* In certain situations, you may assert yourself with someone who has had his or her own way for a long time. She or he may then react to your assertion by looking hurt, claiming precarious health, saying "You don't like me!" crying,

feeling sorry for him or herself, or otherwise attempting to control you or make you feel guilty. Again, you must choose, but it is nearly always best to ignore such behavior.

4. *Psychosomatic Reactions.* Actual physical illness may occur in some individuals if you thwart a long-established habit. Abdominal pains, headaches, and feeling faint are just a few of the symptoms possible. Choose to be firm in the assertion, recognizing that the other person will adjust to the new situation in a short time. You should also be consistent in your assertion whenever the same situation recurs with this individual. If you are inconsistent in asserting your rights, the other person involved will become confused and may eventually just ignore your assertions.

5. *Overapologizing.* On rare occasions after you have asserted yourself, the other party involved will be overly apologetic or humble to you. You should point out that such behavior is unnecessary. If, in later encounters he or she seems to be afraid of you or deferent toward you, do not take advantage. You could help to develop assertiveness in such a person, utilizing the methods we have described.

6. *Revenge.* If you have a continuing relationship with someone with whom you have asserted yourself, that person may seek revenge. At first, it might be difficult to understand what is being attempted; but as time goes on the taunts may become quite evident. Once you are certain that someone is trying to make your life miserable, take steps to squelch the actions immediately. A recommended method is to directly confront the situation. Usually this is enough to get vengeful tactics to cease.

Choosing Not to Assert Yourself

It's worth repeating: *Choice* is the key word in the assertion process. As long as you know in your own mind (from previous, successful assertive encounters) that you *can* assert yourself, you may decide not to do so in a given instance. Following are some circumstances where one may *choose* nonassertiveness:

1. *Overly Sensitive Individuals.* On occasion, from your own observations, you may conclude that a certain person is unable to accept even the slightest assertion. When this is apparent, it is much better to resign yourself to this fact rather than chance an assertion. Although there are overly sensitive types who use their apparent weakness to manipulate others, we are all aware that there are also certain individuals who are so easily threatened that the slightest disagreement causes them to explode, either inwardly (thus hurting themselves) or outwardly (thus hurting others). You could avoid contact with such a person as much as possible, but if you must be around someone like this, it is possible to build up your own tolerance, accept the person, and cause no friction.

2. *Redundancy.* Once in a while, the person who has taken advantage of your rights will notice — before you get a chance to assert yourself — and then remedy the situation in an appropriate way. If the other person recognizes what has happened, it is not appropriate on your part to *then* pipe up and assert yourself. Do not wait for an extended period of time wishing that the other person will notice, however, do not hesitate to be assertive if he or she fails to make the amends which you feel should reasonably be made.

3. *Being Understanding.* Now and then you may choose not to be assertive because you notice that the person is having difficulty; There can be extenuating circumstances. At a restaurant one evening, having ordered our meals a certain way, we noticed that the new cook was having great difficulty with everything. Therefore, when our meals arrived not exactly as we had ordered, we chose not to be assertive rather than "hassle" him further. Another example is when someone you know is having an "off" day and is in a rare bad mood. In these cases, you may *choose* to overlook things that may be going wrong between you, or postpone a confrontation to a more productive time. (*Caution:* It is easy to use "not wanting to hurt the other's feelings" as a rationalization for nonassertiveness when assertion would be more appropriate. If you find yourself doing this more than occasionally, we suggest that you carefully examine your real motives.)

4. *Manipulators and Incorrigible People.* In everyone's life there are those who are just plain difficult! Your best efforts at appropriate assertion may almost always result in one of the undesired reactions listed above. Some people are so unpleasant that it is simply not worth it to confront them. And sometimes the potential gain is not worth the price one must pay in personal pain. We support your *choice* not to assert yourself in such circumstances. Nevertheless, we once again urge you to examine any such situation very carefully; consider the possibility that you may be using "not worth it" as an excuse not to confront a difficult-but-not-impossible situation!

When You Are Wrong

Especially in your early assertions, you may assert yourself when you have incorrectly interpreted a situation. Also, you may assert yourself with poor technique and offend the other person. If either of these situations does occur, be very willing to say that you have been wrong. There is no need to get carried away in making amends, of course; but be open enough to indicate that you know when you have been mistaken. Additionally, do not be apprehensive about future assertions with that person if you again feel that a situation calls for it.

"It's Too Late Now!"

We are often asked about past situations by people who feel they can do nothing about a problem which happened some time ago. Frustrated by the consequences of their earlier lack of assertion, they nevertheless feel helpless to change the situation now.

An example of such a case involved the relationship of Charlene K., a business executive and her secretary, George. The busy executive found herself regularly completing letters and reports late in the day, and asking George to have them typed and duplicated for meetings the following morning. The secretary had, the first time, assumed that the request — which required that he remain after hours to complete the work — was due to unique circumstances at that time. He willingly agreed to help out. Later, he found the "special request" had become an *expectation*, and occurred two or three times a week. Although he enjoyed the work, it interfered with his personal life, and he began to think of quitting the job.

George sought help in an assertiveness training group, where he somewhat tentatively brought the situation up for discussion. He found the therapist and group members very supportive. He selected a relatively assertive woman in the group and "rehearsed" with her a scene in which he confronted Charlene with his feelings. He did poorly at first, apologizing and allowing the "boss" to convince him that such "loyalty to the company" was necessary to the job. With feedback and support from the group, however, he improved his ability to express his feelings effectively and not be cowed by the executive's response. The next day, George confronted Charlene at the office, made his point, and arranged a more reasonable schedule for such projects. In the two months that followed, she made "special requests" only twice, and only when the circumstances clearly *were* unusual. Both were pleased with the result.

The point of this discussion is that it is seldom "too late" for an appropriate assertion — even if a situation has grown worse over some time. Approaching the person involved — yes, even a family member, spouse, lover, boss, employee — with an honest "I've been concerned about...for some time" or "I've been wanting to talk with you about..." can lead to a most productive effort at resolution of an uncomfortable issue. And, as no small side benefit, it can open communication of feelings in the future.

Keep in mind the importance of stating your feelings in such a way as to accept responsibility for them: "I'm concerned..." *not* "You've made me upset..."; "I'm mad..." *not* "You make me mad..."

Another important reason to "go back" and take care of old business with others is that "unfinished business" continues to gnaw away at you. Resentment from experiences which created anger or hurt won't just "go away." Such feelings result in a widening gap between people, and the resulting mistrust and potential grudge are hurtful to both persons.

Even if the old issues cannot be amicably resolved, doing all you can to *attempt* reconciliation is a very healthy and worthwhile step for you. We recognize that opening up old wounds can be painful. And there are certain risks — the outcomes *could* be worse than before. Despite these risks, we have seen so many people gain great rewards from resolving old conflicts that we do not hesitate to encourage you to do all *you* can to work out any such problems in your own life.

One more point: As we have cautioned before, do not attempt to *begin* your journey toward new assertiveness with highly risky relationships (those which are *very* important to you). This is a rather advanced step, and should come after you have mastered the basics.

The Swing Of the Pendulum

A question that often arises from the audience when we conduct an AT workshop:

"I have this friend who went through assertion training and now is unbearable! This person, who used to be peaceful and quiet, is complaining about everything! He (or she) has really gone overboard. Isn't assertion training dangerous at times because it creates monsters?"

If one has considered him or herself the underdog throughout life, and then learns to be assertive, there is the distinct possibility that he or she will swing beyond assertion into verbal aggressiveness. The message may be, "Now I've got my chance, and I'll set a few people straight!" Feelings held down or covered up for so many years often come out with a "bang" when the person begins to learn assertiveness.

The converse of this situation may also be true: The person who has been prone to aggressive behavior, such as manipulating, may go overboard when first learning assertion, becoming "super sweet" to people. It can be flabbergasting to suddenly be treated like a queen or king by someone who was formerly derisive and calculating!

Both of these dramatic shifts in behavior are normal reactions and to be expected under the circumstances. The pendulum was "stuck." Now released, the person seeks to experience the full range of behavior. We have never experienced anyone to have been genuinely harmful in this swing, but such a dramatic change will be upsetting to those personally involved. We suggest patience in these instances. The pendulum returns to the middle range after a relatively brief period of experimentation, and assertion is eventually accepted as the best alternative.

Assertiveness in a Holistic Perspective

Proponents of various systems of therapy generally over-emphasize their particular brand of help and exclude other valuable approaches. Psychologists, for example, often do not look beyond mental treatments into physical and spiritual means of help. However, *there is no one cure for all that ails one psychologically.*

Assertiveness training is an extremely valuable tool for gaining self-confidence and self-control in life, but it is by no means a cure-all. AT works best when used along with other psychological, physical, and spiritual approaches. We espouse a holistic-eclectic treatment system, integrating a variety of psychological methods with physical and spiritual considerations.

Humans are mental-physical-spiritual beings, and we need to look at ourselves as such. There is an inseparable interrelationship among the mental, physical, and spiritual, and it is vital to assess and treat each person as a total unit.

An analysis of psychological functioning should be accompanied by assessment of physical and spiritual areas as well. Medical history, current medical condition, dietary and physical exercise patterns, spiritual strengths and weaknesses — are all important considerations in a thorough assessment of well-being. Do not assume that a lack of assertiveness, for example, will be adequately dealt with by an AT program. The problem could be largely dietary! Examine all the possibilities, and engage medical and/or spiritual as well as psychological professionals if you need their help.

The idea of "holistic health" is something of a fad in our society now, yet the historic roots of holistic procedures are traceable to ancient Egypt. The modern regeneration of these concepts has been stimulated by such factors as increased consumer activism, exhorbitant health care costs, the women's movement, and the assertiveness movement. Despite the continuing tendency for specialization, an increasingly holistic outlook is emerging among health professionals in all fields.

To help place assertiveness in a holistic perspective, then, let us identify those principles of holistic health which are now generally agreed upon among holistic practitioners: (1) Holistic health emphasizes psychological, physical and spiritual wellness; (2) Responsibility for health lies with each individual; (3) Health must be viewed within the context of one's family, community, and culture; (4) No single health system has a monopoly on "truth"; (5) Natural, drugless procedures are to be preferred whenever possible; (6) Total health is dependent upon the curative power of the body, and the inner power of the spirit; (7) Health is a lifelong process involving prevention and cure of illness, maintenance of health, and striving toward optimum well-being.

Should you wish more information regarding holistic treatment methods, we suggest the following material (see the References section): Emmons (1978); Hastings, et al. (1980); Pelletier (1979); Ulene (1979).

We urge you to develop an assertive lifestyle, and to take care of yourself, holistically!

Some Further Thoughts on Assertive Living

We have undertaken this book with continuing awareness of the moral and ethical ramifications of assertive living. The following comments are offered for consideration of these matters, to stimulate the reader's own thinking. The issues are complex and we make no pretense of having arrived at definite answers even for ourselves.

Tolstoy has been credited with the observation that moral acts are distinguished from all other acts by the fact that they operate independently of any predictable advantage to ourselves or to others. This saying can be applied to our thinking about assertive acts. The crucial question is, "Are there times in every life when one must sacrifice her or his own values in order to survive?'' Consider the following situation:

You are nearing the end of three years of difficult preparation for your career. In addition to the time and effort, you have used all of your savings and gone into debt in the process, placing considerable strain on your marriage and two small children. However, it appears to have been worth the sacrifice, since your studies have prepared you to enter a highly respected profession with an excellent salary and fringe benefits.

The final qualifying exam involves a three-hour oral administered by a board of your teachers. As you go through the oral exam, you answer very well until one point toward the end. A question asked by the most powerful and influential member of the board deals with a subject which is presently quite controversial. New scientific information has been discovered only recently; however, this individual rigidly believes that the new knowledge is meaningless and detrimental, and dislikes any challenge of the traditional view. Several candidates have flunked recently for holding opposite views. You have thoroughly studied this new data and believe very strongly that it is relevant, vital, and will replace the older viewpoint.

Should you compromise your values and answer the way the teacher wishes to hear? Should you jeopardize your future by standing up for your beliefs?

If it is legitimate and necessary to compromise one's values in certain instances, should one compromise over an extended period of time?

Other persons must also be taken into consideration. What about the family in the example above? If assertion presents a serious hazard to the welfare of others for whom I am responsible, what are my rights and responsibilities?

I may know certain information about a subject being discussed in an English class that no one else brings up. Am I "non-assertive" if I choose not to seem "know-it-allish" and therefore say nothing of my special knowledge? Does my moral responsibility change if the class is in history? Psychology? Driver training? First aid? Pharmacology? Heart surgery?

Perhaps the key issue is whether or not the assertion which

one feels "morally obligated" to make will actually *make any difference*. It might be better for all to accept the fact that some things are better left as they are. Reinhold Niebuhr said it perhaps best of all: "God, give us serenity to accept what cannot be changed, courage to change what should be changed, and wisdom to distinguish the one from the other."

Beyond Assertiveness

Enough. The rest is up to you.

Keep in mind:

... Assertiveness, as other social behavior, is learned. You *can* change yourself if you wish to do so.

... Change is hard work. It usually comes slowly, and in small steps. Don't try to tackle too much at once. Succeed by taking *achievable* steps!

... There are no magic answers. While assertiveness doesn't always work (for us either!), it sure beats the alternatives — nearly all the time! Don't let failures at first stop you from trying again.

.. Give yourself credit when you bring about changes in your life. Even the smallest accomplishments deserve a pat on the back!

... Don't hesitate to ask for help — including professional help when you need it. Everyone needs help at times.

... Remember, you are working with an infinitely valuable resource — yourself. Take good care!

You are unique, an individual, with your own size, shape, age, ethnic and cultural background, sex, lifestyle, education, ideas, values, occupation, relationships, thoughts, behavior patterns. In this book we have had to generalize a great deal. AT is not all things to all people. *You* must decide what is relevant for you. If you choose to use AT as a tool to help you become the person you want to be, you must also decide how to apply its principles to your own unique life situation.

Remember that assertiveness is *not* a tool for manipulation, or intimidation, or getting your way. It is a means to stand up for your own rights, to express your anger, to reach out to others, to build relationships, to express your affection, to be more direct. Most importantly, it is one means to become the person you want to be, to feel good about yourself, and to demonstrate your respect for the rights of others.

Part Two

15

On Becoming a Professional Trainer

"How do human services professionals learn to be assertiveness trainers?" Since the first edition of *Your Perfect Right* thousands of professionals and students have asked that question. AT is now commonplace in graduate schools of counselor education, social work, psychology, nursing, theology, management and others. Indeed, you may be reading this book in conjunction with such a training program.

As a foundation for offering AT to others, it should be evident that we believe the trainer should be or become personally assertive in his/her *own* life. In addition, we believe the adage, "A therapist must have therapy" applies to the assertive behavior facilitator, and potential assertiveness trainers should have personal training themselves before being allowed to practice.

We consider several steps to be important in becoming a *qualified* facilitator of assertive behavior in others. It is particularly important that professionals prepare themselves adequately to offer a high level of service, since an unfortunately large amount of work called "assertiveness training" is being done by persons who have no qualifications (other than the "assertiveness" to say, "I am going to do assertiveness training")!

The statement of *Principles for Ethical Practice of Assertive Behavior Training* (Appendix B) identifies general and specific qualifications for AT interventions at three levels: assertive behavior *training*; assertive behavior *therapy*; and *training of trainers*. We support and advocate the minimum standards identified in that statement.

In brief, the "General Qualifications" considered to be a minimum requirement for professional facilitators in all settings and at all levels include:

A) Understanding of basic principles of learning and behavior;

B) Understanding of anxiety and its effects upon behavior;

C) Knowledge of limitations, contraindications, and potential dangers of AT;

D) Training as a facilitator under qualified supervision.

Additional "Specific Qualifications" detailed in the statement suggest the need for graduate level training in one of the human services professions (e.g., psychology, education, social work, counseling, HRD, nursing, medicine, human development, theology, public health). The level of training proposed increases as one assumes increasing responsibility: least formal training is required for those who would do non-clinical *training*; more for those who would do AT as *therapy*; and most for those who would *train trainers*. The difference between training and therapy is not always clear, but the ethics statement offers guidelines to help the facilitator in deciding if his/her qualifications are adequate (see 3.2.A, 3.2.B, and 5.A-G).

In 1978, Dr. Pat Jakubowski informed us of her work in developing a set of "competencies" for AT facilitators. It is hoped that such behavioral criteria for qualification of facilitators will make "academic" credentials less important. Nevertheless, at this time, adequate formal training and the other qualifications identified in this chapter and in Appendix B are still the most adequate criteria available. New material is published in the *ASSERT* newsletter.

In addition to the specific recommendations in the ethics statement, we suggest that potential facilitators acquire the following preparation:

Knowledge of Basic Learning Principles. Although this step ordinarily will have been accomplished in formal training as a facilitator, it would be helpful to study such texts as Bandura's (1969) *Principles of Behavior Modification,* and Wolpe's *Practice of Behavior Therapy* (1973).

Familiarity with the Literature. The publication, *Assertiveness Training: An Annotated Bibliography* and the remaining technical literature in the "references" section of this book should be used as guides to study. One should also keep abreast of pertinent material in current journals and books in the field. Perhaps the most comprehensive presentation of AT in print is Alberti's edited volume *Assertiveness: Innovations, Applications, Issues* (1977). Seminars, training courses, workshops, institutes and graduate programs in assertiveness training are being offered currently and should be investigated. Especially helpful in announcing further training for professionals are AABT's *The Behavior Therapist* (420 Lexington Ave., NY, NY 10170), APGA's *Guidepost* (5203 Leesburg Pike, Falls Church, VA 22041), APA's *Monitor* (1200 17th St., N.W., Washington, D.C. 20036), and *ASSERT:The Newsletter of Assertive Behavior and Personal Development* (Box 1094, San Luis Obispo, CA 93406).

Practice with Components. Actually experiencing the full range of the assertive process in a variety of typical situations enables the facilitator more fully to understand what the client experiences. If a client is having difficulty expressing anger in a situation, you will be much more helpful if you yourself have experienced the situation covertly, modeled it, roleplayed, shaped and coached it. One approach is to work with a fellow staff member or a client volunteer. Get together and alternate the roles of client and facilitator, experiment with a variety of situations and techniques. Video tape equipment can be invaluable in your learning process. If available, some type of physiological measuring and feedback device may also provide useful data.

Personal Assertiveness. Anyone who sets out to increase assertiveness in others must first be *actively* assertive. The passive knowledge of assertive behavior gained by reading the first portion of *Your Perfect Right* is only a beginning. In our personal lives we are continually aware of situations in which these principles might be applied. For us this awareness has four benefits: 1) keeping the "air clear" in our own interpersonal functioning; 2) pursuing actual opportunities to practice in the "real world," 3) adding to our on-going examples to report to our individual clients and groups, 4) minimizing cognitive dissonance which could result from "writing the book" on assertive training yet not acting assertively!

By experiencing ourselves the great potential of being in control of our own lives and realizing *how satisfying that feels,* we've become more convincing models and coaches of assertiveness. It is exciting for us to experience changes in our level of assertiveness over a period of years. We both believe we have improved a great deal in all phases of assertiveness as we have continued learning and practicing. (Incidentally, that doesn't mean we are both *more* assertive now; rather we are freer to *choose* in all circumstances!)

Commitment to Ethical Principles: Since AT has become so popular in recent years, we are concerned about high standards of AT practice, and appropriate qualifications and ethics of facilitators. Evaluate your own qualifications in the light of the statement of *Principles for Ethical Practice of Assertive Behavior Training,* and offer only those services for which you are truly qualified. We urge you to become familiar with the statement and, if you are or intend to be an AT facilitator, to support and function within its guidelines.

16

Assessment of Nonassertive, Aggressive, and Assertive Behavior

Preliminary Considerations

The helping person who wishes to facilitate assertiveness must first ascertain as clearly as possible the exact nature of the other person's difficulty, *in order to decide if assertiveness training is appropriate or if it is necessary at all.* Perhaps the client needs support until a crisis blows over, in which case it would be premature to start assertiveness training. Moreover, some individuals may be so shy and withdrawn that even the suggestion of assertiveness training may cause somatic reactions such as flushing and stomach pains. The trainer must be especially careful not to overwhelm this type of client. In such cases, we may administer an anxiety measure, such as the *Willoughby Schedule* (Wolpe, 1958; Hestand, 1971) and/or the *Fear Survey Schedule* (Wolpe, 1969) and often find it necessary for these clients to experience systematic desensitization or other therapeutic measures to reduce fears of criticism and/or rejection. Even when assertiveness training is initiated with such individuals, it is best to start with a one-to-one situation rather than a group setting.

Those individuals whose behavior is frequently aggressive may also be poor candidates for AT until given other types of therapy. Although the actions may imply one who is very brave and very capable, we often find that underneath he or she is easily hurt and has learned not to show it, but rather to bluster or manipulate. For this reason, facilitators may wish to hold these clients out of groups in which they would tend to dominate the nonassertive members, until therapy has helped them to deal less defensively and aggressively with their own anxiety.

Assessment Methods

The primary method we employ in assessing nonassertive or aggressive behavior patterns is simply listening to the individual describe relationships with others who are important in the client's life. One may carefully explore with the person interactions with (depending upon age and lifestyle) parents, peers, co-workers, classmates, spouse, children, bosses, employees, teachers, salesmen, neighbors, relatives. In assessing, one may ask who is dominant in these specific relationships: Is the person easily taken advantage of in dealings with others? Are feelings and ideas openly expressed in most circumstances? Does he or she take advantage of and/or hurt others frequently? What are his/her emotional responses to such events?

In addition Wolpe (1969) and Lazarus (1971) suggest questions which are useful in the process of pinpointing responses which are maladaptive for an individual (e.g., Are you able to contradict a domineering person?). Responses are easily pursued to thoroughly explore the client's nonassertive, aggressive or assertive behavior. Keep in mind your questioning to cover the area of very personal assertions as well as the more traditional areas. Once again, it should be remembered that behavior is person and situation specific, and must be examined in detail, rather than making generalized evaluations about the client's "personality," or falsely attributing a generalized "assertiveness score."

Standardized Tests

Our emphasis is on locating current detailed examples of the client's behavior pattern. For this reason, if we use standardized tests in the diagnostic process, we first look at scores on individual scales, then attempt to discuss item-by-item with the client to find out exactly what was meant by the response. The process yields both insights of value in work with the client and practical experience in the training process.

Abundant standardized testing material is available. Most of the personality tests have scales which could be useful. Among those we have found valuable are the *Omnibus Personality Inventory*, the *Edwards Personal Preference Schedule*, *Eysenck Personality Inventory*, and the *Myers-Briggs Type Indicator*.

Many scales have developed to attempt to assess assertiveness directly. One of the most useful is the Gambrill-Richey "Assertion Inventory" (1975) in which the respondent is asked to report both the "degree of difficulty" in handling a series of situations, and the "response probability" that he or she will actually attempt to confront that scene. A new instrument which offers the most adequate differentiation of different forms of assertiveness is the Interpersonal Behavior Survey (Mauger, et al., 1980).

Instruments which have been reported in the AT literature include the Action Situation Inventory (Friedman, 1971), the Adolescent Assertion Discrimination Test (Shoemaker, 1973 as cited in Bodner, 1975), the Adolescent Self-Expression Scale (McCarthy & Bellucci, 1974), the Adult Assertion Scale (Jakubowski & Wallace, 1975 as cited in Lange & Jakubowski, 1976), the Adult Self-Expression Scale (Gay, Hollandsworth & Galassi, 1975), Anger Self-Report (Doyle & Biaggio, 1981), the Assertion Inventory (Dalali, 1971), the Assertion Inventory (Fensterheim, 1971), The Assertion Inventory (Gambrill & Richey, 1975), Assertive Knowledge Inventory (Bruch, 1981), the Assertiveness Inventory (Alberti & Emmons, 1974), the AQ test (Phelps & Austin, 1975), Children's Emotion Projection Instrument (Bernard, 1980), the Cognition Scale of Assertiveness (Golden, 1981), the College Self-Expression Scale (Galassi, DeLo, Galassi & Bastien, 1974), the Conflict Resolution Inventory (McFall & Lillesand, 1971) which was designed explicitly to measure refusal behavior, the Constriction Scale (Bates & Zimmerman, 1971), Difficulty in Assertiveness Inventory (Leah, Law & Snyder, 1979), Interpersonal Behavior Survey (Mauger, et al., 1980), Interpersonal Problem Solving Assessment Technique (Getter & Nowinski, 1981), Hypothetical Behavioral Role Playing Assertion Test (Bruch, 1981), the Lawrence Assertive Inventory (Lawrence, 1970), the modified Rathus Assertiveness Schedule for the junior high level (Vaal & McCullagh, 1975), Objective Measure of Assertiveness (Gulanick & Howard, 1979), Personal Relations Inventory (Lorr, More & Mansueto, 1981), Personal Report of Communication Apprehension (Pearson, 1979), the Rathus Assertiveness Schedule (Rathus, 1973), the modified Rathus Assertiveness Schedule for Children (d'Amico, 1977), Reduced Behavioral Assertion Test (Bruch, 1981), and the Wolpe-Lazarus Assertiveness Questionnaire (Wolpe and Lazarus, 1966).

We have often been asked about validation studies, scoring procedures, and norms of our *Assertiveness Inventory* (see Chapter 5). The *Inventory* is *not* a validated instrument and has no formalized "scoring" or normative data. It is useful as a clinical tool, primarily when the facilitator reviews each item individually with the trainee.

Keep in mind the situation specific nature of assertiveness, and avoid generalizations based on a "total score" approach!

Note: We consider any assessment of assertiveness to be adequate only insofar as it takes into account the three dimensions we have discussed throughout this book: *attitudes, skills,* and *anxiety.* We know of no single instrument which measures all three!

Behavioral Measures

It can be desirable to incorporate carefully constructed live behavioral tests to determine the degree of one's difficulty with assertiveness. Assessment may be based on post-situation self report, expert judgements of performance, and physiological measures of anxiety. Audio and video tape recording devices are useful in sampling client behaviors in these situations. Examples of applications of such approaches are given in McFall and Marston (1970), Friedman (1971), and Eisler, Miller, and Hersen (1974). Another valuable contribution to behavioral measures is the "unobtrusive" approach of Cummins (1978). At least two recent studies (Gorecki, et al., 1981; Howard, et al., 1980) question the validity of the "behavioral" measures taken in laboratory or therapy settings, suggesting great caution when attempting to assess probable *in vivo* behavior by observing responses in unrealistic environments, such as role play tests.

Vagg (1979) edited a special issue of the *ASSERT* Newsletter on the topic of assessment, and offers a valuable critique of methods and criteria for evaluating an instrument.

Bodner (1975) has provided an excellent review of assessment in AT, including paper-and-pencil, observational, and behavioral measures. Galassi and Galassi (1977) have prepared an extensive discussion of AT assessment, with guidelines for developing an individualized scale.

Any client may need a more thorough treatment program than assertiveness training alone can provide. AT is a very powerful way to help, but the facilitator should be prepared to assess the client's needs in all areas, in order to offer responsible training or referral. AT is *one tool* in an adequate response to client needs. Thorough assessment of those needs, and a careful decision that AT is the most appropriate intervention, are mandatory elements in responsible application of assertiveness training.

The *Principles for Ethical Practice of Assertive Behavior Training* describes seven dimensions which should be evaluated in determining the appropriateness and level of an AT intervention: *client, problem/goals, facilitator, setting, time/duration, method, outcome.* Appendix B, Part 5 spells out this multi-faceted approach to assessment in detail. Trainers are urged to become familiar with these guidelines.

17

Individual and Group Training Procedures

Now that you have thoroughly assessed your client, and decided that AT is called for in this case, you are looking for specific procedures for training. This chapter will help you to apply the material presented in the first part of the book. It is assumed that you are thoroughly familiar with that material and qualified as described in Chapter 15.

Client Preparation

In Chapter 7 we discussed some basic elements of assertive motivation and attitude development. The process of preparation for assertive living is essentially the same for trainer or client. Familiarity with the differences among nonassertive, aggressive, and assertive behaviors is a foundation which is prerequisite for the steps which follow.

To prepare your client/trainee for AT, therefore, we urge you to have him/her read this or another appropriate book on the subject, and to discuss the concepts at some length. Often such a discussion is facilitated by a group orientation to the subject (whether or not the AT will be conducted in a group).

In a few cases, simply the exposure to the AT concepts and the recognition that there *are* alternatives to nonassertion or aggression will get the client started. Nevertheless, we suggest a "trial run" with you, so you may assess the adequacy of the trainee's style before she/he tackles the "real world." Even though some individuals may not need a full training program, it is wise for the facilitator to check it out. The "Method of Contrasted Role Plays" is a valuable technique for confirming the client's level of performance (MacNeilage and Adams, 1977).

Those clients who will be started on a full AT program, whether individual or group, should be informed fully as to the procedures which will be employed, and outcomes to be expected. (Again, refer to the *Principles* in Appendix B.)

Assuming the client has made an informed choice to proceed, (and you are appropriately prepared), you are ready to initiate training.

Individual Training

(Before you go on with this chapter, take a few minutes to return to Chapter 9, and re-read the self-directed "step-by-step" process.)

Here is an example of work with an individual client (you have already completed Steps 1 and 2):

Step 1: Be certain you are adequately prepared as a facilitator
Review Chapter 15 and the statement of *Principles for Ethical Practice of Assertive Behavior Training.* Be sure you have the necessary qualifications before proceeding.

Step 2: Do a thorough preliminary assessment of the needs of the client.
Review chapters 5 and 16. Select an appropriate assessment procedure for the client, and implement it. Avoid generalizations!

Step 3: Identify a situation that needs attention.
Example:
CLIENT: A man has called me twice to ask me out and he just won't take my hints. I don't want to hurt his feelings by telling

him the truth; what should I do when he calls again?

Step 4: Set up the scene.
Work with the client to structure closely the potential situation, in order to present the covert scene accurately and to simulate the feelings one has in the real situation.
Example:
FACILITATOR: You've decided you don't like him?
CL: No, he's a nice person, but we just don't have the same interests. Besides, I'm not attracted to him physically. I can't tell him that though; it would crush him.

Step 5: Present the situation to the person for covert rehearsal.
Example:
FA: Are you sure? I'd like for you to go over the situation in your imagination now. Close your eyes and imagine yourself receiving the next call. Let yourself respond in whatever way you feel.
CL: (Silent, imagines scene.)

Step 6: Help the client develop positive self-statements.
FA: Tell me what you were saying to yourself.
CL: At first I thought, "I *can't* do this!" Then I saw the scene, and thought, "Oh, poor Harold. He really needs me. I *mustn't* tell him no; it would kill him!"
FA: So, first you thought, "I can't," then you thought, "I mustn't."
CL: Yes, that's right.
FA: I want you to try to say just the opposite, the *positive* statement, to yourself. For practice, tell yourself, "I *can* do this," and "I *must* tell Harold the truth about how I feel toward him."
At this point there will probably be some resistance on the part of the client. Be persistent, and urge more than one trial of the positive statements.

Step 7: Model an assertive response for the situation.
Present audio and video models if available. You may wish to tape your modeling here also.

Example:
FA: Now I'll show you *one* way to approach him. Pretend I am you and you are him. Call me.
FA: Hello, this is Dorothy.
CL: Hi, this is Harold...(*small talk*)...Say, there is a great movie playing downtown, and I would love to have you go with me on Friday. I'll be so disappointed if you can't go.
FA: I really am busy on Friday, but I've been wanting to talk to you about us anyway, Harold. I feel I have been misleading you, and I want to straighten things out. I really am concerned about hurting you, but I don't see any future in our relationship.
CL: Why? What have I done wrong?
FA: That's just it; you've done nothing wrong. I feel that our interests aren't the same, and I'm not really attracted to you.
CL: Oh. (Pause).
FA: I hope you aren't too disappointed, but I had to be honest with you, so I wouldn't hurt you more later.
CL: Well, I appreciate that anyway. So, I guess I shouldn't call you anymore.
FA: That would be best...
CL: What if he hangs up halfway through the conversation?
FA: If you are truly assertive, most likely that won't occur; but if it does, that is just the way it has to be.

Step 8: Answer the client's questions about how you handled the situation.
Point out the differences between assertive versus non-assertive and aggressive responses. Stress pertinent non-verbal factors. Discuss philosophical concerns.
Example A:
CL: Wouldn't it be better to tell white lies like, "I have to wash my hair," so he'll get the hint?
FA: You've tried hints already and they haven't worked. Even if they eventually did work, you actually are hurting him and yourself more in the long run by not being honest with your feelings. Believe me, ninety-nine guys out of a hundred would rather you told them the truth, even though it hurts at the time!
Example B:
CL: You sounded so "perfect"! Sometimes I really don't know

what I *want* in a situation. What if I'm not sure?

FA: Not sure whether you want to go out with him?

CL: No, I'm not sure how I feel about him, except I know I don't want to date him.

FA: Could you say that...what you just told me?

CL: You mean tell him I'm not sure how I feel, but I don't want to go out?

FA: Yes.

CL: I guess that's being pretty up-front!

Step 9: Repeat Step 5.

Repeat covert rehearsal, this time encouraging the client to visualize a successful outcome based on effective model.

Step 10: Rehearse the scene once again.

This time the client role-plays him/herself. Audio or video tape if possible.

Step 11: Go over the performance.

Provide feedback and coaching where needed. Don't forget positive reinforcement. Emphasize self-reinforcement.

Example:

FA: You did an excellent job! I liked the way you stuck to your point when he tried to persuade you to let him call again. Your voice was a little soft and somewhat shaky. Let's do it again. Try to use a stronger voice this time. Remind yourself how well you're doing as it goes along.

Step 12: Repeat Steps 6 through 11 as often as needed.

Alternate between modeling and role-playing and provide coaching so as to shape the behavior to the *client's* satisfaction, whenever time allows.

Step 13: The person is now ready to test the new response pattern in the actual situation.

Up to this point the preparation has taken place in a relatively secure environment. Nevertheless, careful training and repeated practice have developed a much more adequate reaction to the situation. The client should thus be reassured if necessary and encourged to proceed *in vivo.* If he/she is unwilling to do so, further rehearsals may be needed. Also, ask to hear the positive self-statements she/he is thinking.

Example:

FA: How do you feel about using your new approach with him when he calls again?

CL: I think I'm ready, and I know he's going to call.

FA: Well, I feel good about how you've handled it here, so I also think you're ready. Tell me what you're telling yourself now...

Step 14: The client should be encouraged to return as soon as practical following the in vivo trial, in order to review the effort.

The therapist should reward whatever degree of success the person experiences, and offer continued assistance, with emphasis on self-management skills.

Example:

FA: I want you to keep a record of how it goes, what he says, what you say, your thoughts, your feelings and so on. Then come in as soon as you can after it is over, so we can review how you did.

CL: O.K.

Further elaboration on Step 14 may be in order:

The client's initial attempts at being assertive should be chosen for their high potential of success, so as to provide reinforcement. This point, of course, is important with all beginning asserters. The more successfully one asserts the more likely one is to do so from then on. Additionally, the individual who reports to the facilitator an instance of successful assertion obtains added reinforcement. The facilitator must be very capable of providing verbal reinforcement for each of the trainee's successful assertive acts, and of helping the trainee to develop self-reinforcing thoughts.

Initially then, the individual should begin with small assertions that are likely to be successful and rewarded, and from there proceed to more difficult assertions. Ideally each step should be explored with the facilitator until the client-trainee is capable of being fully in control of most situations. He or she should be warned against taking initiative to attempt a difficult assertion at first without special preparation. The facilitator also should particularly beware of instigating an assertion where the trainee is likely to fail miserably, thus inhibiting further attempts at assertiveness. If the trainee does suffer a setback, which very well may happen, the facilitator must be ready to help analyze the situation and to help rebuild confidence. Especially in the early stages of assertion, trainees are prone to mistakes either of inadequate technique or of overzealousness to the point of aggression. Either miscue could cause negative returns, particularly if the other individual, the "receiver," becomes hostile and highly aggressive. Therefore, the facilitator must be prepared to serve as a buffer and to help re-establish motivation.

Most trainees will have more than one specific problem with being assertive. In the above case, for example, the woman may have difficulty returning items to a store or gaining her rights with roommates. The same basic process with variations may be used for each situation. The individuality of the client must always be accommodated. Facilitators are encouraged to provide a learning environment in which the trainee may grow in assertiveness, and carefully to avoid "shoving it down the throat."

Long before the end of an assertiveness training process (perhaps ranging from several weeks to several months duration) we point out important factors for the future. First, is the need for continued practice in real-life situations. We point out the desirability for the client to make conscious efforts to practice for at least six months after leaving, and encourage re-reading this book as often as needed to provide continuing motivation and support for assertive ventures.

A key factor in establishing a lasting, independent behavior pattern is to help the trainee understand the need for on-going self-reinforcement. It is necessary for the trainee, in order to maintain newly-developed assertive behavior, to achieve reinforcement within the immediate social environment. Without the benefit of regular reinforcement from the facilitator, the ex-client must provide self-reinforcement and gain rewards for assertiveness from other sources in his/her own unique life situation. Preparation for independent functioning must take place long before the end of the therapeutic intervention, of course.

Group Training Procedures

When the first edition of *Your Perfect Right* was published in 1970, little work had been done on assertiveness training in groups. Since that time the AT group has become the "treatment of choice" for most persons who wish to develop their assertiveness. The process of assertive behavior development may be very effectively applied in a group setting. With many trainees this approach is more effective than one-to-one therapy because of the expanded potential for interaction with others during the training process.

Several specific advantages result from a small group. Trainees typically encounter great anxiety in certain life situations when faced with confronting other people. Learning assertiveness in a group provides a "laboratory" of other people with whom to work. By discovering that they share similar problems, each is less "alone." A group is typically understanding and supportive — a social environment in which each person can be accepted, and thus be comfortable enough to experiment with new behavior.

With several individuals undertaking assertiveness training together, there is a broader base for social modeling. Each trainee sees several others learning to act assertively, and each is able to learn from the strengths and weaknesses of the others.

A group provides more diverse perspectives for feedback than can an individual facilitator. Hearing reactions from several different persons can speed the behavior-shaping process for each trainee.

Social situations involving a number of people are a frequent source of anxiety. Work in a group gives a realistic opportunity to face several people and overcome that difficulty in a relatively safe training environment.

The group is, of course, a powerful source of social reinforcement for each of its members. Knowing several others are "expecting" one's growth and active effort toward assertiveness, each member may be stimulated to greater achievement than when working alone. And, for its part, the group rewards new assertiveness with all the force of its social approval. (This asset can become a liability at the *end* of a group unless the trainer has taken steps to develop independence skills!)

In the use of the small group setting for assertiveness training, it is important to recognize that some trainees are so anxious about their interpersonal contacts that they may be unable to face even a congenial group of others with similar problems. In such cases, of course, individual work is essential, at least until the trainee feels able to enter a group. Obviously group work is not called for in all cases, and the facilitator who works with both group and individual clients will consider the needs and capacities of each person in suggesting one or both approaches. Assessment of individual clients before assignment to group AT is very important.

Preparation of the group for working effectively together will depend upon the institutional setting, the skill and attitudes of the facilitator, and the readiness of group members to respond openly and honestly to one another. Because a discussion of the process of personal interaction in groups is beyond the scope of this book, the interested reader is referred to the excellent treatises of Yalom (1975), and Houts and Serber (1972). It has been our experience with assertive behavior groups that an atmosphere of trust and concern by group members for one another will grow out of the training process, and that growth toward common objectives will provide the cohesiveness necessary to develop an effective working group. The facilitator, acting as model and guide, sets the tone, and by example encourages trust, support and positive regard for each member of the group.

The Makeup and Format of Assertiveness Training Groups

The typical AT group has from five to twelve members. Workshops or classes with greater numbers are not unusual; however, the format is necessarily more didactic and less individualized. Fewer than five restricts the potential for social modeling, limits the sources of feedback, and fails to provide the range of behavior styles needed for each trainee to experience a variety of others as each tries out new assertive behaviors. We prefer, when possible, to balance the number of men and women in our groups, since social relationships with the opposite sex are a frequent source of anxiety for our nonassertive and aggressive clients. A group with equal numbers of each sex has enhanced opportunity for helping its members to deal effectively with social situations involving the opposite sex. We recognize that much work has been done with same-sex groups, particularly for women. There is value in such programs, but our preference is to create a more nearly representative microcosm of the "real world." For some clients, however, work in a same-sex group may be a desirable prerequisite to a mixed group.

Because much AT has been developed in university settings, groups are often designed to coincide with the academic term. It is typical to meet one hour twice each week for eight or nine weeks — a total of sixteen to eighteen hours. We have experimented with alternatives to this approach. We have conducted a group for five or six weeks (10 or 12 one-hour sessions), then suspended meetings for approximately three weeks, reconvening again for a follow-up meeting. This approach can be nearly as successful as our longer groups. The basic concepts of assertion can be covered and practiced within this short period of time. Motivation tends to remain high for both facilitator and members; absenteeism is almost non-existent. The break allows members time to identify any major obstacles which may need more attention. If necessary, further work with assertion on a one-to-one basis can be arranged. In selected cases additional therapeutic measures may also be needed.

We have also worked on a two-hours-once-a-week schedule. The latter has the advantage of a longer and often more intensive session, but the long interval between sessions seems to be a significant loss to the behavior shaping process. Ideally, perhaps one-and-one-half hours twice each week would best achieve the goals of an assertive behavior group (We have no controlled experimental data to support this conclusion, however.) Indeed, one recent study (Berah, 1981) suggests that massed and distributed training formats are equally effective. Brief introductory groups as short as eight one-hour sessions have also been conducted with some success, particularly for those clients who are primarily in need of enhanced awareness of the potential of assertiveness.

Groups led by co-facilitators are, in our experience, more effective environments for client growth than those led by individual facilitators. Attrition is lower, enthusiasm higher, and both self-report and facilitator observation of growth are greater. We have worked with each other, with other psychologists, university staff counselors, and M.A.-level counselor-trainees. Co-facilitators are most effective when they are open and honest with each other and with group members, possess complementary skills and facilitation styles, and are both openly enthusiastic about assertiveness training. In addition, although we have been consistently most effective in assertive groups when working together, we encourage a male-female co-facilitator team. Effective models of assertiveness of each sex are valuable resources for assertive behavior groups.

The Assertiveness Training Process in Groups

First Session. The first session of our training groups is devoted to a didactic presentation on assertive behavior, and to getting acquainted.

Opening with background material on what the group will be all about, we utilize the nonassertive-aggressive-assertive paradigm described in Chapter 2. We call attention to the behavior-attitude cycle, and point out the importance of practice with support and reinforcement from the group. Members are cautioned that assertiveness training is not a panacea, and that they will not discover miraculous changes overnight. They are also told that occasional failure is to be expected, but will not stop long-term progress.

We give several typical examples to illustrate our contention that assertiveness is a better way than the other two alternatives. Next, we indicate how the group will be structured, outlining the exercises in which each will participate. We request that members keep an ongoing log of their progress, emphasizing specific, detailed examples. In summing up, we give a basic pep talk about becoming thoroughly involved in changing, the need for risk-taking, and the progress others have made. Throughout, we encourage the participants to ask questions, even though getting a group of primarily nonassertive people to initiate questions is often difficult. At this time, each member is asked to begin an "AT log" (see Chapter 5) by writing down specific behaviors (within our non-assertive-aggressive-assertive framework) which she/he wishes to change.

Upon completion of these preliminaries, we go around the group for introductions. This initial participation exercise is handled as a demonstration of the process to be used in the group. The trainer asks members to close their eyes and visualize themselves completing the introduction, then models a one-or two-minute introduction, emphasizing personal background and reasons for participating in an AT group. Everyone again repeats the imagery step (with a "successful" outcome this time).

Now the first overt group activity confronts the members. For some, of course, considerable anxiety attends this moment. Trainer sensitivity is important here. The introductions must be seen as a natural activity, not a "performance." No one will be "judged." No rules apply, and there are no expectations to live up to. The length and detail of each introduction is strictly a matter of personal choice by the members. Any feedback which comes up in the discussion which follows should be in the nature of positive reinforcement for success.

In the follow-up discussion after introductions, it can be helpful to inquire about individual thoughts and feelings during the introductions. Most participants will have similar reactions, and the shared impressions will help produce a sense of identi-fication with the group. At this time also the trainer can inform the group that they have just completed the first group exercise, and that the format will be similar in future meetings, with the specific content being different.

Cognitive restructuring, the process of helping clients to change their thinking about themselves and their attitudes toward acting assertively, is introduced at this point. Following the first modeling demonstration, group members inevitably have a host of rationalizations "why it does not work well" in their lives. The reaction offers an ideal training opportunity for presenting the cognitive component. A brief introduction to the concept of positive self-statements (see Chapter 7, and Meichenbaum, 1977), is all there is usually time for in the first meeting. As a homework assignment, however, trainees are asked to write down the negative self-statements they associate with introducing themselves, and to counter each with an opposite positive statement. Again, the AT log is used.

Because we know that anxiety is a major component of the obstacle system for many trainees, we try to end the first group meeting with a brief relaxation exercise. Group members are asked to keep their logs faithfully during the week, including sources of anxiety. If anxiety is a significant problem for many group members, it may be necessary to add a session on anxiety management, or perhaps to regularly include stress inoculation and/or desensitization procedures in group sessions.

Additional Meetings. The format of the first group meeting is essentially followed throughout the life of the group. Each session is divided roughly thus: followup on the homework completed by each individual member; didactic presentation of the "cognitive message" for the session; practice of skills in a specific situation; assignment of homework for the time between sessions.

Homework followup generally consists of inviting each member to describe his/her experiences with assertion since the last meeting, with specific emphasis on the homework exercise. Homework assignments are an extension of the exercises practiced in the group, to facilitate skill development and transfer to "real world" settings.

Didactic presentations are scheduled to emphasize important aspects of the "philosophy" of assertiveness, and to present ideas for expanding the assertive repertoire of participants. Time is devoted to member questions about concepts, but is important to avoid trying to counter all the "Yes, but..." resistances you will find among group members. You simply cannot answer all they can come up with, and you will waste a lot of group time trying!

Skills practice remains the heart of AT. Trainees learn more from doing than from talking about doing, almost universally (those who are more cognitively oriented do gain much from verbal instruction). The practice format is like that described for the introductions exercise in the opening session: a situation is posed; members are asked to fantasize their individual responses; a model (often but not always the facilitator) role-plays the scene; the group briefly discusses the model's performance; individual positive self-statements are developed; a new covert response (with successful outcome) is called for; each member practices and receives feedback. The major facilitative elements of AT (covert rehearsal, modeling, cognitive restructuring, and skill practice) are built in to the group process for each situation covered.

New *homework assignments* are based upon the group's need at the end of each session, and with some awareness of progress toward the stated goals (including those unique to this group, both from the pre-group assessment and from member statements at the first meeting). Most homework is practice of assertive skills learned in the group. Some will include written assignments in the AT log. (Maintaining the log is an ongoing homework assignment.) Often individual members will be asked to follow through on a personal situation which they have presented to the group and practiced during a session. Each member will be expected to report on the assignment at the following meeting. A "buddy system," which pairs group members to support and encourage the completion of homework, can be a very helpful device (Shelton, 1977).

Following this pattern, the first few weeks of group meetings are structured so that each member participates in several fundamental exercises such as (not necessarily in this order):
1. Breaking into a small group of strangers already engaged in conversation at a party.
2. Starting a conversation with a stranger in a classroom, on a bus, at a meeting. Maintaining a conversation.
3. Returning faulty or defective items to a store.
4. Assertiveness with significant others: parents, roommates, boy/girlfriends.
5. Saying "no" to a request for a favor.
6. Assertive anger expression.

7. Asking for a date/refusing a date (telephone and face-to-face).
8. Compliments; caring feelings; "soft assertions."
9. Public speaking.
10. Learning how to argue or stand up for oneself with a dominant dogmatic opinionated person.

We operate with considerable flexibility, and may leave out some situations or add others, according to the apparent needs of a particular group.

After members of the group all have completed the basic exercises, we encourage them to bring to the group current life situations which are troubling them. Although no one is denied the opportunity to present a personal situation earlier in the group process, we find that most participants, as in more traditional forms of group therapy, are reluctant to expose much of themselves very early in the life of the group. Some trainers choose to invite members to present "real life" situations from the beginning of a group. Our experience has been that some others will lose interest if the material is individualized too early. Thus it is usually more valuable to structure the first meetings, and move toward member-initiated activities after the facilitation process is well established, and participants have come to trust one another more fully. At this point individual situations presented in the group frequently relate to intimate relationships: "How can I tell my father to stop nagging me? How can I tell my boyfriend that I don't really love him? My roommate has terrible B.O! My boss keeps making passes at me. I yell at my wife and children every day when I get home from work. No one pays any attention to me."

Such situations strike very close to home, of course, and are more sensitive and difficult to handle than the "clerk-in-the-store" variety, since they involve on-going relationships with a great emotional investment. Sensitivity, patience, and careful attention to the principles of assertiveness — and to the consideration of consequences — are in order here, and the facilitator is cautioned against pat solutions to unique individual problems. Under these conditions other members of a perceptive and caring group are often the most valuable resource to the facilitator. In any event, rehearsing approaches to significant others is usually very worthwhile in the group, if only to gain a better understanding of one's own feelings about the person/situation. It is a rare group which does not offer support and caring in delicate situations.

Practice in the expression of caring for another is, of course, an important goal of an assertiveness training group (Chapter 11 discusses the "soft assertions" in some detail). We focus considerable attention upon the verbal expression of positive feelings toward oneself and others.

Similarly, at another point in the emotional spectrum, putting angry feelings into words is an important group exercise. We encourage group members to practice assertive anger expression (review Chapter 12).

As the assertive behavior group passes the middle of its schedule, we urge each member to sensitize him/herself to sources of continuing reinforcement for assertion in his/her unique individual life environment. The group is an important center of support for the developing assertiveness of each member. However, it will come to an end, and each must take responsibility for identifying and expanding sources of support within his/her own "ecosystem." Internal positive thoughts and self-statements are a key to this step.

The final meeting of our assertiveness training group is usually devoted to a very uplifting emotional experience developed by psychologist Herbert Otto (1969): the "Strength Bombardment." Each member of the group is given approximately one minute to speak about him/herself in only *positive* terms — no qualifiers, no criticisms, no "buts." Immediately thereafter, the rest of the group gives to this member an additional two minutes of *positive* feedback. The time may be varied to suit the group, but caution is urged: don't allow enough for embarrassing — and painful — silence. The "clockwatcher" can be flexible, but the important note is that this must be a positive experience for *each* member. The facilitator needs to be prepared to fill any gaps in the feedback portion for the most "unlovable" group member, and to encourage the too-modest reluctant starter. The facilitator is encouraged to be the first speaker in this exercise, as a model of self-assertion and to demonstrate appropriate positive statements to make about oneself.

On Improving Feedback in Groups

One of the important values of using a group format for AT is the diversity of viewpoints available for providing feedback to participants on the effectiveness of their assertions. Nevertheless, many group members find it difficult to give good feedback, and it is valuable to spend some time training a group in how the members can best help each other.

Toward that goal, it is suggested that a number of qualities of good interpersonal feedback be pointed out to the group. The following list should prove helpful, and the facilitator's experience will provide additional guidelines.

Helpful feedback:

... describes *specific* verbal and non-verbal behaviors in detail;

... avoids telling "how *I* would do it";

... focuses on the *behavior*, not the *person*;

... gives *observations* and *descriptions*, not *opinions* and *judgements*;

... is for the benefit of the *receiver*, not the *giver*;

... gives *information*, not *instructions*, thus allowing the trainee to choose what he or she will do with the information.

One additional comment about feedback which may be of interest. A number of groups in Southern California have utilized poker chips as tokens, encouraging group members to toss a chip at the feet of a member to indicate — by chip color — whether a particular action was assertive, nonassertive, or aggressive. The immediacy of such feedback is valuable, and the chips themselves create a novel source of group interest (and fun!). However, such global feedback needs to be supplemented with specifics about behavior as soon afterward as possible, in order to be of maximum value in aiding the development of more effective behavior.

Other Formats for Assertiveness Training

We have described here in considerable detail an approach to facilitating assertive groups which has worked well for us over a period of years. Our style has modified, of course, as we have found new and better means for achieving the goals of our group participants. Nevertheless, we are under no illusion that there is only one way to conduct effective assertive training groups. We know that many of our colleagues find other styles more appropriate in their own group work, some with more structure, some with less, some more rigorous in application of learning principles, others with a greater humanistic-existential flavor.

Although we have no quarrel with these and other approaches to the development of assertive behavior, we remain convinced that application of the principles detailed in this book will enable clients to achieve their behavioral goals. And that, of course, is the ultimate criterion.

The wide range of interests of AT practitioners, researchers, and theorists, has led to the development of a variety of approaches to meet special needs, and to suit the styles of the professionals involved. We consider this diversity to have been very healthy since the resulting process has been enriched by a relatively free exchange of ideas and discoveries, in contrast to the common experience in which a therapeutic modality has been limited by rigid adherence to "rules" established by its "founding guru."

We have benefited from the excellent work of many colleagues around the world who have helped to develop effective AT procedures. The following material is a very brief overview of some important contributions to AT. Space and time make a fully comprehensive review impractical. Read each of the sources cited, in the process of developing and refining your own style.

General Concepts

Four social myths which are responsible for much non-assertive behavior have been described by *Sherwin Cotler* and *Julio Guerra* (1976). The myths of *anxiety, obligation, modesty,* and the *good friend* help to explain much of the belief system which inhibits self-assertion as it is defined by the popular (pre-AT) culture. Trainee understanding of the false premises inherent in these myths does much to free them to attempt assertions.

AT as a part of the broader framework of behavior therapy has been a theme of *Herbert Fensterheim* (1975), and *Spencer Rathus* (1977). Their work has focused attention on the need to view the clinical client in a broad therapeutic framework, with emphasis on anxiety reduction as well as assertion skills training. Fensterheim has also identified a number of "clinical problem types" which are amenable to AT treatment.

Cognitive restructuring, the process of aiding clients to change their self-defeating thoughts and statements, has been advocated particularly by *Iris Fodor* and *Janet Wolfe* (1975), and *Arthur Lange* and *Patricia Jakubowski* (1976). They have developed (independent but complementary) systems for helping clients to overcome faulty belief systems and to gain more positive and rational conceptions of their life situations. Much of their work has integrated the work of *Donald Meichenbaum* (1977) in cognitive behavior therapy and the Rational Emotive Therapy of *Albert Ellis* (1979, 1980) with AT. Moreover, they have been outspoken advocates of *responsibility* as an element of assertiveness, and high ethical standards for facilitators.

Innovative Procedures

Listening, often overlooked as a component of interpersonal competence, has been incorporated into the AT model espoused by *Lynn Bloom, Karen Coburn*, and *Joan Pearlman* (1975). They suggest that attention to the other person is critical to responsible assertiveness, and present a specific "listening training" procedure. *Scripts*, and a procedure for developing your own assertive messages, is a central feature of the work of *Sharon Bower* (1976). She offers scripts for specific life events, and a general formula (*D*escribe behavior; *E*xpress feelings; *S*pecify desired change; Identify *C*onsequences) for preparing scripts to meet any situation. Her procedures are very systematic and highly detailed.

Cultural differences have been taken into consideration by very few AT practitioners or writers. *Donald Cheek* (1976) offers a thorough analysis of cultural considerations in AT. His material examines the effect on behavior of the psycho-social history of a group (specifically Blacks in America), and presents a new AT methodology designed to accommodate the special needs of Black clients. Of particular note are his emphasis on *language barriers* between black and white, and his concern for adapting the assertive message to the *target person*.

Other important contributions to this area include those of *Brian Grodner* (1977), *Philip Hwang* (1977), *Paula Landau* and *Terry Paulson* (1977), and *Evelyn Yanagida* (1979).

Assessment instruments in AT are plentiful (See Chapter 12). Thoroughly researched instruments, however, are few. *Merna* and *John Galassi* (1977) have been active researchers and practitioners in AT, and have studied assessment devices extensively, including development of their own college and adult "Self Expression Scales." Moreover, they offer a method for devising an individualized assessment scale tailored to the needs of each trainee. They have also been leaders in the move to establish ethical principles for AT practice. See also *Peter Vagg* (1979).

Among other widely used AT measures are the "Rathus Assertiveness Schedule," by *Spencer Rathus* (1973), and the "Assertion Inventory" by *Eileen Gambrill* and *Cheryl Richey* (1975). A promising newcomer is the "Interpersonal Behavior Survey" by *Paul Mauger* et al. (1980).

Sherwin Cotler and *Julio Guerra* (1976) have assembled one of the most comprehensive data collection packages in use in AT. Their concern for client needs includes anxiety measures, assertiveness scales, goal surveys and homework diaries. They have emphasized systematic monitoring of trainee anxiety through use in AT of the numerical "Subjective Unit of Disturbance" scale first presented by *Joseph Wolpe* (See Chapter 8). The "personal effectiveness" skills training program (which parallels AT), developed by *Robert Liberman* and his associates (1976), includes a group procedure which calls for planning, work, and evaluation sessions, so that time is clearly provided for each of those three group tasks.

Specific Techniques

Many techniques have been effectively utilized by AT practitioners and are worthy of mention here. Although we have noted, in the brief summaries below, names of professionals whom we associate with the development of a particular procedure, the exact origin of many techniques is unknown or simultaneous, and we make no claim for the accuracy of our attributions.

Homework Assignments take AT from the training environment into the "life space" of the trainee. Responsible and appropriate assignments are those which would be natural to the client's lifestyle, and would not demand that he or she behave in an embarassing, highly unusual or bizarre fashion. *John Shelton* (1976, 1977) has been a major developer of systematic homework in AT and other forms of therapy.

Contrasted Role Plays, an insight-oriented model for role playing in AT groups, is the work of *Linda MacNeilage* and *Kathleen Adams* (1977). The model incorporates a Gestalt notion of "reconciliaton of opposites" by having the trainee enact three contrasting responses to a situation (unassertive, aggressive, assertive), thus experiencing the full range of emotional and behavioral alternatives.

Verbal Techniques have been widespread and take many forms. The DESC scripts of *Sharon Bower* (see "Innovative Procedures" above) are a very precise guide to assertive language. *Myles Cooley* and *James Hollandsworth* (1977) have devised a "components" strategy for teaching assertive statements, classified in three general areas: saying "no" or taking a stand (position, reason, understanding); asking favors or asserting rights (problem, request, clarification); and expressing feelings (personal expression).

Among the "last resort" techniques used by some trainers are the "broken record," "fog," "selective ignoring," and "critical inquiry," (*Cotler* and *Guerra*, 1976). Each of these is an effort to overcome unfair manipulation or attack, and are considered appropriate only when the trainee has decided that the possible consequence of ending the relationship is worth risking. Briefly, "broken record" involves repetitive expressions of one's position; "fog" is a passive-aggressive agreement with the other person ("Whatever you say, dear"); "selective ignoring" is withholding any response when one feels the other is being unreasonable, unfair, or aggressive; "critical inquiry" is an invitation to the critical person to *be* even more critical, and thus emphasize undesired behavior. Once learned, of course, these techniques may be *used* aggressively and not just in self-defense. Cotler and Guerra are careful to point out the dangers in these "last resort" approaches, and do not advocate their general use (nor do *we*, needless to say!).

Synthesis

There are many ways to grow. Assertiveness training is a complex process comprised of many elements. Goal clarification, skill training, cognitive restructuring, anxiety reduction, emotional expression, and the wide variety of techniques possible to achieve each, weave an intricate web of change mechanisms.

How is the trainer to decide? Surely there is not time in anyone's schedule to include all the possibilities!

AT is something of a paradox. While on the surface it appears among the simplest of behavior change procedures, an in-depth examination makes clear that it must be thoughtfully adapted to the needs of each individual client (or at the least to each client group). Such individualization requires careful assessment, precise selection of procedures, and skilled practice of those techniques which are selected.

A few guides for synthesis:

...assess trainee needs in terms of anxiety/obstacles, behavioral skills, attitudes toward self and toward assertiveness;

...develop professional skills with at least one proven approach in each area. Select carefully from among the many approaches, then learn well those you choose.

...apply your skills with care, continuously monitoring client progress, and putting emphasis where need is greatest. Avoid "canned" training which is the same for everyone!

...keep your practice of AT up to date by regular examination of the literature. Even we are amazed at how fast new procedures are demonstrated valuable, and old ones go out of date.

Cognitive therapies, behavior therapies, and humanistic therapies have all contributed much to the development and practice of assertiveness training. Indeed, AT may be the only procedure where all three may be found as "comfortable bedfellows."

No one has a corner on truth, but those of us whose principal interest is *application* of knowledge may feel confident that "enlightened eclecticism" is still the honorable path:

...Yes, trainees do need to deal with their thoughts, attitudes, and self statements, as the cognitive people have been telling us.

...And yes, overt behavioral skills are the most evident and "trainable" dimension of self expression. The behavior therapists are clearly right in that regard.

...Furthermore, behavioral skills and conditions aside, the client who lacks awareness of his/her feelings and goals will find little to be assertive about, as we have been taught by humanistic psychology.

Each theory/methodology contains some truth. And it is to each that responsible therapists turn for help, *depending upon the needs of the individual client.*

Prepare yourself carefully.

Assess your trainees with equal care.

And practice AT ethically and responsibly.

18

Applications of Assertiveness Training

We have previously suggested that the procedures described here have application in a broad range of human activities. Although most individuals will themselves be better able to identify the usefulness of AT in their own situations, this chapter provides an organized approach to a variety of settings for the assertive behavior development process.

Most of the examples suggested here have been drawn from the experiences of the authors, friends, colleagues, and students, or from professional literature. Others will doubtless occur to the practitioner in his or her own setting. It is recommended that each reader review the entire list. Keep in mind that, although the settings may vary, we consider the general principles of AT — *including the ethical principles noted in Appendix B* — to apply.

Teachers. The classroom teacher will frequently find students who are nonassertive or aggressive, particularly with respect to classroom behavior. Assertiveness training has been shown highly valuable for students who wish to become better able to raise questions in class, to make presentations and reports, to respond to teacher questions, to express opinions, or to participate in group discussions. Similarly, AT is pertinent to helping students who seem to "come on too strong" in asking questions, expressing opinions, and so on. An increasing volume of work with young children indicates tremendous potential for pre-school and early elementary age youngsters. A leader in this work is Dr. Pat Palmer of the Assertiveness Training Institute of Denver, Colorado, who has written two books on AT for children (1977).

Coaches. Every coach of athletic, music, drama or forensic groups has worked with students of considerable potential who were unwilling to try new behavior or to perform individually (e.g., carry the ball, solo) or, conversely, to be "part of the team." For the reluctant student who "wishes" to achieve his or her potential in these areas, assertive training in the area of desired development is suggested. (Indeed, the principles of behavior shaping have been successfully applied in this field for years.) The aggressive individual can also be taught by the coach to temper an approach which seems to be out of line with what is generally accepted. There is great potential in any individual who has all of the necessary qualities, but who hinders results by being aggressive. If the coach can channel these abilities by fostering assertion, both the individual and the team will benefit.

Counselors. The mental health professional will readily recognize the potential of assertiveness training for clients who demonstrate poor social development, inadequate self-confidence, academic disinterest, inability to withstand peer, parental, or teacher pressure. The indecisive individual who wishes to improve decision-making capacity, the non-dater who lacks rudimentary social skills, the student who fears going to see a teacher to ask legitimate questions about the subject matter, the student who eagerly expresses her- or himself but denies others their opportunity, the person who has made a well-considered decision to leave college but is unable to face parents — all of these and many more need to learn how they can more comfortably express themselves as they wish to, and AT can help.

College Student Development Staff. Individuals working in college residence halls, activities-union programs, student health centers, placement offices, special education programs, financial aid offices, minority programs, campus religious programs, and deans' offices have broad contact with college students "where they're at." The perceptive residence hall advisor *knows* the student who cannot stand up to a roommate to ask relief from the stereo's unreasonable noise level. A would-be student leader who lacks the confidence to campaign for office will be recognized by staff members who work with organizations. Medical personnel recognize the rash on a shy student as symptomatic of anxiety over presenting a report in class tomorrow. The placement staff can readily spot in advance the student who will suffer in an upcoming job interview for not knowing how to act in that new and threatening situation. All of these student development staff members are very much aware also of the individual who seems to offend others by being too outspoken, brusque or verbally or physically abusive. Because the assertive behavior shaping process is systematic and straightforward, these staff members can be of direct help *on the spot* to the student with such problems. There are obvious advantages to help offered by a *known* person, with little or no delay, without the need to seek out another office and establish a relationship with a new and unknown person.

Therapists. Interpersonal anxiety is a common symptom in persons who have emotional difficulties. Assertiveness training can be a vital factor in reducing this anxiety The basic principles we have proposed apply, regardless of the setting, be it in correctional work, private therapy practice, alcohol and drug abuse clinics, etc. Persons who lack feelings of self-worth can be helped by facilitating their own development of "worthy person" behaviors (making their own choices, standing up for their rights successfully but nonaggressively). Changing of attitudes and feelings goes hand in hand with changed behavior.

Dr. Arthur Hardy is a California physician who uses AT extensively with severely phobic patients and reports considerable success (1977).

Speech Therapists. Adult stutterers have responaed well to AT by speech therapists in conjunction with other techniques of behavior therapy such as systematic desensitization, in addition to various speech therapy techniques. Stutterers usually have a long history of disfluency beginning in their elementary school years.

Typically they have been "worried over" by parents and teachers, placed in special education classes for therapy, and teased by their peers. As time goes on they learn very well not to expose themselves to situations where attention will be focused on their speech. Essentially, these individuals learn to be very non-demanding of others to the exclusion of their own rights. Often they believe that they are not as good as others, and therefore have no right to be assertive. Because of their dread of interpersonal situations, they can benefit from AT to overcome or inhibit anxiety. Assertive acts such as use of the telephone, talking to sales clerks, asking questions, learning how to disagree, learning to say no, and so on, can be practiced successfully. Thus the long-established pattern of self-denial and lack of spontaneity can be altered significantly.

Social Welfare Workers. The welfare recipient is often a member of a minority group, living in sub-standard housing in the least desirable location in a community. In addition to the oppressive way in which members of minorities have often been treated in our society, the recipient has had to suffer the indignities of the welfare system. Assertiveness training can help to increase self-respect, teach more adaptive ways of behaving in conjunction with gaining rights, help to develop effective community leadership, assist persons in methods for dealing with merchants, insure fair treatment without self-denial or aggressive acts. The frequent use of group work and the practice of family case work provide other opportunities for assertive behavior development in this field.

Inevitable vulnerability to the political system is a particular concern in welfare programs. Assertive community action offers a potential avenue for increasing "clout" and stabilizing fiscal support.

Employment Counselors. Efforts to place persons in productive and rewarding employment are greatly enhanced by the client's ability to demonstrate self-confidence and to communicate effectively with interviewers and employers. Often a simple rehearsal of interviewing behavior provides a client with the tools and confidence needed to gain an appropriate position. Another person may require more extensive help in building up good feelings about self, perhaps by developing assertive behaviors and recognizing that other people acknowledge his or her personhood. One who is *reinforced* for acting like a self-assured person begins to recognize her or his own strengths. Another individual may need awareness of coming across too aggressively and need to learn how to modify that approach.

Marriage Counselors. When a couple comes in for marriage counseling it is almost a foregone conclusion that they are not communicating successfully. Three situations are common: 1) The husband has been the dominant decision-maker throughout the marriage with the woman being the dutiful headnodder; 2) the reverse situation, in which the husband is quiet and indecisive, and the wife is dominant; and 3) neither partner is dominant throughout, but neither has really known the other's thoughts and feelings all these years. All three of these situations are responsive to the assertive training model. As noted earlier, learning assertiveness will change one's relationship with those closest. For this reason it is preferable to have both partners working on the relationship, but if each spouse is truly assertive, the difficulty will not likely balloon into a major crisis.

We are convinced that the more honest and open each partner is about all aspects of the marital relationship the more successful that relationship will be. Similarly, families who encourage freedom of expression on the part of children provide more growth-enhancing environments for young persons *and* their parents (Palmer, 1977).

Pastoral Counselors. One of our clients who had built up fears and doubts about being assertive could still remember from childhood a sign in a Sunday School room: "The formula for *JOY* is: *J*esus first, *O*thers second, *Y*ourself last." Unfortunately, to many youngsters (and oldsters), such messages mean quite pointedly, "don't step out ahead of others," "let others take advantage of you," "turn the other cheek," "keep your feelings inside." There seems to be a religiously-based feeling among many people that they must never feel good about themselves. Because they must never hurt anyone's feelings, they will let others take advantage of them. It is a moot point whether or not is is indeed true that religious education in church or at home fosters ill feelings about one's right to feel good about one's self and to stand up for one's self. The goal is to help the individual to become self-confident. We feel that clients with religious-based barriers towards assertion need re-education about what it truly means to be assertive. There need be no incompatibility between asserting one's perfect (i.e., God-given, natural, inherent) rights and having deep religious convictions.

A number of authors have addressed the area of assertiveness within a religious context. Ethan J. Allen, Jr. (1976) discusses the "nice-guy" syndrome. He states that those being trained to be priests have a reputation for being "too soft" because they are traditionally cheerful in the face of insult and unassertive when others disregard their rights. Allen feels that these characteristics lead others to regard the seminarian as a "Caspar Milquetoast."

Randy K. Sanders (1976) speaks of a theologically oriented approach to assertiveness training. He feels that devout Christians are likely to feel that their commitment to Christ requires such behavior as passively "turning the other cheek." Because of such conceptions, Sanders suggests that a religious AT facilitator may need to employ a method of teaching assertion which uses "scriptures exemplifying assertiveness."

Edward W. C. McAllister (1975), a member of the Psychology Department of Russell Sage College, advocates assertiveness training for Christian therapists as a useful tool to help their clients grow, relieve anxiety, and function better in interpersonal relationships. He feels that many Christians are in need of assertion training *because* they view being nonassertive as part of their Christianity.

Two books discussing assertiveness and religion have recently been published. David Augsburger has written *Anger and Assertiveness in Pastoral Care* (1979) and Michael Emmons and David Richardson have written *The Assertive Christian* (1981). Augsburger illustrates how pastors can handle anger and aggression in constructive ways. Emmons and Richardson discuss several vital issues: meekness, anger, guilt, the assertiveness of Jesus.

A special issue of *ASSERT* (June, 1980) was devoted to assertiveness and religion, with articles by ministers, nuns, social workers, psychologists, and others who have been trained both in psychology and religion. (Incidentally, we are aware of no work relating assertiveness to religions other than Christian. Readers who are familiar with such work are *urged* to submit reports for possible publication in the *ASSERT* newsletter.)

Nurses and Allied Medical Personnel. Health care delivery systems have long been controlled in near-despotic fashion (albeit perhaps benevolent!) by physicians. Recently, however, nurses and other health care professionals have assumed more important roles in delivery of services to patients. As both cause and result, these health care staff are developing greater independence and personal/professional assertiveness. The Nurse Practitioner, for example, proceeds independently under only limited physician supervision. Assertiveness training has become a vital part of nursing education programs throughout the country (Herman, 1977, 1978; Faily, Hensley, Rich, 1979). And many health care professionals are advocating greater *patient* assertiveness as well! In a very important and therapeutic way, health care delivery is becoming a cooperative venture, involving physician, staff, and patient, and AT is a valuable tool in that process.

Rehabilitation Counselors. A particularly exciting area of AT application has evolved in work with handicapped and retarded persons. Although results are highly variable, and the work very difficult, a number of professionals have reported success in training for employment interviews, obtaining medical, educational and social services, dealing with relatives who treat the handicapped adult "like a child," gaining enough confidence to enroll in college, and developing skills in general social interaction. Issue 13 of the *ASSERT* newsletter described several such programs. Markel and Greenbaum (1979) provide a step-by-step guide for parents of handicapped children, teaching them assertiveness with schools and agencies.

Management and Human Resources Development. Individuals who are concerned with staff development in industrial and/or governmental organizations may find that a systematic effort to train management and sales personnel in assertiveness will pay big dividends. Group training methods will be useful in large organizations, and assertive training can be effectively incorporated into other management development or staff training programs. Supervisorial personnel who understand, and can apply the assertive (nonaggressive) model to their interactions with subordinates are too few, and more effective management teams can be developed utilizing AT as a key to recognition of the rights and organizational parameters of each employee. For example, a supervisor who can firmly reprimand a subordinate's *error* without devastating that *person* is a valuable asset in any organization. Also, of course, the lower-level employee who can honestly and constructively criticize supervisors or the operation — in an assertive fashion — without fear on the one hand, or aggressive attack on the other, can be a significant contributor to organizational productivity, and a happier person (Shaw, 1979). (Issue 19 of the *Assert* newsletter featured AT in management.)

Teacher Education. Among the chief complaints we hear from teachers are difficulty in "handling the kids" (discipline), lack of communication with supervisors, and fear of parent conferences. If a teacher is nonassertive, the students will typically take advantage of the weakness. On the other hand, a tyrant, the overly aggressive teacher, will be feared but not respected, a counter-productive situation. Assertive communication with the principal is essential for teachers. Teachers must also learn that children and parents are people, their equals as human beings, and should be approached accordingly.

A teacher described to us the experience at her school district with an assertive training program. A faculty group set out to learn assertive techniques for helping their students. After a short time, they recognized many of their own nonassertive or aggressive responses to students, administrators, and parents, and began to focus upon their own need for assertiveness. The result was a highly-enthusiastic report about their growth in personal and professional assertiveness.

It is our opinion that student teachers should take part in assertiveness training as a routine segment of their preparation for classroom teaching.

Leadership Training for Community Organizations. Effective leadership at all levels is perhaps the greatest single area of difficulty facing volunteer community groups. School-parent associations, service clubs, auxiliaries, women's clubs, interest groups, churches, youth activities, social clubs, even community action agencies and political parties suffer from a lack of persons willing and able to assume key responsibilities. While it is obvious that lack of time for such involvement is an important reason for the dearth of willing individuals, it is also true that many persons simply consider themselves inadequately prepared to accept responsibility for a committee, or a club, or a community activity (Lawson, et al., 1976). Leadership development in such groups — from securing volunteers for an arrangements committee to convincing candidates to accept the nominating committee's call to the presidency or chairmanship — can be enhanced by including a program of assertive behavior development for the "rank and file" membership as well as for those who have already attained identified leadership roles.

Youth Workers. Adult leaders in such organizations as YM and YWCA's, YM and YWHA's, Boy and Girl Scouts, 4-H, Future Farmers, community recreation programs, church and church school youth groups, and summer camps have considerable opportunity to observe the behavior of young people, notably in social settings where the youngsters are working and/or playing with their fellows. The apathetic, disinterested or asocial youth who is observed in such a group may well be nonassertive, may fear failure and subsequent rejection, refuse to try anything, or attempt to dominate peers by being brash and abrasive. The sensitive adult who notes such behavior may be able to help this young person by providing a non-threatening, secure environment (perhaps on a one-to-one basis at first) in which the youth can feel safe in trying some new activity. The process of shaping more confident behavior may be slow, but it can provide the youngster with opportunities to make choices among alternative ways of acting. This step toward independence is an important quality of all such youth-oriented programs.

Journalism. A university journalism instructor noticed the potential use of AT with photography students and asked us to make presentations and give demonstrations in his classes. We have found that assertive concepts can be important in the improvement of photographic skills. If the photographer is either overly shy and cautious or too overbearing and pushy, the results will be affected. By being assertive rather than aggressive one may be able to avoid the physical abuse and even law suits that press photographers experience.

Another application for journalists is in development of interviewing skills. For instance, how do you assertively approach the subject and obtain the story you need? How do you handle a domineering person who wants to take over the interview? What should you say if you deeply disagree with the person's views? Is there a way to put at ease a subject who is anxious or is trying too hard? Or to confront the person who feeds you information which you already know is false? All of these situations are natural opportunities for the assertive processes.

Human Liberation. Many women have learned not to feel good about themselves and their abilities for a variety of reasons. Women, like men, have a perfect right to feel good about their real selves and to be able assertively to stand up for themselves in life. Most of us are familiar with the aggressive female who has a "cause" which she pushes fanatically. Conversely, we are equally put off by her nonassertive counterpart, the frail female with little spunk and independence.

There now exist many broadly-based community programs of treatment for persons typically denied access to therapeutic services: the poor, minorities, working people. Women's consciousness efforts are growing in large and small communities throughout the world (Phelps and Austin, 1975).

Application of assertive behavior principles is useful to any oppressed group; ethnic minorities, students, children, laborers, the poor, the aged, all have much to gain from assertion of their rights in accordance with the fundmental processes described in this book.

Others. AT with juvenile delinquents, consumers, the divorced, alcohol and substance abusers, senior citizens, families, and in weight control programs are among other applications of which we are aware. The *ASSERT* newsletter regularly carries reports of new AT programs. The examples given in this chapter are by no means all-inclusive. The reader is encouraged to consult the literature, colleagues and friends, and to reflect on his/her own experience for other relevant applications of assertiveness training.

It should be noted, however, that although AT may have been utilized with a particular population — even successfully — there are no assurances that it will be of benefit to any individual or group. Facilitators are urged to thoroughly *assess* the needs of their clients — including those in "public" workshops — to determine the appropriateness of their interventions.

As a final comment, we urge professionals to integrate AT into a comprehensive approach to total client needs, and to operate within principles which advocate responsible self-expression which is non-hurtful to others.

Selected Annotated Bibliography*

General Reports

Alden, L. & Cappe, R. Nonassertiveness: Skill deficit or selective self-evaluation? *Behavior Therapy*, 1981 (Jan), *12* (1), 107-114.

College students were videotaped in assertion role-plays, and the tapes were rated by trained observers. Students were also asked to evaluate themselves. Nonassertive participants rated themselves more anxious, less assertive, and less effective than assertive subjects. Observers noted no difference between the groups. Nonassertives also endorsed Ellis' irrational beliefs more than assertives. (Assertiveness measured on Gambrill-Richey.) Perhaps assertiveness is more a function of self-evaluation than skill?

Bandura, A. Psychotherapy based upon modeling principles. In A.E. Bergin & S.L. Garfield (Eds.) *Handbook of psychotherapy and behavior change: an empirical analysis*. New York: Wiley & Sons, 1971.

Essential reading for anyone using modeling procedures. A comprehensive chapter covers a variety of topics such as: vicarious extinction, graduated modeling, multiple modeling, live vs. symbolic modeling, etc. He found that modeling with guided participation is the best method discovered so far for reducing fears of various kinds. A component analysis of this method is given.

*Galassi, J.P., Kosta, M.P. & Galassi, M.D. Assertive training: a one year follow-up. *Journal of Counseling Psychology*, 1975, 22, 451-452.

This study reports the results of a one-year follow-up on group AT with nonassertive college students. One year after training, experimental and control Ss were significantly different on two self-reports

* A number of items in this bibliography were prepared by Donna Stringer-Moore (*Ph.D.*), Director of the Office for Women's Rights, City of Seattle, for publication in *Assertive Behavior Training. An Annotated Bibliography* (794 items), published by Impact Publishers, Inc. (1981).

(The College Self-Expression Scale and the Subjective Unit of Disturbance Scale) and two of four behavior measures (assertive content and scene length). No differences were found on eye contact or response latency. The results indicated the long term effects of assertive training. (Authors' abstract) This is a particularly important study since it is one of the few which successfully measures long-term effects of AT. The authors suggest two possible reasons for their success: first, their original training was longer, more intensive and more complex than other researchers had used, and secondly, their follow-up procedure was conducted in the laboratory whereas other researchers had used *in vivo* follow-up (self-report diaries or phone calls). Although *in vivo* reports may be strong assessments of assertiveness, they are also strongly confounded by other variables which make them difficult to interpret.

Hoffman, R.A.; Kirwin, P.M. & Rouzer, D.L. Facilitating generalization in assertiveness training. *Psychological reports*, 1979 (aug), *45* (1), 27-30.

Experimental studies of catharsis and studies on the inability to express anger adequately are reviewed. A constructive method for expression of anger is needed, with distinctions between anger and aggression and between destructive and constructive expression of anger. Describes how constructive expression of anger can be employed in assertive training.

* Lazarus, A.A. On assertive behavior: A brief note. *Behavior Therapy*, 1973, 4, 697-699.

The author begins by stating that people who need assertive training are usually deficit in one or more of the following areas: the ability to say no, the ability to ask for favors or make requests, the ability to express positive and negative feelings, the ability to initiate, continue or terminate general conversations. In order for AT to be successful, he believes it must be specific to the area in which the client is having difficulty because there is very little generalization across areas. The author then expresses his concern that most assertive training has focused on negative aspects (e.g., saying no, expressing displeasure, etc.) which have too often been aggression under the guise of assertiveness. He suggests that AT should give more attention to the positive aspects of assertion (e.g., expressing affection, appreciation, etc.).

Shelton, J.L. Assertive training: Consumer beware. *Personnel and Guidance Journal*, 1977 (Apr), 55 (8), 465-468.

General discussion of AT, with caveats. Underscores importance of trained, competent facilitators. Suggests procedures to improve effectiveness of AT: Screen clients in advance; Inform clients of training procedures and expected outcomes; Use least coercive methods; Be sure leaders are trained and knowledgeable; Supervise trainers; Monitor effects on clients.

* Wolfe, J.L., & Fodor, I.G. A cognitive-behavioral approach to modifying assertive behavior in women. *Counseling Psychologist*, 1975, 5 (4), 45-52.

Beginning with a typical discussion of the sex-role socialization which occurs for women, thus leading to non-assertion, the authors continue by giving the outline for an AT group which first attempts to dispute irrational attitudes and beliefs, and then gives members of the group practice in new forms of behavior. A very nice chart of traditional beliefs with ways of disputing irrational ideas is included. Lengthy scripts for role played situations are also included. Discussion of what to do with assertive failures, why homework is important, differences between AT and consciousness raising groups. A nice chart on typical assignments which is divided into target problem, behavioral assignment and cognitive assignment sections. This is a useful article for persons thinking about working with women in AT groups.

Measurement of Assertiveness

Andrasik, et al. Assessing the readability levels of self-report assertion inventories. *Journal of Consulting & Clinical Psychology*, 1981 (Feb), 49 (1), 142-144.

Reading levels were obtained for 11 commonly used assertion inventories by a standard formula. *Directions* ranged from the 7th to college-graduate reading grade level; *inventory items* were more readable, with scores from the 7th to the 12th grade level. Consider reading difficulty when selecting assertion scales!

* Galassi, J.P. & Galassi, M.D. Relationship between assertiveness and aggressiveness. *Psychological Reports*, 1975, 36, 352-354.

In recognition of the importance of differentiating assertive behavior from aggressive behavior, this study administered the College Self Expression Scale (the authors' measure of assertiveness) and the Buss-Durkee Inventory (a measure of eight types of aggressiveness) to 100 female and 71 male college students. Male and female Ss were treated separately for analysis. The only significant positive relationship found was between the assertiveness scale and the verbal aggression scale for females. This led the authors to conclude that the College Self Expression Scale is not tapping aggressiveness as operationalized by the Buss-Durkee Inventory. There is nothing in this article of specific interest to trainers but it is one of the few studies which have looked at sex differences and also the only research to date looking at the relationship between aggression and assertion — a distinction which most trainers make.

* Gambrill, E.D. & Richey, C.A. An assertiveness inventory for use in assessment and research. *Behavior Therapy*, 1975, 6, 550-561.

The inventory, a 40-item self-report measure, permits respondents to indicate their degree of discomfort, probability of engaging in the behavior, and situations they would like to handle better. Normative data include college students and women taking part in AT groups. The inventory is reported to have value in both clinical settings and research. A particularly useful instrument for research on assertiveness, especially as a pre-post test to establish effectiveness of AT procedures between groups. Caution must be used regarding the population tested because the response instructionsmight make the test difficult to use with younger or less sophisticated populations.

ANNOTATED BIBLIOGRAPHY

Gorecki, P.R., et al. Relationship between contrived *in vivo* and role-play assertive behavior. *Journal of Clinical Psychology*, 1981 (Jan), 37 (1), 104-107.

Role play situations were compared with actual life situations to determine validity of role-play as a measure of assertiveness. Undergraduates were selected as high or low assertive by Conflict Resolution Inventory. A positive relationship was found between role-play performance and self report scores, however, self-report scores did not predict *in vivo* performance. Suggests caution in generalizing from role-play or self-report scores to natural settings.

Hartwig, W.H., et al. Conflict Resolution Inventory: Factor-analytic data. *Psychological Reports*, 1980 (Jun), *46* (3, Pt 1), 1009-1010.

The Conflict Resolution Inventory (ability to refuse unreasonable requests) was administered to 159 students. The results were factor analyzed, and the resulting 12 factors suggest that assertion is situation-specific even within one class of responses.

Lorr, M., and More, W.W. Four dimensions of assertiveness. *Multivariate Behavioral research*, 1980 (Apr), *15* (2). 127-138.

Directiveness, Social Assertiveness, Defense of One's Interests, and *Independence*, are dimensions of assertiveness which resulted from factor analytic studies of 479 subjects (average age, 21). Extensive statistical analysis was made of item sets developed to measure several postulated kinds of assertiveness. Dimensions found were positively correlated with self-esteem, and were independent of hostility and social desireability.

Nesbitt, E.B. Rathus Assertiveness Schedule and College Self-Expression Scale scores as predictors of assertive behavior. *Psychological Reports*, 1979 (Dec), *45* (3), 855-861.

Forty male undergraduates were tested on Rathus Assertiveness Schedule (RAS) and College Self-Expression Scale (CSES). Scores were correlated with performance ratings in situations requiring positive assertion. Total RAS scores, total CSES scores, and scores on items that purport to measure ability to respond appropriately in situations requiring positive assertive responses were poor predictors

of ability to perform in realistic situations. The best predictor of actual performance was an individual's assessment of his or her overall level of assertiveness!

Vagg, P.R. Assessment in AT: How to choose an instrument. *ASSERT 28*, 1979, 28, 1 & 3.

Discusses importance of careful measurement, and criteria for selection of assessment instruments. Notes that test users need to determine information required, review available test materials and relevant data, and examine adequacy of tests in terms of construction and validation methods. Users are cautioned regarding difficulties and hazards of casual attempts at test construction.

* Rathus, S.A. A 30-item schedule for assessing assertive behavior. *Behavior Therapy*, 1973, *4*, 398-406.

A 30-item schedule for measuring assertiveness is shown to have moderate to high test-retest reliability and split-half reliability. Validity in terms of the impressions respondents make on other people and in terms of their indication of how they would behave in specific situations in which assertive, outgoing behavior can be used with profit is satisfactory. Item analysis shows good correlation with the total scale score and with external criteria. A shorter version of the scale is discussed. Also, it was found that assertiveness varies negatively with impressions of niceness. This is one of the few scales which has been experimentally tested for validity and reliability and should be considered if one is doing assertiveness research. Norms are available with males scoring higher than females. Additionally, the items are general enough to be useful for pre-post testing with non-college or college populations if assertiveness trainers wish to test the effectiveness of their groups.

Cultural & Sex Differences

Cheek, D.K., Landau, P., Paulson, T., Hwang, P.O., and Grodner, B.S. Assertiveness across cultures (Four papers). In Alberti, R.E. (Ed.) *Assertiveness: Innovations, Applications, Issues*. San Luis Obispo, CA: Impact Publishers, 1977, pp. 111-147.

Cheek's paper discusses assertive behavior and black lifestyles, including problems of using "white approach" with black clients. Landau and Paulson describe a treatment program using group AT with Spanish speaking Mexican-American mothers. Hwang's paper places self-assertion in juxtaposition to Oriental myths, noting that AT can be used as an effective procedure to counter self-defeating beliefs. Grodner studies assertiveness and anxiety in cross-cultural and socioeconomic perspective, finding that socio-economic differences outweigh cultural differences as factors in assertion and anxiety.

Kelly, J.A., et al. Reactions to assertive versus unassertive behavior: Differential effects for males and females and implications for assertiveness training. *Behavior Therapy*, 1980 (Nov), *11* (5), 670-682.

Examined evaluation of assertiveness by men and women, by having 258 students rate male and female models acting either assertively or unassertively. An interpersonal attraction inventory was used to assess models on various characteristics. Assertive models were seen as less likeable, although more skilled and able. Assertiveness by females yielded more negative evaluations than the same behavior in males.

Romano, J.M. & Bellack, A.S. Social validation of a component model of assertive behavior. *Journal of Consulting and Clinical Psychology*, 1980 (Aug), *48* (4), 478-490.

Videotape was used to allow trained male and female raters to evaluate social skill of 20 adult women AT trainees. Important results: nonverbal behaviors were best predictor of overall performance; complex verbal behaviors were best predictor of of skill over variety of situations; clear sex differences between male and female judges in cues which were influential in ratings.

Yanagida. E.H. Cross-cultural considerations in the application of assertion training: A brief note. *Psychology of Women Quarterly*, 1979 (Sum), *3* (4), 400-402.

Case study of AT with a Japanese-American woman, illustrating difficulties in cross cultural work. Particularly noted: lack of social

baseline data, ethnic variations in essential components of behavior.

Experimental Studies

Berah, E.F. Influence of scheduling variations on the effectiveness of a group assertion-training program for women. *Journal of Counseling Psychology*, 1981 (May), *28* (3), 265-268.

Explored effects of massed vs. distributed practice to an applied situation. Four types of groups were compared: massed practice, distributed practice, combination massed and distributed practice AT groups, and no-treatment control groups. 66 college students participated. Assertiveness was assessed by College Self Expression Scale, a role-play test, and peer ratings before, immediately after, and 4 wks following AT. AT produced greater increases in assertiveness than no treatment. There were no differences between the different types of AT groups. At least for the type of program and Ss involved in the study, scheduling of sessions can be guided by the convenience of group leaders and participants without loss of effectiveness.

Eisler, R.M., Hersen, M., and Miller, P.M. Effects of modeling on components of assertive behavior. *Journal of Behavior Therapy and Experimental Psychiatry*, 1973, *4*, 1-6.

Measured the effects of videotaped modeling on eight verbal and non-verbal aspects of assertive behavior. 30 male psychiatric patients with an average age of 44 years. Two additional groups were utilized: 1) practice-control and 2) test — retest. The modeling and practice groups participated in a behavioral assertiveness test (devised by the authors) six times during a three-day period. Video tapes of performances were rated by judges for duration of looking, loudness of speech, etc. Results showed the modeling group had significantly more change than the other two groups. Specifically, the modeling participants showed greater changes in five of the eight variables studied: 1) longest duration of reply, 2) greatest number of requests for new behavior, 3) greater affect, 4) louder speech, and 5) greatest overall assertiveness.

* Eisler, R.M., Hersen, M., Miller, P.M., and Blanchard, E.B. Situational determinants of assertive behaviors. *Journal of Consulting and Clinical Psychology*, 1975, *43*, 330-40.

The purposes of this study were to extend earlier findings regarding negative assertion to the area of positive assertion, to look at the effects of the social context of interpersonal behavior on assertion and to delineate behaviors differentiating high and low assertiveness with regard to three variables: male or female interaction partner, positive or negative responses, and familiar or unfamiliar interaction partner. Combining the three variables into 8 categories, 4 scenes were developed for roleplaying in each category, yielding 32 role play scenes. Assertiveness was measured by the Wolpe-Lazarus self report inventory and behavior ratings by two judges. Categories for behavior ratings were 5 verbal and 7 nonverbal behaviors in addition to an overall assertiveness score. Subjects were 60 male psychiatric patients. Results yielded significant interactions between the three variables substantiating the hypothesis that assertive behavior is functionally related to the social context of interpersonal interaction. Significant differences were found on 6 of 7 nonverbal variables when positive and negative assertive situations were compared. Subjects exhibited greater assertion toward women than toward men in both positive and negative situations. In general, the results support a stimulus-specific theory of assertiveness as well as demonstrating the behavioral complexity of assertiveness.

* Hirsch, S.M. An experimental investigation of the effectiveness of assertion training with alcoholics. *Dissertation Abstracts International*, 36/06, 3044-B. Texas Technical University. Order No. 75-26843, 133 pgs.

In an attempt to delineate parameters of unassertiveness in alcoholics, 123 state hospitalized alcoholics were chosen as a standardization normalization group for the Rathus Assertiveness Scale. Comparing these patients with a group of college students, no significant differences were found in assertiveness of the two groups on the RAS. The second part of the study attempted to demonstrate that AT could be effective in working with alcoholic patients. 102 chronic alcoholics at two state hospitals were assigned to three groups: minimal assertive training (received regular state hospital

program plus 2 hours of didactic presentation and group discussion on assertiveness); full scale AT (received regular state hospital program plus 2 hours of didactic presentation and group discussion on assertiveness); full scale AT (received regular state hospital program plus 10 hours of AT utilizing all the components of AT); and control group (received only the regular hospital treatment program). At the end of two weeks, all Ss were post-tested with the RAS, a tape-recorded situational test of assertive behavior and *in vivo* rating scale of assertiveness. The full scale AT group improved significantly on the RAS, the tape recorded situational test, and staff assessments of assertiveness.

McFall, R.M. & Twentyman, C.T. Four experiments on the relative contributions of rehearsal, modeling and coaching to assertion training. *Journal of Abnormal Psychology*, 1973.

Experiment 1 — examined the effects of six treatment conditions: 1) rehearsal, modeling, coaching; 2) rehearsal and modeling; 3) rehearsal and coaching; 4) rehearsal only; 5) modeling and coaching; 6) control. Subjects were seen for two 45-minute sessions one week apart. The laboratory set-up was similar to the procedure used in McFall et al. above. The modeling was on audio tape and the coaching was live, administered by a non-therapist. Results showed that rehearsal and coaching treatment on assertive behavior both were effective and that these effects were independent and additive. Also, audio modeling added very little if anything to successful treatment.

Experiment 2 — three treatments were investigated: a) covert rehearsal, modeling, coaching; b) covert rehearsal, coaching; c) covert rehearsal only. The set-up was essentially the same as above. Again modeling added little, if any, to the increase in assertiveness gained by rehearsal and coaching.

Experiment 3 — compared the effect of the old audio models with a set of audio models who were more tactful, more hesitant and less extreme in their responses. Also compared overt with covert rehearsal under several conditions. The results still supported that audio modeling, either old or new, didn't add to successful treatment effects. Results also made clearer the effects of overt and covert rehearsal, finding no differences between overt and covert when the playback component was eliminated. This indicates that the playback of response may be the variable causing earlier differences.

Experiment 4 — compared audio modeling with audio-visual modeling. A professional TV video tape involved student actors. stage sets, three-camera dramatizations, etc. The sound track was utilized for the audio modeling subjects. Two treatments of 40-minute duration were given in refusal behavior. Results showed that the video tape of models did *not* improve the treatment results. Includes excellent extensive discussion of the results of the four experiments and limitations of the treatment approach.

* Percell, L.P., Berwick, P.T. & Beigel, A. The effects of assertive training on self-concept and anxiety. *Archives of General Psychiatry*, 1974, *31*, 502-504.

Two separate studies were conducted to test the relationships between assertiveness. self-esteem and anxiety. In the first study 50 male and 50 female outpatient psychiatric patients were given the Lawrence Interpersonal Behavior Test, the Self-Acceptance Scale of the California Psychological Inventory and the Taylor Manifest Anxiety Scale. Findings indicated a substantial positive relationship between assertiveness and self-acceptance for both males and females and a strong negative correlation between assertiveness and anxiety for women only. In the second study, 24 patients were assigned to either an AT group or a relationship control group for eight sessions. Ss in the At group showed significant increases in assertiveness. self-acceptance and significant decreases in anxiety relative to controls. This is a particularly significant study for those who wish to explore the relationship between assertiveness and other factors (notably anxiety and self-esteem) which have often been assumed by trainers to be related. The weaknesses of the research (e.g., use of only psychiatric Ss, inability to get valid follow-up data) are well noted and discussed by the authors. Particularly interesting is the finding of negative relationships between assertiveness and anxiety for women only which is the opposite of what has been postulated by many authors due to cultural sex role expectations and should be explored further with larger, non-clinical populations.

Marriage/Family/Child Studies with AT

* Eisler, R.M., Miller, P.J., Hersen, M. & Alford, H. Effects of assertive training on marital interaction. *Archives of General Psychiatry*, 1974, *30*, 643-649.

Three passive-avoidant husbands were given short but intensive assertiveness training (four 45-minute sessions). AT was aimed at very specific difficulties each man was having in his marital relationship but was found to generalize to other areas of marital interaction. The three couples were video-taped in maritalinteractions pre- and post-training and the interactions rated by observers for behavioral deficits. Findings indicated that the husbands became more assertive. marital interactions improved in productivity and the wife's manner of relating to her husband changed as he became more assertive. Although the research gives support to the advantages of assertiveness training for family interaction, its outstanding weaknesses (e.g., no follow-up to test long-term effects, no self-reports of feelings about interactions, and small number of Ss) make it most valuable as an impetus for further research.

Gittelman, M. Behavior rehearsal as a technique in child treatment. *Journal of Child Psychology and Psychiatry*, 1965, *6*, 251-255.

This treatment procedure involved first finding out the situations which have caused the child to be aggressive in the past. The child acts out situations with other group members. This approach is scored by other members with a system that gives more value to assertive rather than aggressive behavior. Gittelman describes one group of seven boys ages 12-14 which met once a week for two hours. One specific aggressive behavior was successfully modified in 12 group sessions.

Mummery, D.V. Family backgrounds of assertive and non-assertive children. *Child Development*, 1954, *25*, 63-80.

In an early review of the literature looking for information regarding what might lend to assertive/nonassertive children, and what makes for socially acceptable or socially unacceptable assertiveness, this author found that democratic homes which give guidance and control, nurturance, consideration for others and channel behavior into socially acceptable forms are most related to socially acceptable assertiveness. Children who are reared in a freedom-giving, exploration accepting, participatory, non-sheltering home appear to be most assertive. The author states that other factors which should be explored are parental attitudes regarding the acceptability of children's ascendant methods, parental modeling, quality of guidance a child receives regarding his peer relationships, and the child's first-hand experiences in participating in democratic attitudes and practices in daily home living. Overall, the conclusion seems to be that a sense of security and adequacy underlies both the capacity for assertiveness and the ability to determine methods of assertiveness which show concern for others. This review is important because it is one of the few which look at antecedent conditions for assertiveness rather than methods for reversing nonassertion. It would be important to do some current studies and reviews in this same manner.

Johnson, T., Tyler, V., Thompson, R. and Jones. Systematic desensitization and assertive training in the treatment of speech anxiety in middle-school students. *Psychology in the Schools,* 1971, *8* (3), 263-267.

Compared systematic desensitization with a type of assertive training (speech practice) for speech-anxious eighth graders. Groups met twice per week for a total of nine sessions. The group speech practice required members to give short talks before the group. These talks were audio-taped and immediately played back, after which the subject re-presented the talk. Some coaxing to speak plus information given about speech and anxiety was utilized. Interestingly enough, no difference between the two groups was noted on a post-measure of speech anxiety which showed that both groups improved.

References

Alberti, R.E. Was that *assertive* or *aggressive*? *ASSERT: The Newsletter of Assertive Behavior*, 1976, *1* (7), 2.

Alberti, R.E. and Emmons, M.L. Assertion training in marital counseling, *Journal of Marriage and Family Counseling*, January 1976, 49-54. Also in R.E. Alberti (Ed.), *Assertiveness: Innovations, Applications, Issues.* San Luis Obispo, California: Impact Publishers, Inc., 1977.

Alberti, R.E. & Emmons, M.L. *Your Perfect Right: A Guide to Assertive Behavior.* San Luis Obispo, California: Impact Publishers, Inc., 1970 (1st edition), 1974 (2nd edition).

Alden, L. & Cappe, R. "Non-assertiveness: Skill Deficit or Selective Self-Evaluation?" *Behavior Therapy*, 1981, *12* (2), 107-114.

Alden, Lynn & Safran, Jeremy. Irrational beliefs and nonassertive behavior. *Cognitive Therapy & Research*, 1978 (Dec), Vol 2 (4), 357-364.

Allen, E.J., Jr. Repression-sensitization and the effect of assertion on anxiety. Senior Research Paper. St. Meinrad College, St. Meinrad, Indiana, May, 1976.

Arrick, M. Carole; Voss, Jacqueline & Rimm, David C. The relative efficacy of thought-stopping and covert assertion. *Behaviour Research & Therapy*, 1981, Vol 29 (1), 17-24.

Augsberger, D. *Anger and Assertiveness in Pastoral Care.* Philadelphia: Fortress Press. 1979.

Averill, J. Studies on anger and aggression. Paper presented at the American Psychological Association Convention, Los Angeles, 1981.

Bandura, A. *Aggression: A Social Learning Analysis.* Englewood Cliffs: Prentice-Hall, 1973.

Bandura, A. *Psychological Modeling: Conflicting Theories.* Chicago: Aldine-Atherton, 1971.

Bandura, A. *Principles of Behavior Modification.* New York: Holt, Rinehart, Winston, 1969.

Bandura, A. Psychotherapy based upon modeling principles. In A.E. Bergin & S.L. Garfield (Eds.), *Handbook of Psychotherapy and Behavior Change.* New Wiley & Sons, 1971.

Bach, G. and Wyden, P. *The Intimate Enemy: How to Right Fair in Love and Marriage.* New York, William Morrow and Company, Inc., 1968.

Baer, J. *How to Be an Assertive* (not Aggressive) *Woman in Life, in Love, and on the Job.* New York: Signet (New American Library), 1976.

Bates, H.D. and Zimmerman, S.F.Toward the development of a screening scale for assertive training. *Psychological Reports, 1971, 28,99-107.*

Bates, P. The effectiveness of interpersonal skills training on the social skill acquisition of moderately and mildly retarded adults. *Journal of applied behavior Analysis, 1980,13,* 237-248.

Berah, E.F. Influence of scheduling variations on the effectiveness of a group assertion training program for women. *Journal of Counseling Psychology*, 1981 (May), *28*(3), 265-268.

Berkowitz, L. The concept of aggressive drive:some additional considerations. In L. Berkowitz (Ed.), *Advances in Experimental Social Psychology*, Vol.2. New York: Academic Press, 1965.

Berkowitz, L. *Roots of Aggression: A Re-Examination of the Frustration-Aggres sion Hypothesis.* New York:Atherton Press, 1969.

Berkowitz, L. What ever happened to the frustration-aggression hypothesis? *American Behavioral Scientist,* 1978, *21,* 691-708.

Bernard, J.M.Assertiveness in children. *Psychological Reports,*1980,*46,*935-938.

Biaggio, M.K. Assessment of anger arousal. *Journal of Personality Assessment,* 1980, *44,* 289-298.

Blanchard, E.B. & Ahles, T.A. Behavioral treatment of psychophysical disorders. *Behavior Modification,* 1979 (Oct), *3,* 518-549.

Bloom, L.Z., Coburn, K. and Pearlman, J.*The New Assertive Woman.* New York: Delacorte Press, 1975.

Bodner, G. The role of assessment in assertion training. *The Counseling Psychologist,* 1975,*5,* 90-96.

Bohart, A.C. Toward a cognitive theory of catharsis. *Psychotherapy:Theory, Research and Practice,* 1980, *17,* 192-201.

Bordewick, M.C. & Bornstein, P.H. Examination of multiple cognitive response dimensions among differentially assertive individuals. *Behavior Therapy,* 1980, *11,* 440-448.

Bornstein, M. et al. Social skills training for highly aggressive children:Treatment in an inpatient psychiatric setting. *Behavior Modification,* 1980,*4,* 173-186.

Boulette, T.R. Determining needs and appropriate counseling approaches for Mexican-American women:A comparison of therapeutic listening and behavioral rehearsal. Unpublished dissertation,University of California, Santa Barbara, 1972

Bower,S.A. & Bower,G.H.*Asserting Yourself.* Reading:MA:Addison-Wesley,1976

Bourque, P. & Ladouceur,R. Self-report and behavioral measures in the assessment of assertive behavior. *Journal of behavior Therapy and Experimental Psychiatry,* 1979 (Dec), *10,* 287-292.

Bowman, C. & Spadoni, A. Assertion therapy: the nurse and the psychiatric patient in an acute, short-term hospital setting. *Journal of Psychiatric Nursing,* 1981, *19* (6), 7-21.

Brown, S. Videotape feedback: Effect on assertive performance and subject's perceived competence and satisfaction. *Psychological Reports,* 1980, *47,* 455-461.

Bruch, M.A. A task analysis of assertive behavior revisted: Replication and extension. *Behavior Therapy,* 1981 (Mar), *12,* 217-230.

Buss, A. & Durkee. An inventory for assessing different kinds of hostility. *Journal of Consulting Psychology,* 1957, *21,* 343-348.

Cameron, D.E. The conversion of passivity into normal self-assertion. *American Journal of Psychiatry,* 1951, *108,* 98.

Carducci, D.J. Positive peer culture and assertiveness training: Complementary modalities for dealing with disturbed and disturbing adolescents in the classroom. *Behavioral Disorders,* 1980 (May), *5* (3), 156-162.

Cautela, J.R. Covert reinforcement. *Behavior Therapy,* 1970, *1,* 33-50.

Cautela, J.R. Covert sensitization. *Psychological Reports,* 1967, *20,* 459.

Cautela, J.R. & Wisocki, P.A. The use of the reinforcement survey schedule in behavior modification. In Rubin, R.D., Fensterheim, H., Lazarus, A.A. & Franks, C.M. (Eds.), *Advances in behavior therapy,* N.Y.: Academic Press, 1971.

Cheek, D.K. Assertive behavior and black lifestyles. In R.E. Alberti (Ed.), *Assertiveness: Innovations, Applications, Issues.* San Luis Obispo, California: Impact Publishers, Inc., 1977.

Cheek, D.K. *Assertive Black...Puzzled White.* San Luis Obispo, California: Impact Publishers, Inc., 1976.

Chittenden, G.E. An experimental study in measuring and modifying assertive behavior in young children. *Monographs of the Society for Research in Child Development,* 1942, *7* (1, Serial #31).

Christmann, F. & Sommer, G. Behavior therapy of fingernail biting: Assertive training and self-control. (Germ) *Praxis der Kinderpsychologie und Kinderpsychiatrie*, 1976 (May-Jun), *25* (4), 139-146.

Combs, M.L. & Lahey, B.B. A cognitive social skills training program: Evaluation with young children. *Behavior Modification*, 1981, *5* (1), 39-60.

Cooley, M. A model for assertive statements. *ASSERT: The Newsletter of Assertive Behavior*, 1976, *1* (6), 2.

Cooley, M.L. and Hollandsworth, J.G., Jr. A strategy for teaching verbal content of assertive responses. In R.E. Alberti (Ed.), *Assertiveness: Innovations, Applications, Issues.* San Luis Obispo, California: Impact Publishers, Inc., 1977.

Cooper, J. Reducing fears and increasing assertiveness: The role of dissonance reduction. *Journal of Experimental Social Psychology*, 1980 (May), *16* (3), 199-213.

Corsini, R.J. *Roleplaying in psychotherapy: A manual*, Chicago: Aldine, 1966.

Corsini, R.J., et al. *Roleplaying in business and industry*, New York: Free Press, 1961.

Cotler, S.B. and Cotler, S.M. Four myths of nonassertiveness in the work environment. In R.E. Alberti (Ed.), *Assertiveness: Innovations, Applications, Issues.* San Luis Obispo, California: Impact Publishers, Inc., 1977.

Cotler, S.B. and Guerra, J.J. *Assertion Training: A Humanistic-Behavioral Guide to Self-Dignity.* Champaign: Research Press, 1976.

Craighead, L. & Craighead, W.E. Implications of persuasive communication research for the modification of self-statements. *Cognitive Therapy and Research*, 1980, *4* (2), 117-134.

Crassini, B., Law, H.G. & Wilson, E. Sex differences in assertive behavior? *Australian Journal of Psychology*, 1979 (Apr), *31* (1), 15-19.

Cummins, D.E. On the use of unobtrusive measures of assertion. *ASSERT: The Newsletter of Assertive Behavior and Personal Development*, February, 1978, p. 1.

Curran, J.P., et al. Social skill and social anxiety: Self-report measurement in a psychiatric population. *Behavior Modification*, 1980, *4* (4), 493-512.

D'Amico, W. Case studies in assertive training with adolescents. In R.E. Alberti (Ed.), *Assertiveness: Innovations, Applications, Issues.* San Luis Obispo, California: Impact Publishers, Inc., 1977.

D'Amico, W. *Revised Rathus Assertiveness Scale for Children, Grades 3-8.* Marblehead, Mass.: Educational Counseling and Consulting Services, 1976.

Dalali, I.D. The effect of active-assertion and feeling clarification training on factor analyzed measures of assertion. Doctoral dissertation, University of California, Los Angeles, 1971. *Dissertation Abstracts International*, 1971, *32*, 1B-1291B, University Microfilms No. 71-21, 322.

Davis, M., Eshelman, E., McKay, M. *The Relaxation and Stress Reduction Workbook.* New Harbinger Publications, 1980.

Derksen, J.J. Theory, technique and practice of rational therapy in a critical perspective. (Dutch) *Tijdschrift voor Psychotherapie*, 1979 (Nov) *5* (6), 327-342.

Doherty, J. & Ryder, G. Locus of control, interpersonal trust, and assertive behavior among newlyweds. *Journal of Personality & Social Psychology*, 1979 (Dec), *37* (12), 2212-2220.

Doyle, A. & Biaggio, M.K. Expression of anger as a function of assertiveness and sex. *Journal of Clinical Psychology*, 1981 (Jan), *37* (1), 154-157.

Dunn, M, Lloyd, E. & Phelps, G.H. Sexual assertiveness in spinal cord injury. *Sexuality & Disability*, 1979 (Win), *2* (4), 293-300.

Dunn, M., Van Horn, E. & Hermann, H. Social skills and spinal cord injury: A comparison of three training procedures. *Behavior Therapy*, 1981 (Mar), *12* (2), 153-164.

Eisler, R.M., Miller, P.M., and Hersen, M. Components of assertive behavior. *Journal of Clinical Psychology*, 1973, *29*, 295-299.

Eisler, R.M., Hersen, M., and Agras, W.S. Videotape: a method for the controlled observation of nonverbal interpersonal behavior. *Behavior Therapy*, 1973, *4*, 420-425.

Eisler, R.M., Hersen, M., and Miller, P.M. Effects of modeling components of assertive behavior. *Journal of Behavior Therapy and Experimental Psychiatry*, 1973, *4*, 1-6.

Ekman, P. Differential communication of affect by head and body cues. *Journal of Personality and Social Psychology*, 1965, *2*, 726-735.

Elder, J.P., Edelstein, B.A. & Fremouw, W.J. Client by treatment interactions in response acquisition and cognitive restructuring approaches. *Cognitive Therapy & Research*, 1981 (Jun), *5* (2), 203-210.

Ellis, A. Rational Emotive Therapy and Cognitive Behavior Therapy: Similarities and differences. *Cognitive Therapy and Research*, 1980, *4* (4), 325-340.

Emmons, M.L. Assertion training within an holistic-eclectic framework. In. R.E. Alberti (Ed.), *Assertiveness: Innovations, Applications, Issues*. San Luis Obispo California: Impact Publishers, Inc., 1977.

Ellis, A. & Harper, R. *A New Guide to Rational Living*. Englewood Cliffs, New Jersey: Prentice-Hall; Hollywood: Wilshire Brooks/Cole, 1979.

Emmons, M.L. *The Inner Source: A Guide to Meditative Therapy*. San Luis Obispo, California: Impact Publishers, Inc., 1978.

Emmons, M. & Richardson, D. *The Assertive Christian*. Minneapolis: Winston Press, 1981.

Epstein, N. Social consequences of assertion, aggression, passive aggression, and submission: Situational and dispositional determinants. *Behavior Therapy*, 1980 (Nov), *11* (5).

Eriksen, L., Mossige, S. & Johansen, K.G. Behavior therapy methods with alcoholics: Assertiveness, self control and systematic desensitization/relaxation. (Norg) *Scandanavian Journal of Behaviour Therapy*, 1979, *8* (2), 69-82.

Faily, et al. *Leadership Development: Assertive Training for Nurses*. Chapel Hill, North Carolina: School of Nursing, 1977, 1979 (2nd Edition).

Fensterheim, H. Personal communication. January, 1977.

Fensterheim, H. Assertive methods and marital problems. In R. Rubin, H. Fensterheim, J. Henderson, and L. Ullmann (Eds.), *Advances in Behavior Therapy*. New York: Academic Press, 1972.

Fensterheim, H. "Behavior therapy: assertive training in groups" in C.J. Sayer & H.S. Kaplan (Eds.), *Progress in Group and Family Therapy*. New York: Brunner/Mazel, 1972.

Fensterheim, H. *Help Without Psychoanalysis*. New York: Stein and Day, 1971.

Fensterheim, H. and Baer, J. *Don't Say Yes When you Want To Say No*. New York: Dell, 1975.

Feshback, S. Dynamics of morality of violence and aggression: Some psychological considerations. *American Psychologist*, 1971, *26*, 281-291.

Firth, P.M. & Snyder, C.W. Three-mode factor analysis of self-reported difficulty in assertiveness. *Australian Journal of Psychology*, 1979 (Aug), *31* (2), 125-135.

Flowers, J. and Guerra, J. The use of client-coaching in assertion training with a large group. *Journal of Community Health*, 1974.

Fodor, I.G. and Wolfe, J.L. Assertiveness training for mothers and daughters. In R.E. Alberti (Ed.), *Assertiveness: Innovations, Applications, Issues*. San Luis Obispo, California: Impact Publishers, Inc., 1977.

Franzini, L.R. Review of *The Assertive Woman*. *Behavior Therapy*, 1976, 7, 418-419.

Freedman, J.L. & Fraser, S.C. Compliance without pressure: The foot-in-the-door technique. *Journal of Personality and Social Psychology*, 1966, *4*, 195-202.

Freud, S. *Civilization and Its Discontents.* London: The Hogarth Press, Ltd., 1962.

Friedman, P.H. The effects of modeling and role playing on assertive behavior. In R. Rubin, A. Lazarus, H. Fensterheim, and C. Franks (Eds.), *Advances in Behavior Therapy.* New York: Academic Press, 1971.

Friedman, P.H. The effects of modeling, role playing, and participation on behavior change. In B.A. Maher (Ed.), *Progress in Experimental Personality Research,* Vol. 6. New York: Academic Press, 1972.

Fromm, E. *The Art of Loving.* New York: Harper and Row, 1956.

Galassi, J.P. *Assertive Training in Groups Using Video Feedback.* Final progress report in National Institute of Mental Health Small Research Grant MH22392-01, 1973.

Galassi, J.P., DeLo, J.S., Galassi, M.D., and Bastien, S. The College self-expression scale: a measure of assertiveness. *Behavior Therapy,* 1974, *5,* 165-171.

Galassi, J.P. and Galassi, M.D. Assessment procedures for assertive behavior. In R.E. Alberti (Ed.), *Assertiveness: Innovations, Applications, Issues.* San Luis Obispo, California: Impact Publishers, Inc., 1977.

Galassi, J.P. and Galassi, M.D. Relationship between assertiveness and aggressiveness. *Psychological Reports,* 1975, *36,* 352-354.

Galassi, J.P. and Galassi, M.D. Validity of a measure of assertiveness. *Journal of Counseling Psychology,* 1974, *21,* 248-250.

Galassi, J.P., Galassi, M.D., and Litz, C.M. Assertive training in groups using video feedback. *Journal of Counseling Psychology,* 1974, *21,* 390-394.

Galassi, M.D. and Galassi, J.P. A critical review of assertive behavior: definition and assessment. *Psychotherapy: Theory, Research and Practice,* 1976, in press.

Galassi, M.D. and Galassi, J.P. *Assert Yourself! How to Be Your Own Person.* New York: Human Sciences Press, 1977.

Gambrill, E.D. and Richey, C.A. An assertion inventory for use in assessment and research. *Behavior Therapy,* 1975, *6,* 550-561.

Gambrill, E.D. and Richey, C.A. *It's up to You: The Development of Assertive Social Skills.* Millbrae, California: Les Femmes, 1976.

Garnett, L. Assertion training with juvenile delinquents. In R.E. Alberti (Ed.), *Assertiveness: Innovations, Applications, Issues.* San Luis Obispo, California: Impact Publishers, Inc., 1977.

Gay, M.L., Hollandsworth, J.G. Jr., and Galassi, J.P. An assertiveness inventory for adults. *Journal of Counseling Psychology,* 1975, *22,* 340-344.

Getter, H. & Nowinski, J.K. A free response test of interpersonal effectiveness. *Journal of Personality Assessment,* 1981 (Jun), *45* (3), 301-308.

Gilmour, D.R., McCormick, I.A. & de Ruiter, C.A. Group assertion training for adult male offenders: Internal validity. *Behavior Therapy,* 1981 (Mar), *12* (2), 274-279.

Gittelman, M. Behavior rehearsal as a technique in child treatment. *Journal of Child Psychology and Psychiatry,* 1965, *6,* 251.

Goddard, R.C. Increase in assertiveness and actualization as a function of didactic training. *Journal of Counseling Psychology,* 1981 (Jul), *28* (4), 279-287.

Golden, M. A measure of cognition within the context of assertion. *Journal of Clinical Psychology,* 1981 (Apr), *37* (2), 253-262.

Goldstein, A.J., Serber, M., & Piaget, G. Induced anger as a reciprocal inhibitor of fear. *Journal of Behavior Therapy & Experimental Psychiatry.* 1970, 67-70.

Goldstein, A.P. The use of modeling to increase independent behavior. *Behavior Research and Therapy,* 1973, *11,* 31-42.

Goodman, J. (Ed.). *Turning Points.* Saratoga Springs, New York: Creative Resources. Press, 1979.

Gordon, T. *Parent Effectiveness Training.* New York: Wyden, 1970.

Gorecki, P.R., Dickson, A.L., Anderson, H.N. & Jones, G.E. Relationship between contrived *in vivo* and role-play assertive behavior. *Journal of Clinical Psychology*, 1981 (Jan), *37* (1), 104-107.

Greenwald, D.P., et al. Differences between social skills therapists and psycho-therapists in treating depression. *Journal of Consulting and Clinical Psychology*, 1981, *49* (5), 757-759.

Gresham, F.M. & Nagle, R.J. Social skills training with children: Responsiveness to modeling and coaching as a function of peer orientation. *Journal of Consulting and Clinical Psychology*, 1980, *48* (6), 718-729.

Grodner, B.S. Assertiveness and anxiety: a cross-cultural and socio-economic perspective. In R.E. Alberti (Ed.), *Assertiveness: Innovations, Applications, Issues.* San Luis Obispo, California: Impact Publishers, Inc., 1977.

Grunebaum, H. Middle age and marriage: Affiliative men and assertive women. *American Journal of Family Therapy*, 1979 (Fal), *7* (3), 46-50.

Guerra, J.J. and Taylor, P.A. The four assertive myths: a fable. In R.E. Alberti (Ed.), *Assertiveness: Innovations, Applications, Issues.* San Luis Obispo, California:Impact Publishers, Inc., 1977.

Gulanick, N.A. & Howard, G.S. Evaluation of a group program designed to increase androgyny in feminine women. *Sex Roles*, 1979 (Dec), *5* (6), 811-827.

Hammen, C.L., Jacobs, M., Mayol, A. & Cochran, S.D. Dysfunctional cognitions and the effectiveness of skills and cognitive behavioral assertion training. *Journal of Consulting & Clinical Psychology*, 1980 (Dec), *48* (6), 685-695.

Haney, M. & Boenisch, E. *Stress Relief.* San Luis Obispo, California: Impact Publishers, Inc., 1982.

Hardy, A.B. Assertive training in the treatment of phobias. In R.E. Alberti (Ed.), *Assertiveness: Innovations, Applications, Issues.* San Luis Obispo, California: Impact Publishers, Inc., 1977.

Harrell, T., et al. Didactic persuasion techniques in cognitive restructuring. *American Journal of Psychotherapy*, 1981, *35* (1), 87-92.

Hart, E.W. Levels of assertiveness. *Transactional Analysis Journal*, 1977 (Apr), *7* (2), 173-165.

Hastings, A., Fadiman, J., Gordon, J. *Health for the Whole Person.* Boulder, Colorado: Westview Press, 1980.

Hautzinger, M. Assertive training procedure in the treatment of obesity. *Behavior Therapist*, 1979 (Jan-Feb), *2* (1), 23-24.

Heimberg, R.G. & Harrison, D.F. Use of the Rathus assertiveness schedule with offenders: A question of questions. *Behavior Therapy*, 1980, *11* (2), 278-281.

Heller, K. Effects of modeling procedures in helping relationships. *Journal of Consulting and Clinical Psychology*, 1969, *33*, 522-526.

Henderson, J.M. The effects of assertiveness training on self-actualization in women. Unpublished doctoral dissertation, University of Northern Colorado, 1976.

Herman, S.J. Assertiveness: One answer to job dissatisfaction for nurses. In R.E. Alberti (Ed.), *Assertiveness: Innovations, Applications, Issues.* San Luis Obispo, California: Impact Publishers, Inc., 1977.

Hersen, M., Eisler, R.M., and Miller, P.M. An experimental analysis of generali-zation in assertive training. *Behavior Research and Therapy*, 1974, *12*, 295-310.

Hersen, M., Eisler, R.M., and Miller, P.M. Development of assertive responses: clinical, measurement and research considerations. *Behavior Research and Therapy*, 1973, *2*, 505-521.

Hersen, M., et al. Effects of practice, instructions, and modeling on components of assertive behavior. *Behaviour Research and Therapy*, 1973, *11*, 443-451.

Hersen, M., Bellack, A.S. & Himmelhoch, J.M. Treatment of unipolar depression with social skills training. *Behavior Modification*, 1980 (Oct), *4* (4), 547-556.

Hess, E., et al. Situational determinants in the perception of assertiveness: Gender-related influences. *Behavior Therapy*, 1980, *11* (1), 49-58.

Hestand, R., et al. The Willoughby schedule: A replication. *Journal of Behavior Therapy and Experimental Psychiatry*, 1971, *2*, 111-112.

Hewes, D.D. On effective assertive behavior: a brief note. *Behavior Therapy*, 1975, *6*, 269-271.

Hirsch, S.M. Assertiveness training with alcoholics. In R.E. Alberti (Ed.), *Assertiveness,: Innovations, Applications, Issues.* San Luis Obispo, California: Impact Publishers, Inc., 1977.

Hobbs, N. The role of insight in behavior change: A commentary. *American Journal of Orthopsychiatry*, 1981 (Oct), 632-635.

Hoffman, R.A., et al. Facilitating generalization in assertiveness training. *Psychological Reports*, 1979, *45*, 27-30.

Hokanson, J.E. Psychophysiological evaluation of the catharsis hypothesis. In E.I. Megargee and J.E. Hokanson (Eds.), *the Dynamics of Aggression.* New York: Harper and Row, 1970.

Hollandsworth, J.G., Jr., Galassi, J.P., and Gay, M.L. The adult self-expression scale: Validation using the multitrait-multimethod procedure. *Journal of Clinical Psychology*, 1976, in press.

Houts, P. and Serber, M. *After The Turn-On, What?* Champaign, Illinois: Research Press, 1972.

Howard, G.S., et al. Is a behavioral measure the best estimate of behavioral parameters? Perhaps not. *Applied Psychological Measurement*, 1980 (Sum), *4* (3), 293-311.

Hung, J., et al. Social comparison standards spur immediate assertion: So you think you're submissive? *Cognitive Therapy and Research*, 1980, *4* (2), 223-234.

Hwang, P.O. Assertion training for Asian-Americans. In R.E. Alberti (Ed.), *Assertiveness: Innovations, Applications, issues.* San Luis Obispo, California: Impact Publishers, Inc., 1977.

Ivey, A.E., Normington, C.J., Miller, D., and Morrill, W.H. Microcounseling and attending behavior, *Journal of Counseling Psychology*, 1968, *15* (5), 1-12.

Kaufmann, H. Definitions and methodology in the study of aggression. *Psychological Bulletin*, 1965, *64*, 351-361.

Kaufmann, L.M. and Wagner, B.R. Barb: a systematic treatment technology for temper control disorders. *Behavior Therapy*, 1972, *3*, 84.

Kazdin, A.E. Covert and overt rehearsal and elaboration during treatment in the development of assertive behavior. *Behaviour Research & Therapy*, 1980, *18* (3), 191-201.

Kelly, J.A., et al. Reaction to assertive versus unassertive behavior: differential effects for males and females and implications for assertiveness training. *Behavior Therapy*, 1980, *11* (5), 670-682.

Kern, M. & MacDonald, M.L. Assessing assertion: An investigation of construct validity and reliability. *Journal of Consulting and Clinical Psychology*, 1980 (Aug), *48* (4), 532-534.

Kienhorst, I., Van Ijzendoorn-Schmitz, R.M. & Diekstra, R. Assertiveness training: A survedy study. (Duth) *Tijdschrift voor Psychotherapie*, 1980 (May), *6* (3), 159-171.

Kolotkin, R.A. Situation specificity in the assessment of assertion: Considerations for the measurement of training and transfer. *Behavior Therapy*, 1980 (Nov), *11* (5), 651-661.

L'Abate, L. Toward a theory and technology for social skills training: Suggestions for curriculum development. *Academic Psychology Bulletin*, 1980 (Jun), *2* (2), 207-228.

196   YOUR PERFECT RIGHT

La Greca, A.M. & Santogrossi, D.A. Social skills training with elementary school students: A behavioral group approach. *Journal of Consulting and Clinical Psychology*, 1980, *48* (2), 220-227.

Landau, P. and Paulson, T. COPE: A wilderness workshop in AT. In R.E. Alberti (Ed.), *Assertiveness: Innovations, Applications, Issues*. San Luis Obispo, California: Impact Publishers, Inc., 1977.

Landau, P. and Paulson, T. Group assertion training for Spanish speaking Mexican-American mothers. In R.E. Alberti (Ed.), *Assertiveness: Innovations, Applications, Issues*. San Luis Obispo, California: Impact Publishers, Inc., 1977.

Lange, A.J. and Jakubowski, P. *Responsible Assertive Behavior: Cognitive/Behavioral Procedures for Trainers*. Champaign: Research Press, 1976.

Lang, A.J. and Jakubowski, P. *The Assertive Option*. Champaign: Research Press, 1978.

LaPointe, K.A. & Rimm, D.C. Cognitive, assertive, and insight-oriented group therapies in the treatment of reactive depression in women. *Psychotherapy: Theory, Research & Practice*, 1980 (Fall), *17* (3), 312-321.

Lawrence, P.S. The assessment and modification of assertive behavior. Doctoral dissertation, Arizona State University, 1970. *Dissertation Abstracts International*, 31, 1B-1601B &University Microfilms No. 70-11, 888).

Laws, D.R. and Serber, M. Measurement and evaluation of assertive training. Paper presented at the meeting of the Association for Advancement of Behavior Therapy, Washington, D.C., September, 1971.

Laws, D.R. and Serber, M. Measurement and evaluation of assertive training with sexual offenders. In R.E. Hosford and S. Moss (Eds.), *The Crumbling Wall: Treatment and Counseling of the Youthful Offender*, 1972.

Lawson, J.D., Griffin, L.G., and Donant, F.D. *Leadership is Everybody's Business*. San Luis Obispo, California: Impact Publishers, Inc., 1976.

Lazarus, A.A. Behavior rehearsal vs. non-directive therapy vs. advice in effecting behavior change. *Behavior Research and Therapy*, 1966, *4*, 209-212.

Lazarus, A.A. *Behavior Therapy and Beyond*. New York: McGraw-Hill, 1971.

Lazarus, A.A. Behavior therapy in groups. In G.M. Gazda (Ed.), *Basic Approaches to Group Psychotherapy and Group Counseling*. Springfield, Illinois: Charles C. Thomas, 1968.

Lazarus, A.A. Behavior therapy, incomplete treatment, and symptom substitution. *The Journal of Nervous and Mental Disease*, 1965, *140*, 180.

Lazarus, A.A. Broad-spectrum behavior therapy and the treatment of agoraphobia. *Behavior Research and Therapy*, 1966, *4*, 95.

Lazarus, A.A. (Ed.), *Clinical Behavior Therapy*. New York: Brunner/Mazel, 1972.

Lazarus, A.A., and Fay A. *I Can If I Want To*. New York: William Morrow and Company, Inc., 1975.

Lehman-Olson, D. Assertiveness training: theoretical and clinical implications. In D. Olson (Ed.), *Treating Relationships*. Lake Mills, Iowa: Graphics Publishing Co., 1976.

Lewinsohn, P.M., Weinstein, M.S. & Shaw, D.S. Depression: A clinical-research approach. In R.D. Rubin & C.M. Franks (Eds.), *Advances in behavior therapy*. New York: Academic Press, 1969.

Liberman, R. Behavioral approaches to family and couple therapy. *American Journal of Orthopsychiatry*. 1970, *40*, 106-118.

Liberman, R.P., King, L.W., DeRisi, W.J., and McCann, M. *Personal Effectiveness*. Champaign, Illinois: Research Press, 1976.

Liberman, R.P. & Eckman, T. Behavior Therapy vs. insight-oriented therapy for repeated suicide attempts. *Archives of General Psychiatry*, 1981,*38*(10) 1126-1130.

Lomont, J.F., Gilner, F.H., Spector, N.J., & Skinner, K.K. Group assertive training and group insight therapies. *Psychological Reports*, 1969, *25*, 463-470.

Loo, R.M.Y. The effects of projected consequences and overt behavior rehearsal on assertive behavior. Unpublished doctoral thesis. University of Illinois, Urbana, 1971.

Lorenz, K. *On Aggression.* New York: Harcourt, Brace and World, 1966.

Lorr, M., More, W.W. & Mansueto, S. The structure of assertiveness: A confirmatory study. *Behaviour Research & Therapy,* 1981, *19* (2), 153-156.

Maass, M. Situational role playing: a technique for learning to be more loving. *Marriage and Family Counselors Quarterly,* 1972, *7,* 34-39.

MacDonald, M.L. A behavioral assessment methodology applied to the measurement of assertion. Doctoral dissertation, University of Illinois, Urbana, 1974.

MacNeilage, L.A. and Adams, K.A. The method of contrasted role-plays: An insight-oriented model for role playing in assertiveness training groups. Paper presented at the American Psychological Association, 1977.

Markel, G. & Greenbaum, J. *Parents Are To Be Seen and Heard.* San Luis Obispo, California: Impact Publishers, Inc., 1979.

Marshall, P.G., et al. Anxiety reduction, assertive training, and enactment of consequences. *Behavior Modification,* 1981, *5* (1), 85-102.

Martin, O.V. Social skill development in delinquent adolescent patients. *Corrective & Social Psychiatry & Journal of Behavior Technology, Methods & Therapy,* 1980, *26* (1), 35-36.

Marzillier, J. Cognitive Therapy and Behavioural Practice. *Behaviour Research & Therapy,* 1980, *18,* 249-258.

Matson, J. and Senatore, V. A comparison of traditional psychotherapy and social skills training for improving interpersonal functioning of mentally retarded adults. *Behavior Therapy,* 1981, *12* (3), 369-382.

Mauger, P., et al. *Interpersonal Behavior Survey.* Los Angeles: Western Psychological Service, 1980.

Maultsby, M.C. Systematic, written homework in psychotherapy. *Psychotherapy: Theory, Research and Practice,* 1971, *8,* 195-198.

McAllister, E.W. Assertive training and the Christian therapist. *Journal of Psychology and Theology,* Winter, 1975, p. 19-24.

McFall, R.M. Assertion training. In B.B. Wolman (Ed.), *International Encyclopedia of Neurology, Psychiatry, Psychoanalysis, and Psychology.* In press, 1977.

McFall, R.M. and Lillesand, D.B. Behavior rehearsal with modeling and coaching in assertive training. *Journal of Abnormal Psychology,* 1971, *77* (3), 313-323.

McFall, R.M. and Marson, A.R. An experimental investigation of behavior rehearsal in assertiveness training. *Journal of Abnormal Psychology,* 1970, *76,* 295-303.

McFall, R.M. and Twentyman, C.T. Four experiments on the relative contributions of rehearsal, modeling, and coaching to assertion training. *Journal of Abnormal Psychology,* 1973, *81,* 199-218.

McMillan, M. Assertiveness as an aid to weight control. In R.E. Alberti (Ed.), *Assertiveness: Innovations, Applications, Issues.* San Luis Obispo, California: Impact Publishers, Inc., 1977.

McPhail, G.W. Developing adolescent assertiveness. In R.E. Alberti (Ed.), *Assertiveness: Innovations, Applications, Issues.* San Luis Obispo, California: Impact Publishers, Inc., 1977.

Meichenbaum, D. *Cognitive Behavior Modification.* New York: Plenum, 1977.

Meichenbaum, D. and Cameron, R. Stress-inoculation training: a skills approach to anxiety measurement. Unpublished manuscript, University of Waterloo, 1973.

Meichenbaum, D. and Turk, D. Stress-inoculation training. In P.O. Davidson (Ed.), *The Behavioral Management of Anxiety, Depression, and Pain.* New York: Brunner/Mazel, 1976.

Meredith, R.L., Sason, S., Doleys, D.M. & Syzer, B. Social skills training with mildly retarded young adults. *Journal of Clinical Psychology*, 1980 (Oct.), *36* (4), 1000-1009.

Michelson, L. & Wood, R. A group assertive training program for elementary schoolchildren. *Child Behavior Therpy*, 1980 (Spr), *2* (1), 1-9.

Miller, P.M., Hersen, M., Eisler, R.M., and Hilsman, G. Effects of social stress on operant drinking of alcoholics and social drinkers. *Behavior Research and Therapy*, 1974, *12*, 67-72.

Mischel, W. *Personality and Assessment*. New York: Wiley, 1968.

Moore, D. *Assertive Behavior Training: An Annotated Bibliography*. San Luis Obispo, California: Impact Publishers, Inc., 1977.

Monti, P.M., et al. Effects of social skills training groups and sensitivity training groups with psychiatric patients. *Journal of Consulting and Clinical Psychology*, 1980, *48* (2), 241-248.

Moreno, J.L. *Psychodrama: Vol. I*. New York: Beacon House, 1971.

Morrow, W.R. *Behavior Therapy Bibliography: 1950-1969*. Columbia: University of Missouri Press, 1971.

Mowrer, O.H. The behavior therapies with special reference to modeling and imitation. *American Journal of Psychotherapy*, 1966, *20*, 439-461.

Nachman, G. Squeak up! *Newsweek*, April 5, 1977, p. 13. Also in R.E. Alberti (Ed.), *Assertiveness: Innovations, Applications, Issues*. San Luis Obispo, California: Impact Publishers, Inc., 1977.

Neuman, D. Using assertive training. In J. Krumboltz and C. Thoreson (Eds.), *Behavioral Counseling: Cases and Techniques*. New York: Holt, Rinehart and Winston, 1969.

Norton-Ford, J.D. & Hogan, D.R. Role of nonverbal behaviors in social judgments of peers' assertiveness. *Psychological Reports*, 1980 (Jun), *46* (3, Pt 2), 1085-1086.

O'Connor, R.D. Modification of social withdrawal through symbolic modeling. *Journal of Applied Behavior Analysis*, 1969, *2*, 15-22.

Osborn, S.M. and Harris, G.G. *Assertive Training for Women*. Springfield, Illinois: Charles C. Thomas, 1975.

Otto, H. *More Joy in Your Marriage*. New York: Hawthorn Books, Inc., 1969.

Palmer, P. *Liking Myself*. San Luis Obispo, California: Impact Publishers, Inc., 1977.

Palmer, P. *The Mouse, the Monster, and Me: Assertiveness for Young People*. San Luis Obispo, California: Impact Publishers, Inc., 1977.

Patterson, G.R. *Families: Applications of social learning to family life*. Champaign, Ill.: Research Press, 1971.

Patterson, R. Time-out and assertive training for a dependent child. *Behavior Therapy*, 1972, *3*, 466-468.

Paulson, T.L. and Landau, P. Divorce recovery: Assertion training for the divorced. In R.E. Alberti (Ed.), *Assertiveness: Innovations, Applications, Issues*. San Luis Obispo, California: Impact Publishers, Inc., 1977.

Pearson, J.C. A factor analytic study of the items in the Rathus assertiveness schedule and the personal report of communication apprehension. *Psychological Reports*, 1979 (Oct), *45* (2), 491-497.

Pelletier, K. *Holistic Medicine*. New York: Delacorte Press/Seymour Lawrence, 1979.

Peniston, E. & Burman, W. Relaxation and assertive training as treatment for a psychosomatic American Indian patient. *White Cloud Journal*, 1978 (Spr), *1* (1), 7-10.

Percell, L.P. Assertive behavior training and the enhancement of self-esteem. In R.E. Alberti (Ed.), *Assertiveness: Innovations, Applications, Issues*. San Luis Obispo, California: Impact Publishers, Inc., 1977.

Percell, L.P., Berwick, P.T., and Beigel, A. The effects of assertive training on self-concept and anxiety. *Archives of General Psychiatry*, 1974, 502-504.

Perls, F.S. *Gestalt Therapy Verbatim*. Lafayette, California: Real People Press, 1969.

Perls, F., Hefferline, R.F., and Goodman, P. *Gestalt Therapy*. New York: Dell, 1951.

Phelps, S. and Austin, N. The assertive woman: developing an assertive attitude. In R.E. Alberti (Ed.), *Assertiveness: Innovations, Applications, Issues*. San Luis Obispo, California: Impact Publishers, Inc., 1977.

Phelps, S. and Austin, N. *The Assertive Woman*. San Luis Obispo, California: Impact Publishers, Inc., 1975.

Piaget, G.W. and Lazarus, A.A. The use of rehearsal-desensitization. *Psychotherapy: Theory, Research and Practice*, 1969, *6*, 264.

Piercy, F.P. Birth of a person: One woman's reflections on survival and growth. *Personnel & Guidance Journal*, 1980 (Oct), *59* (2), 74-78.

Pitcher, S.W. & Meikle, S. The topography of assertive behavior in positive and negative situations. *Behavior Therapy*, 1980, *11* (4), 532-547.

Rahaim, S., Lefebvre, C. & Jenkins, J.O. The effects of social skills training on behavioral and cognitive components of anger management. *Journal of Behavior Therapy & Experimental Psychiatry*, 1980 (Mar), *11* (1), 3-8.

Rathus, S.A. A 30-item schedule for assessing assertive behavior. *Behavior Therapy*, 1973, *4*, 398-406.

Rathus, S.A. An experimental investigation of assertive training in a group setting. *Journal of Behavior Therapy and Experimental Psychiatry*, 1972, *3*, 81-86.

Rathus, S.A. and Nevid, J.S. *BT: Behavior Therapy*. New York: Doubleday, 1978.

Rathus, S.A. Principles and practices of assertive training: an eclectic overview. *Counseling Psychologist*, 1975, *5* (4), 9-20.

Rehm, L.P. & Marson, A.R. Reduction of social anxiety through modification or self-reinforcement. *Journal of Consulting and Clinical Psychology*, 1968, *32*, 565-574.

Replogle, W., et al. Locus of control and assertive behavior. *Psychological Reports*, 1980, *47*, 769-770.

Rich, A.R. and Schroeder, H.E. Research issues in assertiveness training. *Psychological Bulletin*, 1976, *83*, 6, 1081-1096.

Rickel, A.U., Dudley, G. & Berman, S. An evaluation of parent training. Evaluation Review, 1980 (Jun), *4* (3), 389-403.

Rimm, D.C. Assertive training and the expression of anger. In R.E. Alberti (Ed.), *Assertiveness: Innovations, Applications, Issues*. San Luis Obispo, California: Impact Publishers, Inc., 1977.

Rimm, D.C., Hill, G.A., Brown, N.N., and Stuart, J.E. Group assertive training in the treatment of inappropriate anger expression. *Psychological Reports*, 1974, *34*, 791-798.

Rimm, D.C. and Masters, J.C. *Behavior Therapy: Techniques and Empirical Findings*. New York: Academic Press, 1974.

Rimm, D.C., Snyder, J.J., Depue, R.A., Haanstad, M.J., and Armstrong, D.P. Assertive training versus rehearsal, and the importance of making an assertive response. *Behavior Research and Therapy*, 1976.

Ringer, R. *Winning Through Intimidation*. New York: Funk & Wagnalls, 1976.

Rock, D.L. The confounding of two self-report assertion measures with the tendency to give socially desirable responses in self-description. *Journal of Consulting and Clinical Psychology*, 1981, *49* (5), 743-744.

Rodriguez, R., et al. Sex role orientation and assertiveness among female college students. *Behavior Therapy*, 1980, *11* (3), 353-367.

Rogers, C.R. *On Becoming a Person*. Boston: Houghton-Mifflin, 1961.

Rose, Y.J. & Tryon, W.W. Judgments of assertive behavior as a function of speech loudness, latency, content, gestures, inflection, and sex. *Behavior Modification*, 1979 (Jan), *3* (1), 112-123.

Rosenblum, L. Telephone therapy. *Psychotherapy: Theory, Research nd Practice*, 1969, *6*, 241-242.

Rotter, J.B. Generalized expectancies for internal versus external control of reinforcement. *Psychological Monographs*, 1966, *80*, 1-28.

Safran, J.D., Alden, L.E. & Davidson, P.O. Client anxiety level as a moderator variable in assertion training. *Cognitive Therapy & Research*, 1980 (Jun), *4* (2), 189-200.

Salter, A. *Conditioned Reflex Therapy*. New York: Farrar, Straus, and Girous, 1949 (Capricorn Books edition, 1961).

Salter, A. On assertion. In R.E. Alberti (Ed.), *Assertiveness: Innovations, Applications, Issues*. San Luis Obispo, Californi: Impact Publishers, Inc., 1977.

Sanchez, V. and Lewinsohn, P.M. Assertive behavior and depression. *Journal of Consulting and Clinical Psychology*, 1980 *48* (1), 119-120.

Sanders, J.L., Thomas, M.A., Suydam, M. & Petri, H. Use of an auditory technique in personal space measurement. *Journal of Social Psychology*, 1980 (Oct), *112* (1), 99-102.

Sanders, R. The effectiveness of a theologically oriented approach to assertive training for refusal behaviors. Masters Thesis. S.F. Austin State University, 1976. *Masters abstracts*, 1976, *14*, 252. (University Microfilm No. 13-08786).

Sarason, I.G., and Ganzer, V.J. Modeling and group discussion in the rehabilitation of juvenile delinquents. *Journal of Counseling Psychology*, 1973, *20*, 442.

Seligman, M.E. Fall into helplessness. *Psychology Today*, 1973, June, 43.

Seligman, M.E. For helplessness: Can we immunize the weak? *Psychology Today*, 1969, June, 42.

Serber, M. Book review of *Your Perfect Right*. *Behavior Therapy*, 1971, *2*, 253-254.

Serber, M. Teaching the non-verbal components of assertive training. *Journal of Behavior Therapy and experimental Psychiatry*, 1971, *3*, 1-5. Also in R.E. Alberti (Ed.), *Assertiveness: Innovations, Applications, Issues*. San Luis Obispo, California: Impact Publishers, Inc., 1977.

Sgan, M.L. & Pickert, S.M. Cross-sex and same-sex assertive bids in a cooperative group task. *Child Development*, 1980 (Sep), *51* (3), 928-931.

Shaffer, C.S., Shapiro, J., Sank, L.I. & Coghlan, J. Positive changes in depression, anxiety, and assertion following individual and group cognitive behavior therapy intervention. *Cognitive Therapy & Research*, 1981 (Jun), 5 (2).

Shaw, M. *Assertive-Responsive Management*. Reading, Mass.: Addison-Wesley, 1979.

Sheehy, G. *Passages: Predictable Crises of Adult Life*. New York: E.P. Dutton and Company, 1976.

Shelton, J.L. Homework inAT: promoting the transfer of assertive skills to the natural environment. In R.E. Alberti (Ed.), *Assertiveness: Innovations, Applications, Issues*. San Luis Obispo, California: Impact Publishers, Inc., 1977.

Shelton, J. and Ackerman, M. *Homework in Counseling and Psychotherapy: Examples of Systematic Assignments for Therapeutic Use by Mental Health Professionals*. Springfield, Illinois: Charles C. Thomas, 1974.

Shoemaker, M.E. Developing assertiveness: training or therapy? In R.E. Alberti (Ed.), *Assertiveness: Innovations, Applications, Issues*. San Luis Obispo, California: Impact Publishers, Inc., 1977.

Shoemaker, M.E. and Paulson, T.L. Group assertion training for mothers: a family intervention strategy. In E.J. Mash, L.C. Handy, and L.A. Hamerlynck (Eds.), *Behavior Modification Approaches to Parenting*. New York: Brunner/Mazel, Inc., 1976.

Shilling, C.S. The relationship between the assertive behavior of parents and the behavior of their children. *American Journal of Family Therapy*, 1979 (Fal) 7 (3), 59-64.

Simon, S.B. *Values Clarification*. New York: Hart Publishing Co., 1972.

Smaby, M.H.and Tamminen, A.W. Counselors can be assertive. *Personnel and Guidance Journal*, 1976, *54*, 420-424.

Smith, M. *When I Say No, I Feel Guilty.* New York: Dial Press, 1975.

Tanabe-Endsley, P. *Project Write.* El Cerrito, California, 94530: 1421 Arlington, 1974, 1979 (2nd edition).

Taubman, B. *How To Become An Assertive Woman.* New York: Pocket Books (Simon and Schuster), 1976.

Taylor, J.A. A personality scale of manifest anxiety. *Journal of Abnormal and Social Psychology*, 1953, *48*, 285-290.

Thoft, J.S. Developing assertiveness in children. In R.E. Alberti (Ed.), *Assertiveness: Innovations, Applications, Issues.* San Luis Obispo, California: Impact Publishers, Inc., 1977.

Trower, P. Situational analysis of the components and processes of behavior of socially skilled and unskilled patients. *Journal of Consulting and Clinical Psychology*, 1980, *48* (3), 327-339.

Ulene, A. *Feeling Fine.* New York: St. Martin's Press, 1977.

Vaal, J.J. and McCullagh, J. The Rathus assertiveness schedule: reliability at the junior high school level. *Behavior Therapy*, 1975, *6*, 566-567.

Vagg, P. (Ed.). Assessment in assertiveness training. San Luis Obispo, California: Impact Publishers, Inc., *ASSERT Newsletter*, 1979.

Van Egeren, L.F., et al. Cardiovascular consequences of expressing anger in a mutually dependent relationship. *Journal of Psychosomatic Research*, 1978, *22*, 537-548.

Van Erven, Tom. Assertiveness: A review. (Duth) *Tijdschrift voor Psychotherapie* 1980 (Jan), *6* (1), 33-43.

Videback, L. Self-conception and the reaction of others. *Sociometry*, 1960, *23*, 351-359.

Wallander, J.L. & Albion, M.N. Modification of social interaction behaviors with primary focus on social skills and assertion training: A bibliography. *Catalog of Selected Documents in Psychology*, 1981 (Feb), *11*.

Walters, R.H. and Brown, M. Studies of reinforcement of aggression: III. Transfer of responses to an interpersonal situation. *Child Development*, 1963, *24*, 563-571.

Weinman, B., et al. Inducing assertive behavior in chronic schizophrenics. *Journal of Consulting and Clinicla Psychology*, 1972, *37* (2), 246-252.

Wells, W.P. Relaxatin-Rehearsal: A variant of systematic desensitization. *Psychotherapy: Theory, Research and Practice*, 1970, *7*, 224-225.

West, Against our will: Male interruptions of females in cross-sex conversation. *Annals of the New York Academy of Sciences*, 1979, *327*, 81-97.

Westefeld, J.S., Galassi, J., Galassi, M. Effects of role-playing instructions on assertive behavior: A methodological study. *Behavior Therapy*, 1980, *11* (2), 271-277.

Wheeler, K. Assertiveness and the job hunt. In R.E. Alberti (Ed.), *Assertiveness: Innovations, Applications, Issues.* San Luis Obispo, California: Impact Publishers, Inc., 1977.

White, R.W. The concept of healthy personality: What do we really mean? *The Counseling Psychologist*, 1973, *4*, 3.

Winship, B.J. and Kelley, J.D. A verbal response model of assertiveness. *Journal of Counseling Psychology*, 1976, *23*, 215-220.

Wolfe, J. and Fodor, I. A cognitive/behavior approach to modifying assertive behavior in women. *The Counseling Psychologist*, 1975, *5* (4), 45-52.

Wolfe, J. and Fodor, I. Modifying assertive behavior in women: a comparison of three approaches. *Behavior Therapy*, 1976.

Wolpe, J. *Psychotherapy by Reciprocal Inhibition.* Stanford: Stanford University Press, 1958.

Wolpe, J. *The Practice of Behavior Therapy.* New York: Pergamon Press, 1969, 1973.

Wolpe, J. The instigation of assertive behavior: Transcripts from two cases. *Journal of Behavior Therapy and Experimental Psychiatry,* 1970, *1* (2), 145-151.

Wolpe, J. & Lange, P. A fear survey schedule for use in behavior therapy. *Behavior Research and Therapy,* 1964, *2,* 27-30.

Wolpe, J. & Lang, P. *The Fear Survey Schedule.* San Diego, California: Knapp, 1969.

Wolpe, J. and Lazarus, A.A. *Behavior Therapy Techniques.* New York: Pergamon Press, 1966 (Now out of print).

Woodward, R. & Jones, R. Cognitive restructuring treatment: A controlled trial with anxious patients. *Behavior Research and Therapy,* 1980, *18,* 401-407.

Yalom, I.D. *The Theory and Practice of Group Psychotherapy.* New York: Basic Books, 1970, 1975 (Second Edition).

Yanagida, E.H. Cross cultural considerations in the application of assertion training: A brief note. *Psychology of Women Quarterly,* 1979 (Sum), *3* (4), 400-402.

Appendix A

The Universal Declaration of Human Rights

WHEREAS recognition of the inherent dignity and of the equal and inalienable rights of all members of the human family is the foundation of freedom, justice and peace in the world,

WHEREAS disregard and contempt for human rights have resulted in barbarous acts which have outraged the conscience of mankind, and the advent of a world in which human beings shall enjoy freedom of speech and belief and freedom from fear and want has been proclaimed as the highest aspiration of the common people,

WHEREAS, it is essential, if man is not to be compelled to have recourse, as a last resort, to rebellion against tyranny and oppression, that human rights should be protected by the rule of law,

WHEREAS it is essential to promote the development of friendly relations between nations,

WHEREAS the peoples of the United Nations have in their Charter reaffirmed their faith in fundamental human rights, in the dignity and worth of the human person and in the equal rights of men and women and have determined to promote social progress and better standards of life in larger freedom,

WHEREAS Member States have pledged themselves to achieve, in cooperation with the United Nations, the promotion of universal respect for and observance of human rights and fundamental freedoms,

WHEREAS a common understanding of these rights and freedoms is of the greatest importance for the full realization of this pledge,

NOW, THEREFORE, THE GENERAL ASSEMBLY PROCLAIMS this Universal Declaration of Human Rights as a common standard of achievement for all peoples and all nations, to the end that every individual and every organ of society, keeping this Declaration constantly in mind, shall strive by teaching and education to promote respect for these rights and freedoms and by progressive measures, national and international, to secure their universal and effective recognition and observance, both among the peoples of Member States themselves and among the peoples of territories under their jurisdiction.

Article 1. All human beings are born free and equal in dignity and rights. They are endowed with reason and conscience and should act towards one another in a spirit of brotherhood.

Article 2. Everyone is entitled to all the rights and freedoms set forth in this Declaration, without distinction of any kind, such as race, colour, sex, language, religion, political or other opinion, national or social origin, property, birth or other status.

Furthermore, no distinction shall be made on the basis of the political, jurisdictional or international status of the country or territory to which a person belongs, whether it be independent, trust, non-self-governing or under any other limitation of sovereignty.

Article 3.   Everyone has the right to life, liberty and security of person.

Article 4.   No one shall be held in slavery or servitude; slavery and the slave trade shall be prohibited in all their forms.

Article 5.   No one shall be subjected to torture or to cruel, inhuman or degrading treatment or punishment.

Article 6.   Everyone has the right to recognition everywhere as a person before the law.

Article 7.   All are equal before the law and are entitled without any discrimination to equal protection of the law. All are entitled to equal protection against any discrimination in violation of this Declaration and against any incitement to such discrimination.

Article 8.   Everyone has the right to an effective remedy by the competent national tribunals for acts violating the fundamental rights granted him by the constitution or by law.

Article 9.   No one shall be subjected to arbitrary arrest, detention of exile.

Article 10.   Everyone is entitled in full equality to a fair and public hearing by an independent and impartial tribunal, in the determination of his rights and obligations and of any criminal charge against him.

Article 11.   (1) Everyone charged with a penal offence has the right to be presumed innocent until proved guilty according to law in a public trial at which he has had all the guarantees necessary for his defence.

(2) No one shall be held guilty of any penal offence on account of any act or omission which did not constitute a penal offence, under national or international law, at the time when it was committed. Nor shall a heavier penalty be imposed than the one that was applicable at the time the penal offence was committed.

Article 12.   No one shall be subjected to arbitrary interference with his privacy, family, home or correspondence, nor to attacks upon his honour and reputation Everyone has the right to the protection of the law against such interference or attacks.

Article 13.   (1) Everyone has the right to freedom of movement and residence within the borders of each state.

(2) Everyone has the right to leave any country, including his own, and to return to his country.

Article 14.   (1) Everyone has the right to seek and to eenjoy in other countries asylum from persecution.

(2) This right may not be invoked in the case of prosecutions genuinely arising from non-political crimes or from acts contrary to the purposes and principles of the United Nations.

Article 15.   (1) Everyone has the right to a nationality.

(2) No one shall be arbitrarily deprived of his nationality nor denied the right to change his nationality.

Article 16.   (1) Men and women of full age, without any limitation due to race, nationality or religion, have the right to marry and to found a family. They are entitled to equal rights as to marriage, during marriage and at its dissolution.

(2) Marriage shall be entered into only with the free and full consent of the intending spouses.

(3) The family is the natural and fundamental group unit of society and is entitled to protection by society and the State.

Article 17. (1) Everyone has the right to own property alone as well as in association with others.
(2) No one shall be arbitrarily deprived of his property.
Article 18. Everyone has the right to freedom of thought, conscience and religion; this right includes freedom to change his religion or belief, and freedom, either alone or in community with others and in public or private, to manifest his religion or belief in teaching, practice, worship and observance.
Article 19. Everyone has the right to freedom of opinion and expression; this right includes freedom to hold opinions without interference and to seek, receive and impart information and ideas through any media and regardless of frontiers.
Article 20. (1) Everyone has the right to freedom of peaceful assembly and association.
(2) No one may be compelled to belong to an association.
Article 21. (1) Everyone has the right to take part in the government of his country, directly or through freely chosen representatives.
(2) Everyone has the right of equal access to public service in his country.
(3) The will of the people shall be the basis of the authority of government; this will shall be expressed in periodic and genuine elections which shall be by universal and equal suffrage and shall be held by secret vote or by equivalent free voting procedures.
Article 22. Everyone, as a member of society, has the right to social security and is entitled to realization, through national effort and international cooperation and in accordance with the organization and resources of each State, of the economic, social and cultural rights indispensable for his dignity and the free development of his personality.
Article 23. (1) Everyone has the right to work, to free choice of employment, to just and favourable conditions of work and to protection against unemployment.
(2) Everyone, without any discrimination, has the right to equal pay for equal work.
(3) Everyone who works has the right to just and favourable remuneration ensuring for himself and his family an existence worthy of human dignity, and supplemented, if necessary, by other means of social protection.
(4) Everyone has the right to form and to join trade unions for the protection of his interests.
Article 24. Everyone has the right to rest and leisure, including reasonable limitation of working hours and periodic holidays with pay.
Article 25. (1) Everyone has the right to a standard of living adequate for the health and well-being of himself and of his family, including food, clothing, housing and medical care and necessary social services, and the right to security in the event of unemployment, sickness, disability, widowhood, old age or other lack of livelihood in circumstances beyond his control.
(2) Motherhood and childhood are entitled to special care and assistance. All children, whether born in or out of wedlock, shall enjoy the same social protection.
Article 26. (1) Everyone has the right to education. Education shall be free, at least in the elementary and fundamental stages. Elementary education shall be compulsory. Technical and professional education shall be made generally available and higher education shall be equally accessible to all on the basis of merit.
(2) Education shall be directed to the full development of the human personality and to the strengthening of respect for human rights and fundamental freedoms. It shall promote understanding, tolerance and friendship among all nations, racial or

religious groups, and shall further the activities of the United Nations for the maintenance of peace.

(3) Parents have a prior right to choose the kind of education that shall be given to their children.

Article 27. (1) Everyone has the right freely to participate in the cultural life of the community, to enjoy the arts and to share in scientific advancement and its benefits.

(2) Everyone has the right to the protection of the moral and material interests resulting from any scientific, literary or artistic production of which he is the author.

Article 28. Everyone is entitled to a social and international order in which the rights and freedoms set forth in this Declaration can be fully realized.

Article 29. (1) Everyone has duties to the community in which alone the free and full development of his personality is possible.

(2) In the exercise of his rights and freedoms, everyone shall be subject only to such limitations as are determined by law solely for the purpose of securing due recognition and respect for the rights and freedoms of others and of meeting the just requirements of morality, public order and the general welfare in a democratic society.

(3) These rights and freedoms may in no case be exercised contrary to the purposes and principles of the United Nations.

Article 30. Nothing in this Declaration may be interpreted as implying for any State, group or person any right to engage in any activity or to perform any act aimed at the destruction of any of the rights and freedoms set forth herein.

Appendix B

Principles for Ethical Practice of Assertive Behavior Training

As AT gained in popularity during the mid-1970's, an increasing concern developed among responsible practitioners for the misuse of the process: unqualified trainers, illegitimate purposes, contraindicated clients. At the December 1975 meeting of the Association for Advancement of Behavior Therapy in San Francisco, a group of nationally recognized AT professionals met to initiate work on a statement of ethical principles. The following statement is the result of their work.

Further discussion of this proposal occurred at the First International Conference on Assertive Behavior Training in Washington, D.C., in August, 1976, and at the Association for Advancement of Behavior Therapy in New York City, December, 1976. Although no amendments to the original statement have been formalized, considerable concern has been expressed about the academic credentials suggested herein for qualifying facilitators. It is likely that a competency based criterion for qualification will emerge.

Moreover, AABT itself is preparing a statement of ethics for the practice of behavior therapy generally, which may have direct application to AT, although AT is not considered solely a ''behavior therapy'' by a considerable number of its practitioners.

Meanwhile, however, this statement remains the only public declaration by a group of professionals which is directed toward greater ethical responsibility in the practice of AT. Practitioners are urged to consider its implications for their own work.

With the increasing popularity of assertive behavior training, a quality of "faddishness" has become evident, and there are frequent reports of ethically irresponsible practices (and practitioners). We hear of trainers who, for example, do not adequately differentiate assertion and aggression. Others have failed to advocate proper ethical responsibility and caution to clients—e.g., failed to alert them to and/or prepare them for the possibility of retaliation or other highly negative reactions from others.

The following statement of "Principles for Ethical Practice of Assertive Behavior Training" is the work of the professional psychologists and educators listed below, who are actively engaged in the practice of facilitating assertive behavior (also referred to as "assertive therapy," "social skills training," "personal effectiveness training," and "AT"). We don't intend by this statement to discourage untrained individuals from becoming more assertive on their own, and we don't advocate that one must have extensive credentials in order to be of help to friends and relatives. Rather, these principles are offered to help foster responsible and ethical teaching and practice by human services professionals. Others who wish to enhance their own assertiveness or that of associates are encouraged to do so, with awareness of their own limitations, and of the importance of seeking help from a qualified therapist/trainer when necessary.

We hereby declare support for and adherence to the statement of principles, and invite responsible professionals in our own and other fields who use these techniques to join us in advocating and practicing these principles.

Robert E. Alberti, Ph.D.
San Luis Obispo, CA

Michael L. Emmons, Ph.D.
San Luis Obispo, CA

Iris G. Fodor, Ph.D.
Associate Professor, Educational Psychology
New York University, Washington Square
New York, NY

John Galassi, Ph.D.
School of Education
University of North Carolina
Chapel Hill, NC

Merna D. Galassi, Ed.D.
Meredith College
Raleigh, NC

Lynne Garnett, Ph.D.
Counseling Psychologist
University of California
Los Angeles, CA

Patricia Jakubowski, Ed.D.
Associate Professor, Behavioral Studies
University of Missouri
St. Louis, MO

Janet L. Wolfe, Ph.D.
Director of Clinical Services
Institute for Advanced Study in Rational
   Psychotherapy
New York, NY

1. Definition of Assertive Behavior

For purposes of these principles and the ethical framework expressed herein, we define assertive behavior as that complex of behaviors, emitted by a person in an interpersonal context, which express that person's feelings, attitudes, wishes, opinions or rights directly, firmly, and honestly, while respecting the feelings, attitudes, wishes, opinions and rights of the other person(s). Such behavior may include the expression of such emotions as anger, fear, caring, hope, joy, despair, indignance, embarrassment, but in any event is expressed in a manner which does not violate the rights of others. Assertive behavior is differentiated from aggressive behavior which, while expressive of one person's feelings, attitudes, wishes, opinions or rights, does not respect those characteristics in others.

While this definition is intended to be comprehensive, it is recognized that any adequate definition of assertive behavior must consider several dimensions:

A. *Intent:* behavior classified as assertive is not intended by its author to be hurtful of others.

B. *Behavior:* behavior classified as assertive would be evaluated by an "objective observer" as itself honest, direct, expressive and non-destructive of others.

C. *Effects:* behavior classified as assertive has the effect upon the receiver of a direct and non-destructive message, by which a "reasonable person" would not be hurt.

D. *Socio-cultural Context:* behavior classified as assertive is appropriate to the environment and culture in which it is exhibited, and may not be considered "assertive" in a different socio-cultural environment.

2. Client Self-Determination

These principles recognize and affirm the inherent dignity and the equal and inalienable rights of all members of the human family, as proclaimed in the "Universal Declaration of Human Rights" endorsed by the General Assembly of the United Nations.

Pursuant to the precepts of the Declaration, each client (trainee, patient) who seeks assertive behavior training shall be treated as a person of value, with all of the freedoms and rights expressed in the Declaration. No procedure shall be utilized in the name of assertive behavior training which would violate those freedoms or rights.

Informed client self-determination shall guide all such interventions:

A. the client shall be fully informed in advance of all procedures to be utilized;
B. the client shall have the freedom to choose to participate or not at any point in the intervention;
C. the client who is institutionalized shall be similarly treated with respect and without coercion, insofar as is possible within the institutional environment.
D. the client shall be provided with explicit definitions of assertiveness and assertive training.
E. the client shall be fully informed as to the education, training, experience or other qualifications of the assertive trainer(s).
F. the client shall be informed as to the goals and potential outcomes of assertive training, including potentially high levels of anxiety, and possible negative reactions from others.
G. the client shall be fully informed as to the responsibility of the assertion trainer(s) and the client(s).
H. the client shall be informed as to the ethics and employment of confidentiality guidelines as they pertain to various assertive training settings (e.g. clinical vs. non-clinical).

3. Qualifications of Facilitators
Assertive behavior training is essentially a therapeutic procedure, although frequently practiced in a variety of settings by professionals not otherwise engaged in rendering a "psychological" service. Persons in any professional role who engage in helping others to change their behavior, attitudes, and interpersonal relationships must understand human behavior at a level commensurate with the level of their interventions.

3.1 General Qualifications
We support the following minimum, general qualifications for facilitators at all levels of intervention (including "trainers in training"—preservice or inservice—who are preparing for professional service in a recognized human services field, and who may be conducting assertive behavior training under supervision as part of a research project or practicum):
A. Fundamental understanding of the principles of learning and behavior (equivalent to completion of a rigorous undergraduate level course in learning theory);
B. Fundamental understanding of anxiety and its effects upon behavior (equivalent to completion of a rigorous undergraduate level course in abnormal psychology);
C. Knowledge of the limitations, contraindications and potential dangers of assertive behavior training; familiarity with theory and research in the area.
D. Satisfactory evidence of competent performance as a facilitator, as observed by a qualified trainer, is strongly recommended for all professionals, particularly for those who do not possess a doctorate or an equivalent level of training. Such evidence would most ideally be supported by:
   1) participation in at least ten (10) hours of assertive behavior training as a client (trainee, patient); and
   2) participation in at least ten (10) hours of assertive behavior training as a facilitator under supervision.

3.2 Specific Qualifications
The following additional qualifications are considered to be the minimum expected for facilitators at the indicated levels of intervention:
A. *Assertive behavior training*, including non-clinical workshops, groups, and individual client training aimed at teaching assertive skills to those persons who

require only encouragement and specific skill training, and in whom no serious emotional deficiency or pathology is evident.

1) For trainers in programs conducted under the sponsorship of a recognized human services agency, school, governmental or corporate entity, church, or community organization:

   a) An advanced degree in a recognized field of human services (e.g. psychology, counseling, social work, medicine, public health, nursing, education, human development, theology/divinity), including at least one term of field experience in a human services agency supervised by a qualified trainer; *or*

   b) certification as a minister, public school teacher, social worker, physician, counselor, nurse, or clinical, counseling, educational, or school psychologist, or similar human services professional, as recognized by the state wherein employed or by the recognized state or national professional society in the indicated discipline; *or*

   c) one year of paid counseling experience in a recognized human services agency, supervised by a qualified trainer; *or*

   d) qualification under items 3.2B or 3.2C below.

2) For trainers in programs including interventions at the level defined in this item (3.2A), but without agency/organization sponsorship:

   a) An advanced degree in a recognized field of human services (e.g. psychology, counseling, social work, medicine, public health, nursing, education, human development, theology/divinity) including at least one term of field experience in a human services agency supervised by a qualified trainer; *and*

   b) certification as a minister, social worker, physician, counselor, nurse, or clinical, counseling, educational, or school psychologist, or similar human services professional, as recognized by the state wherein employed or by the recognized state or national professional society in the indicated discipline; *or*

   c) qualification under items 3.2B or 3.2C below.

B. *Assertive behavior therapy*, including clinical interventions designed to assist persons who are severely inhibited by anxiety, or who are significantly deficient in social skills, or who are controlled by aggression, or who evidence pathology, or for whom other therapeutic procedures are indicated:

1) For therapists in programs conducted under the sponsorship of a recognized human services agency, school, governmental or corporate entity, church, or community organization:

   a) An advanced degree in a recognized field of human services (e.g. psychology, counseling, social work, medicine, public health, nursing, education, human development, theology/divinity) including at least one term of field experience in a human services agency supervised by a qualified trainer; *or*

   b) certification as a minister, social worker, physician, counselor, nurse, or clinical, counseling, educational, or school psychologist, as recognized by the state wherein employed or by the recognized state or national professional society in the indicated discipline; *or*

   c) qualification under item 3.2C below.

2) For therapists employing interventions at the level defined in this item (3.2B), but without agency/organization sponsorship

   a) An advanced degree in a recognized field of human services (e.g. psychology, counseling, social work, medicine, public health, nursing, education, human development, theology/divinity) including at least one term of field experience in a human services agency supervised by a qualified trainer; *and*

b) certification as minister, social worker, physician, counselor, nurse, or clinical, counseling, educational, or school psychologist, as recognized by the state wherein employed or by the recognized state or national professional society in the indicated discipline; *and*

c) at least one year of paid professional experience in a recognized human services agency, supervised by a qualified trainer; *or*

d) qualification under item 3.2C below.

C. *Training of trainers*, including preparation of other professionals to offer assertive behavior training/therapy to clients, in school, agency, organization, or individual settings.

1) A doctoral degree in a recognized field of human services (e.g. psychology, counseling, social work, medicine, public health, nursing, education, human development, theology/divinity) including at least one term of field experience in a human services agency supervised by a qualified trainer; *and*

2) certification as a minister, social worker, physician, counselor, nurse, or clinical, counseling, educational, or school psychologist, as recognized by the state wherein employed, or by the recognized state or national professional society in the indicated discipline; *and*

3) at least one year of paid professional experience in a recognized human services agency, supervised by a qualified trainer; *and*

4) advanced study in assertive behavior training/therapy, including at least two of the following:

a) At least thirty (30) hours of facilitation with clients;

b) participation in at least two different workshops at professional meetings or professional training institutes:

c) contribution to the professional literature in the field.

3.3 We recognize that counselors and psychologists are not certified by each state. In states wherein no such certification is provided, unless contrary to local statute, we acknowledge the legitimacy of professionals who: A) are otherwise qualified under the provisions of items 3.1 and 3.2; and B) would be eligible for certification as a counselor or psychologist in another state.

3.4 We do not consider that participation in one or two workshops on assertive behavior, even though conducted by a professional with an advanced degree, is adequate qualification to offer assertive behavior training to others, *unless the additional qualifications* of items 3.1 and 3.2 are also met.

3.5 These qualifications are presented as *standards* for professional facilitators of assertive behavior. No "certification" or "qualifying" agency is hereby proposed. Rather, it is incumbent upon each professional to evaluate himself/herself as a trainer/therapist according to these standards, and to make explicit to clients the adequacy of his/her qualifications as a facilitator.

4. Ethical Behavior of Facilitators

Since the encouragement and facilitation of assertive behavior is essentially a *therapeutic* procedure, the ethical standards most applicable to the practice of assertive behavior training are those of psychologists. We recognize that many persons who practice some form of assertive behavior training are not otherwise engaged in rendering a "psychological" service (i.e. teachers, personnel/training directors). To all we support the statement of "Ethical Standards for Psychologists" as adopted by the American Psychological Association as the standard of ethical behavior by which assertive behavior training shall be conducted.

We recognize that the methodology employed in assertive behavior training may include a wide range of procedures, some of which are of unproven value. It is the responsibility of the facilitators to inform clients of any experimental procedures. Under no circumstances should the facilitator "guarantee" a specific outcome from an intervention.

5. Appropriateness of Assertive Behavior Training Interventions

Assertive behavior training, as any intervention oriented toward helping people change, may be applied under a wide range of conditions, yet its appropriateness must be evaluated in each individual case. The responsible selection of assertive behavior training for a particular intervention must include attention to at least the following dimensions:

A. *Client:* The personal characteristics of the client in question (age, sex, ethnicity, institutionalization, capacity for informed choice, physical and psychological functionality).

B. *Problem/Goals:* The purpose for which professional help has been sought or recommended (job skills, severe inhibition, anxiety reduction, overcome aggression).

C. *Facilitator:* The personal and professional qualifications of the facilitator in question (age, sex, ethnicity, skills, understanding, ethics—see also Principles 3 and 4 above).

D. *Setting:* The characteristics of the setting in which the intervention is conducted (home, school, business, agency, clinic, hospital, prison). Is the client free to choose? Is the facilitator's effectiveness systematically evaluated?

E. *Time/Duration:* The duration of the intervention. Does the time involved represent a brief word of encouragement, a formal training workshop, an intensive and long-term therapeutic effort?

F. *Method:* The nature of the intervention. Is it "packaged" procedure or tailored to client needs? Is training based on sound principles of learning and behavior? Is there clear differentiation of aggressiveness, assertiveness and other concepts? Are definitions, techniques, procedures and purposes clarified? Is care taken to encourage small, successful steps and to minimize punishing consequences? Are any suggested "homework assignments" presented with adequate supervision, responsibility, and sensitivity to the effect upon significant others of the client's behavior change efforts? Are clients informed that assertiveness "doesn't always work?"

G. *Outcome:* Are there follow-up procedures, either by self-report or other post-test procedures?

6. Social Responsibility

Assertive behavior training shall be conducted within the law. Trainers and clients are encouraged to work assertively to change those laws which they consider need to be changed, and to modify the social system in ways they believe appropriate—in particular to extend the boundaries of human rights. Toward these ends, trainers are encouraged to facilitate responsible change skills via assertive behavior training. All those who practice, teach, or do research on assertive behavior are urged to advocate caution and ethical responsibility in application of the technique, in accordance with these Principles.

We hope you have enjoyed reading this book. For more books with *Impact* we invite you to order the following titles...

YOUR PERFECT RIGHT
A Guide to Assertive Living
by Robert E. Alberti, Ph.D. and
Michael L. Emmons, Ph.D.

The book that started the assertiveness training movement! Build equal, satisfying relationships through "honest-but-not-pushy" self-expression that respects the rights of others. Step-by-step procedures, examples and exercises. With over 400,000 sold, a positive, practical and readable bestseller!
Paper $6.95/Hardcover $8.95   Order Code YPR

THE ASSERTIVE WOMAN
by Stanlee Phelps, M.S.W. and Nancy Austin, M.B.A.

Assertiveness (NOT aggressiveness!) training for women! The original book that applies assertiveness principles to all phases of a woman's life...individual, feminist, mother, student, lover. Full of examples, checklists and helpful procedures. Over 200,000 copies sold and still going strong!
Paper $5.95   Order Code TAW

REBUILDING
When Your Relationship Ends
by Bruce Fisher, Ed.D.

A book for those who are putting their lives back together after divorce or after other crises. Rebuilding includes aids for coping with the fifteen "building blocks" that mark the path to recovery: denial, loneliness, guilt, rejection, grief, anger, letting go, self concept, friendships, leftover love, trust, sexuality, responsibility, singleness and freedom.
Paper $5.95   Order Code R

THE COUPLE'S JOURNEY
Intimacy as a Path to Wholeness
by Susan M. Campbell, Ph.D.

"Coupling, like life, is a continually changing process." Dr. Campbell guides us on the five-stage path of growth traveled by every intimate relationship—romance, power struggle, stability, commitment and co-creation. Here is help in discovering new meaning in the often confusing process of living intimately with another person.
Paper $5.95   Order Code CJ

PLAYFAIR
Everybody's Guide to Non-Competitive Play
by Matt Weinstein and Joel Goodman, Ed.D.

Now you can play games where EVERYONE wins! Sixty non-competitive games for large and small groups: adults, young adults, schools, children, families. Detailed descriptions with complete instructions for "play-leaders." A delightful book that takes play seriously and makes it a way of life; filled with playful photographs!
Paper $8.95   Order Code PF

SURVIVING WITH KIDS
A Lifeline for Overwhelmed Parents
by Wayne Bartz, Ph.D. and Richard Rasor, Ed.D.

A jargon-free, practical book for parents! Thirty proven principles of behavior applied to parent-child interaction. Clearly written, down-to-earth, and delightfully illustrated with cartoon-style examples of everyday situations. A solid guide for first-time parents and those who sometimes feel overwhelmed...and isn't that everybody?
Paper $4.95   Order Code SWK

NO MORE SECRETS
Protecting Your Child from Sexual Assault
by Caren Adams and Jennifer Fay

A supportive, conversational guide for parents who wish to teach their young children how to prevent sexual advances. Points out that most offenders are not strangers but relatives and "friends." This important resource encourages open discussion—"no secrets" —between parents and children. Dialogue, games and other tools to help parents instruct children, 3 and up.
Paper $3.95   Order Code NMS

LIKING MYSELF
by Pat Palmer, Ed.D.
Illustrated by Betty Schondeck

A child-size introduction to concepts of feelings, self-esteem and assertiveness for youngsters 5-9. Delightful drawings help convey its message to young readers. Liking Myself is widely used by parents and teachers to help children learn and appreciate the good things about themselves, their feelings and their behavior.
Paper $4.50;w/Teacher Guide $5.50   Order Code LM

THE MOUSE, THE MONSTER & ME!
Assertiveness for Young People
by Pat Palmer, Ed.D.

Assertiveness concepts for youngsters 8 and up explained in an entertaining way. Non-assertive "mice" and aggressive "monsters" offer young persons an opportunity to develop a sense of personal rights and responsibilities, to become appropriately assertive and to gain a greater sense of self-worth.
Paper $4.50;w/Teacher Guide $5.50 Order Code MMM

STRESSMAP: Finding Your Pressure Points
by Michele Haney, Ph.D. and Edmond Boenisch, Ph.D.

A personal guidebook for pinpointing sources of stress — and finding stress relief! Questionnaire-"maps" help readers survey people, money, work, body, mind and leisure stress areas. Worksheets permit an individualized plan for relief.
Paper $5.95   Order Code SM

LEAD ON! The Complete Handbook For Group Leaders
by Leslie G. Lawson, M.A., Franklyn Donant, M.A. and John Lawson, Ed.D.

Comprehensive guide for leaders of volunteer groups. Twenty-four easy to follow chapters make it easy to lead. Describes essentials for novices and experienced leaders. Indispensable for leaders of youth clubs, church programs, and other "new volunteerism" organizations.
Paper $5.95   Order Code LO

Please see following page for information on how to order

Impact Publishers' books are available at booksellers throughout the U.S.A. and in many other countries. If you are not able to find a title of interest at a nearby bookstore, we would be happy to fill your direct order. Please send us:
1. Complete name, address and zip code information
2. The full title of the book(s) you want
3. The number of copies of each book
4. California residents add 6% sales tax
5. $1.00 shipping for the first book; $.25 for each additional book.
VISA and MasterCard are acceptable; be sure to include complete card number, expiration date and your authorizing signature. Send your order to **Impact Publishers, Post Office Box 1094, San Luis Obispo, CA 93406**, or call us at **805-543-5911.**